Varieties of Democracy

Varieties of Democracy is the essential user's guide to the Varieties of Democracy project (V-Dem), one of the most ambitious data collection efforts in comparative politics. This global research collaboration sparked a dramatic change in how we study the nature, causes, and consequences of democracy.

This book is great in scope and ambition. More than a reference guide, it raises standards for causal inferences in democratization research and introduces new, measurable concepts of democracy and many political institutions.

Varieties of Democracy enables anyone interested in democracy – teachers, students, journalists, activists, researchers, and others – to analyze V-Dem data in new and exciting ways. This book creates opportunities for V-Dem data to be used in education, research, news analysis, advocacy, policy work, and elsewhere. V-Dem is rapidly becoming the preferred source for democracy data.

Michael Coppedge is Professor of Political Science at the University of Notre Dame and co-Principal Investigator of Varieties of Democracy (V-Dem). He is the author of *Democratization and Research Methods*, published by Cambridge University Press.

John Gerring is Professor of Government at the University of Texas at Austin and co-Principal Investigator of Varieties of Democracy (V-Dem). His work extends across comparative politics, political history, and methodology.

Adam N. Glynn is Associate Professor of Political Science and Quantitative Theory and Methods at Emory University and Project Manager for Methodology of Varieties of Democracy (V-Dem). His research examines causal inference and sampling/survey designs for political science applications.

Carl Henrik Knutsen is Professor of Political Science at the University of Oslo and co-Principal Investigator of Varieties of Democracy (V-Dem). His research examines the economic effects of political institutions and regimes, policy making in autocracies, and processes of regime change.

Staffan I. Lindberg is Director of the V-Dem Institute and Professor of Political Science at University of Gothenburg and co-Principal

Investigator of Varieties of Democracy (V-Dem). His research examines topics ranging from elections, democratization, and civil society to women's representation and voting behavior.

Daniel Pemstein is Associate Professor of Political Science at North Dakota State University and Project Manager for Measurement Methods of the Varieties of Democracy (V-Dem). He specializes in measurement and builds statistical tools to study political institutions, parties, and careers.

Brigitte Seim is Assistant Professor of Public Policy at the University of North Carolina, Chapel Hill, and Project Manager for Experiments of Varieties of Democracy (V-Dem). Her research examines the relationship between citizens and political officials.

Svend-Erik Skaaning is Professor of Political Science at Aarhus University and Project Manager for Varieties of Democracy (V-Dem). His research examines the conceptualization, measurement, and explanation of democracy and other governance-related phenomena.

Jan Teorell is Professor of Political Science at Lund University and co-Principal Investigator for Varieties of Democracy (V-Dem). His research interests include political methodology, comparative politics and democratization, corruption, and state-making.

Anagon 9/20/24

Varieties of Democracy

Measuring Two Centuries of Political Change

MICHAEL COPPEDGE
University of Notre Dame

JOHN GERRING
University of Texas at Austin

ADAM N. GLYNN
Emory University

CARL HENRIK KNUTSEN
University of Oslo

STAFFAN I. LINDBERG
University of Gothenburg

DANIEL PEMSTEIN
North Dakota State University

BRIGITTE SEIM
University of North Carolina at Chapel Hill

SVEND-ERIK SKAANING
Aarhus University

JAN TEORELL
Lund University

CAMBRIDGE
UNIVERSITY PRESS

CAMBRIDGE
UNIVERSITY PRESS

Shaftesbury Road, Cambridge CB2 8EA, United Kingdom

One Liberty Plaza, 20th Floor, New York, NY 10006, USA

477 Williamstown Road, Port Melbourne, VIC 3207, Australia

314–321, 3rd Floor, Plot 3, Splendor Forum, Jasola District Centre, New Delhi – 110025, India

103 Penang Road, #05–06/07, Visioncrest Commercial, Singapore 238467

Cambridge University Press is part of Cambridge University Press & Assessment, a department of the University of Cambridge.

We share the University's mission to contribute to society through the pursuit of education, learning and research at the highest international levels of excellence.

www.cambridge.org
Information on this title: www.cambridge.org/9781108440967

DOI: 10.1017/9781108347860

First published 2020
First paperback edition 2022

A catalogue record for this publication is available from the British Library

Library of Congress Cataloging-in-Publication data
Names: Coppedge, Michael, 1957– author.
Title: Varieties of democracy : measuring two centuries of political change / edited by Michael John Coppedge, John Gerring, Staffan I. Lindberg, Svend Erik Skaaning, Jan Teorell, Daniel Pemstein, Brigitte Seim, Adam Glynn, Carl Henrik Knutsen.
Description: Cambridge, United Kingdom ; New York, NY : Cambridge University Press, 2020. | Includes bibliographical references and index.
Identifiers: LCCN 2019040390 (print) | LCCN 2019040391 (ebook) | ISBN 9781108424837 (hardback) | ISBN 9781108347860 (ebook)
Subjects: LCSH: Democracy – History. | Democratization – History. | Democracy – Research – Methodology. | Democratization – Research – Methodology. | Democracy – Mathematical models. | Democratization – Mathematical models.
Classification: LCC JC421 .V3155 2020 (print) | LCC JC421 (ebook) | DDC 321.8–dc23
LC record available at https://lccn.loc.gov/2019040390
LC ebook record available at https://lccn.loc.gov/2019040391

ISBN   978-1-108-42483-7   Hardback
ISBN   978-1-108-44096-7   Paperback

Contents

Figures

Tables

Contributors

Altman, David
Bernhard, Michael
Bizzarro, Fernando
Coppedge, Michael
Gerring, John
Glynn, Adam N.
Knutsen, Carl Henrik
Krusell, Joshua
Lindberg, Staffan I.
Maguire, Matthew
Marquardt, Kyle
McMann, Kelly
Mechkova, Valeriya
Miri, Farhad
Pemstein, Daniel
Pernes, Josefine
Seim, Brigitte
Skaaning, Svend-Erik
Staton, Jeffrey
Stepanova, Natalia
Teorell, Jan
Tzelgov, Eitan
Wang, Yi-ting

Acknowledgments

Just like the *Varieties of Democracy* project (V-Dem), this first V-Dem book is the result of so much effort over several years that it is impossible to provide an adequate recognition of the people and institutions to which we are indebted. Nevertheless, it is important to try. The unusually large number of coauthors is a reflection of this fact. All of the principal investigators and most of the project managers are coauthors, as well as the project coordinators and several of the research fellows and doctoral research assistants, precisely because there are so many whose contributions were indispensable. We describe their specific contributions, and those of others, in more detail in Chapter 1, which tells the story of the project, and here and there in other chapters. Below we recognize the other students, staff, postdocs, and affiliated scholars who have made so many important contributions to the development and expansion of the V-Dem venture. Nonetheless, our efforts on this score are certain to fall short. Ideas and inputs have flowed so freely and generously that it is impossible to reconstruct every one of them and adequately appreciate everyone. We ask all undergraduate and graduate students, postdocs, and visiting and affiliate scholars who at some point were involved to know that we appreciate all of your contributions and extend our sincerest gratitude.

Several project managers did not directly work on this book but made fundamental contributions to the project: Steven Fish at the University of California, Berkeley, who, with Matthew Kroenig, wrote the survey questions on legislatures; Allen Hicken at the University of Michigan, who developed all the questions on political parties; Patrik Lindenfors at the University of Stockholm, who designed genetic models testing evolutionary theories of democratization; Pamela Paxton at the University of Texas at Austin, who oversaw the development of questions on formal and descriptive representation; Rachel Sigman at the Naval Postgraduate School, who now oversees data collection on exclusion and state capacity; and Steven Wilson at the University of Nevada, Reno, who, as project manager for computational infrastructure, reworked the V-Dem research database and website, including its expert survey interface and all the online analysis tools. Former project managers Megan Reif and Holli Semetko contributed valuable expertise on election fraud and violence and the Middle East and on the media in Western Europe, respectively.

At the V-Dem Institute at the University of Gothenburg, those who are not coauthors but who have made significant contributions to the research that led to this book include data managers Moa Olin, Laura Saxer, Johannes von Römer, and Lisa Gastaldi. The project has benefited enormously from collaboration with many top-notch postdoctoral research fellows who are not coauthors: Anna Lührmann (who is now Deputy Director of the V-Dem Institute and Assistant Professor at the University of Gothenburg), Matthew Wilson, Richard Morgan, Juraj Medzihorsky, Laura Maxwell, Constanza Sanhueza Petrarca, and Sirianne Dahlum; and with Research Associates Aksel Sundström, Carolien van Ham, Abdalhadi Alijla, Marina Povitkina, and Petrus Sundin. We also wish to recognize doctoral students Yaman Berker Kavasoglu and Marcus Tannenberg and research assistant Sandra Grahn.

The Kellogg Institute for International Studies at the University of Notre Dame served as the second institutional home of the project until 2018. Until 2014, a series of doctoral students (Cecilia Lero, Sandra Botero, Krystin Krause, and Chad Kiewiet de Jonge) and then full-time administrator Elizabeth Andrews also worked as project coordinators, overseeing data collection in the Western Hemisphere. Other doctoral students (Rodrigo Castro Cornejo, Lucía Tiscornia, Benjamin Denison, M. Tahir Kilavuz, Richard Price, and Paul Friesen) and several undergraduates (Haixiao Wang, Caroline Simpson, and Austin Metheny-Kawisch) provided additional research assistance. Nicholas Ottone deserves special thanks for helping Coppedge pull the final manuscript of this book together: proofreading and reformatting the text and references, updating many tables and graphs, and undertaking the thankless job of compiling the index. Two dozen undergraduates at Notre Dame also identified more than a thousand potential country experts and did some preliminary A-coding on legislative chambers. Notre Dame's Center for Research Computing developed our initial research database and website despite our constantly evolving requirements even while data collection was fully under way. The Kellogg Institute hosted various V-Dem events and provided generous start-up funding for the project, as did Notre Dame's Vice President for Research, Bob Bernhard.

Numerous people, located at different institutions, also deserve special thanks for contributing to the Historical V-Dem part of the data collection. First and foremost, a special thanks to Agnes Cornell (Aarhus University, then Lund University), Haakon Gjerløw (University of Oslo), Tore Wig (University of Oslo), and Daniel Ziblatt (Harvard University), who have been a part of the core team for historical data collection over several years, but also to Sirianne Dahlum and Luca J. Uberti, who were part of the core historical team for shorter periods of time when employed as researchers at the University of

Oslo. Furthermore, we gratefully acknowledge coding efforts and other research assistance specifically related to the historical data collection by Solveig Bjørkholt, Ben Chatterton, Vlad Ciobanu, Lee Cojocaru, Vilde Lunnan Djuve, Linda Eitrem Holmgren, Kristian Frederiksen, Sune Orloff Hellegaard, Bernardo Isola, Sindre Haugen, Haakon Haugevik Jernsletten, Claudia Maier, Swaantje Marten, Selemon Negash, Moa Olin, Konstantinos Skenteri, and Katharina Sibbers. Talib Jabbar ably assisted the project as a whole with data collection and data management while at Lund University.

At Aarhus University, a number of research assistants were instrumental in the collection of data on suffrage and state institutions, including Filip Ask Von Ubisch, Frederik Lasserre, Kristian Vrede Skaaning Frederiksen, and Sune Orloff Hellegaard. Furthermore, Agnes Cornell (member of the group behind the historical extension of V-Dem), David Delfs Erbo Andersen, Jakob Tolstrup, Lasse Lykke Rørbæk, and Merete Bech Seeberg have provided valuable feedback and other kinds of input. Jørgen Møller deserves special thanks for his help on various occasions and for supporting V-Dem via joint research projects (DEDERE and CODE).

At Emory University, Nancy Arrington, Leann Bass, Brian Delgado, Rick Morgan, and Jane Sumner provided research assistance, and Bethany Nanamaker, Stephanie Dean Kearce, Lauren Webb, Dorothy Dlugolecki, Hossein Fazilatfar, Stephane Mundel, Patrick Toure, Julie-Marie Dalbello, Brandon Sibilia, Katerina Dvlishvili, Amaya Phillips, Mark Davies, Derek Quindry, and Emma Foley did judicial coding. Former Project Manager Drew Linzer provided guidance on an initial measurement model. Myungwoo Lee provided research assistance at North Dakota State University, as did Lee Cojocaru at Boston University.

At the University of North Carolina, Chapel Hill, Carolyne Barker provided invaluable assistance in writing, editing, and testing the V-Dem anchoring vignettes. Andre Assumpcao contributed analytical expertise in refining validation tests of V-Dem indices.

At Case Western Reserve University, Andrew Slivka provided critical research assistance with the development, validation, and use of the subnational indicators; Cara Brown, Lucas Flowers, Brandon Mordue, Mark Patteson, Hayley Rassuchine, Hannah Steele, and Abigail Whisler were invaluable research assistants, and the Department of Political Science and Social Justice Institute provided time and financial support to complete the work.

V-Dem and its large team have benefited from numerous grants and awards over the years that have contributed to making the project possible. Chapter 1 seeks to recognize all agencies and foundations that have provided support over the years. Special recognition is deserved by the Swedish foundation Riksbankens Jubileumsfond, which provided the team with a $5.7 million research grant as well as $1.1 million in grants in support of workshops and the research infrastructure. These grants, along with many others, have required cofunding, without which we could not have accepted them. To this end, we are grateful that University of Gothenburg's Office of the Vice Chancellor, the College of Social Sciences, and the Department of Political Science together have provided $6.5 million in cofunding and direct support to V-Dem's research infrastructure and for research.

Finally, various aspects of V-Dem examined in the following chapters have been the subject of deliberations during some 200 or more talks and workshops, occurring in countries across the world over a time span of more than a decade. Every one of these consultations has contributed to what V-Dem is today and thus to the contents of this book. We kindly ask all participants in those talks, seminars, and workshops who generously offered their critical conjectures and refutations to feel appreciated and acknowledged. We are grateful to each and every one of you who donated your time to listen, reflect, and provide your thoughts and critiques. Without you, V-Dem would not have become what it is today.

This manuscript was completed on January 30, 2019, and therefore does not reflect events that transpired after that date.

1

Introduction

*The Story of Varieties of Democracy**

Varieties of Democracy, or "V-Dem," is a global research project producing new measures of hundreds of attributes of democracy as far back as 1789 for many countries and for almost all countries around the world from 1900 to the present. This book is a reference guide for anyone who wants to use V-Dem data wisely. It provides full information about the concepts that the data measure, what we know about the validity and reliability of the data, what they reveal about the structure of democracy and the general trends in democratization over the past 229 years, and why this explosion of information is likely to raise the standards for causal inferences in democratization research. The V-Dem team and others are already producing a series of publications and papers leveraging the distinctive strengths of these new data, so this book also calls attention to some of those first fruits.

V-Dem draws on expertise and a network of several thousand scholars across almost every country on earth to examine the nature, causes, and consequences of democracy. It radically alters the way scholars can address these questions. There has always been a severe trade-off between providing detailed, rich, nuanced evidence about a few countries based on thick concepts and generalizing about many countries with thinly defined models.[1] V-Dem makes this trade-off much less severe because V-Dem data are fine grained: they

---

* The primary authors of this chapter were Michael Coppedge and Staffan I. Lindberg, with contributions from Carl Henrik Knutsen.
[1] Well-known examples of qualitative studies include Collier and Collier (1991), Diamond et al. (1989), Luebbert (1987), O'Donnell et al. (1986), Rueschemeyer et al. (1992), and innumerable case studies. Important quantitative contributions include Jackman (1973), Hannan and Carroll (1981), Bollen and Jackman (1985), Hadenius (1992), Burkhart and Lewis-Beck (1994), Przeworski and Limongi (1997), Ross (2001), Gleditsch and Ward (2006), Finkel et al. (2007), and Teorell (2010). Some scholars have also used multiple methods, fleshing out regressions with case studies or testing the conclusions of small-*N* research quantitatively in large samples (e.g., Lieberman 2005).

include hundreds of specific indicators typically measuring differences of degree that collectively depict hundreds of qualitative differences, and at the same time, the data rate most countries back to 1900 or – as is the case for 91 polities, including all large, sovereign states at the time – the late eighteenth or early nineteenth century. They therefore capture both qualitative and quantitative distinctions without sacrificing geographic or historical scope. V-Dem data thus make it possible to test general hypotheses concerning democracy quantitatively without neglecting crucial qualitative distinctions.

V-Dem is distinctive in three other respects as well. First, we recognize and respect multiple conceptions of democracy that have long and distinguished intellectual pedigrees. We therefore provide five indices of democracy – and dozens of indices of separate components of these – that are specifically designed to map onto the most prevalent theories of democracy. The core index measures electoral democracy as "polyarchy," the seminal concept defined by Robert Dahl (1971, 1989, 1998), and its seven core constitutive components.[2] The other four indices measure liberal, deliberative, participatory, and egalitarian democracy. A second distinctive feature is captured by the V-Dem slogan, "Global standards, local knowledge": we rely on more than 3000 academics and other experts to code countries. Of these, more than 64 percent of the Country Experts are nationals of or residents in the countries they code. In a real sense, each country's experts rate their own country, while at the same time, our broad concepts and complex methods to blend in-country and cross-national ratings help ensure international comparability. Finally, V-Dem is one of the very few democracy measurement programs that takes measurement error seriously. We do not pretend to have measured the attributes of democracy without error. Rather, we estimate how certain we can be about each data point, and we make this information freely available to the public.

The project is of unprecedented scope in the social sciences. The data set, which contains more than 27 million observations and continues to grow, is the world's largest data set on democracy, human rights, and civil liberties. Behind the data set is a complex research infrastructure and many years of effort by a large organization comprising (past and present) 6 Principal Investigators, 19 Project Managers, 19 Postdoctoral Research Fellows and Research Associates, 7 Program and Data Managers, many graduate and undergraduate research assistants, 37 past and present Regional Managers, more than 160 Country Coordinators, and more than 3200 Country Experts. About 20 of these people, and the data research infrastructure, are based at the V-Dem Institute at the

---

[2] In *Democracy and Its Critics*, Dahl's (1989) short list of the institutions necessary for polyarchy was elected officials, free and fair elections, inclusive suffrage, the right to run for office, freedom of expression, alternative [sources of] information, and associational autonomy (222). In *On Democracy* (Dahl 1998), he treated the right to run for office as an implicit part of "free, fair, and [now] frequent elections." He also expanded inclusive suffrage into "inclusive citizenship" (85).

University of Gothenburg, which has become the project's de facto headquarters; the rest are dispersed all over the world.

In the early years of V-Dem, the Kellogg Institute for International Studies at the University of Notre Dame was one of the two founding institutions and institutional homes for the project. It was initially responsible for data collection in the Western Hemisphere, hosted workshops, and funded many students who worked on the project, as well as one of the project coordinators. In addition, the Center for Research Computing at Notre Dame developed the research database and the web interfaces that were used from 2011 to fall 2014. As the project grew, the V-Dem Institute in Gothenburg progressively assumed responsibility for these functions and became, in effect, the headquarters for the project. Recognizing the shifting roles, in 2018, the Kellogg Institute formalized its current role as the V-Dem Regional Center in North America, which supports research projects using V-Dem data and hosts speakers and occasional conferences and workshops. V-Dem regional centers had already been established in Estonia for Eastern Europe and Russia, in Kyrgyzstan for Central Asia, in Lusaka for southern Africa, and in Portugal for Southern Europe. Our networks of Regional Managers and Country Coordinators in places like Burkina Faso, Japan, Colombia, Liberia, Mozambique, the Philippines, and South Africa are also currently working to create additional regional centers.

We believe that many users of the data will be curious about how a project of this scale came together and why it has succeeded. This chapter tells that story. In the beginning, we expected that the project could be accomplished over two to three years with a few research assistants, Excel spreadsheets, and less than $1 million. This was a miscalculation. We ended up having to create a complex research infrastructure consisting of several custom-designed web interfaces for data collection, a complex relational database for handling data, an administrative database for managing thousands of coders and hundreds of country questionnaires, a website for both internal use and social media, a custom-designed Bayesian item response theory (IRT) measurement model, many specially designed data quality control and cleaning protocols, and a V-Dem Institute with specially trained Program and Data Managers with assistants. We spent more than $4.5 million between 2010 and 2016 to make this happen, plus an additional $0.5 million for Historical V-Dem 2015–17, not counting the thousands of working hours invested by Principal Investigators, Project Managers, and associated researchers supported by their own universities.

Five main factors were responsible for V-Dem's success: timing, inclusion, deliberation, administrative centralization, and fund-raising. First, planning for V-Dem began at a time when both social scientists and practitioners were realizing that they needed better democracy measures. This made it possible to recruit collaborators and find funding. Second, the leaders of the project were always eager to expand the team to acquire whatever expertise they lacked and share credit with everyone who contributed. Third, the project leaders practiced an intensely deliberative decision-making style to ensure that all points of view were consulted and only decisions that won wide acceptance were adopted. Fourth, centralizing the execution of the agreed-upon tasks helped tremendously by streamlining processes and promoting standardization, documentation, professionalization, and coordination of a large number of intricate steps. Finally, successful fund-raising from a mix of both research foundations and bilateral and multilateral organizations has been critical.

1.1   TIMING: V-DEM EMERGED TO ADDRESS THE NEED FOR BETTER MEASURES OF DEMOCRACY

The planning for V-Dem began in 2007. Before that time, there were already hundreds of measures of democracy or aspects of democracy. Two of them – the Polity IV Index and Freedom House ratings of political rights and civil liberties – were frequently used by political scientists and practitioners who needed broad measures of democracy.[3] However, practitioners such as national development agencies, international organizations, and NGOs needed metrics for assessing the effectiveness of their democracy and governance programs, which typically target specific institutions, such as elections, the courts, legislatures, political parties, and civil society organizations. Among practitioners and government representatives outside the US, and especially in parts of the Global South, there was also some wariness about whether these measures were biased toward a US-centric understanding of democracy because they have been mostly or completely funded by US government agencies.

Social scientists also needed finer-grained measures of democracy. After several decades of quantitative research on democracy, social scientists had found several robust empirical relationships, most famously the positive association between democracy and per capita income and the "democratic peace" – the idea that democracies do not make war against other democracies. However, there were unresolved debates about why these associations existed. Does high income cause democratization (Boix and Stokes 2003)? Are rich democracies more likely to survive (Przeworski et al. 2000)? Or, is the income–democracy relationship a spurious one (Acemoglu et al. 2008)? Does democracy promote economic growth (Gerring et al. 2005)? Does democracy make states less war prone, or is the democratic peace a by-product of military alliances, trade, or other international ties (Reiter 2017)? One way to resolve such debates is to test competing hypotheses about the specific causal mechanisms that link these phenomena; but without measures of specific attributes of democracy, there was no way to perform such tests in large samples (Seawright 2007). And unlike practitioners, who tended to be interested mostly in the present and recent past, researchers needed very large

---

[3] See Chapter 6 for a more complete inventory of other democracy measures.

samples, preferably all countries, going back into history as far as possible. In addition, both practitioners and social scientists needed more transparency about how data are generated and how reliably they measure what they purport to measure (Munck and Verkuilen 2002; Trier and Jackman 2008).

The limitations of Freedom House, Polity, and other measures of democracy were widely known and often discussed among social scientists and between social scientists and practitioners. There were some efforts to produce better indices.[4] Chapters 2 and 6 describe and evaluate many of these. As the number of democracy measures proliferated, several scholars stepped forward to critique them.[5] There were also many professional conferences and panels to address these issues.[6]

The surge of democracy measurement activity by many researchers makes it hard to pinpoint the beginning of V-Dem in an unambiguous way.[7] However, a reasonable starting point is the beginning of sustained collaboration between researchers who are now among the leaders of the project. In this sense, the collaboration was sparked by 2006–7 National Research Council (NRC) consultations that concluded that no democracy indicators existed that were sufficiently fine grained and reliable to assess the impact of democracy-promotion programs. The NRC's thinking was summarized in its final report (which John Gerring coauthored): "Current aggregate national indicators of

---

[4] Bollen (1993), Vanhanen (1990), Coppedge and Reinicke (1990), Hadenius (1992), Cingranelli and Richards (2004), Gasiorowski (1996), ACLP (1997), Bernhard et al. (2001), Mainwaring et al. (2001), Altman and Pérez-Liñán (2002), Reich (2002), UNDP (2004), Bowman et al. (2005), and Coppedge et al. (2008), to name a few.

[5] For example, Beetham (1994), Collier and Levitsky (1997), Gleditsch and Ward (1997), Coppedge (1999), Bollen and Paxton (2000), Elkins (2000), Foweraker and Krznaric (2000), McHenry (2000), Beetham et al. (2001), Munck and Verkuilen (2002), Berg-Schlosser (2004), Diamond and Morlino (2005), and Hadenius and Teorell (2005).

[6] Conference on Measuring Democracy, the Hoover Institution, Stanford University, May 1988; Workshop on Indicators of Progress toward Democracy and Improved Governance, sponsored by the National Research Council, Washington, DC, May 1991; Seminar on Assessing Progress toward Democracy and Good Governance, National Research Council, Washington, DC, April 1992; panel on Concepts and Causation, co-sponsored by the Committee on Conceptual and Terminological Analysis, at the annual meeting of the American Political Science Association, Atlanta, September 1999; panel on Big Concepts and Fine-Grained Measurement at the 2000 annual meeting of the American Political Science Association, Washington, DC; Methodological Foundations for the Statistical Compendium of the Report on Democratic Development in Latin America, UNDP Regional Bureau for Latin America and the Caribbean, Inter-American Development Bank, and International IDEA, New York, NY, August 15–16, 2002; Calidad de la democracia y desarrollo humano en América Latina, sponsored by the Proyecto Estado de la Nación and the United Nations Development Program, San José, Costa Rica, February 1–2, 2002.

[7] A possible demarcation is the conversation between Lindberg, Coppedge, Teorell, and Altman in Santiago, Chile, in 2003 during a workshop on democracy co-organized by Axel Hadenius and David Altman. This was the first conversation on this topic among several of the future leaders of the V-Dem team. That conference finished with the ambiguous but still powerful idea that something had to be done, even though it was several years before anything concrete materialized.

democracy, such as Freedom House or Polity scores, are neither at the right level for identifying the impacts of particular USAID DG [democracy and governance] projects nor accurate and consistent enough to track modest or short-term movements of countries toward or away from greater levels of democracy." The group therefore advocated "developing more transparent, objective, and widely accepted indicators of changes in democratic behavior and institutions at the sectoral level" (National Research Council 2008: 4). Following up on that conclusion, the NRC and USAID asked Gerring to convene a January 27–28, 2007, workshop at Boston University to discuss whether better democracy measurement would be feasible, and if so, how it could be done. In preparation for that workshop, Gerring wrote a think piece that became the first draft of V-Dem's 2011 *Perspectives on Politics* article. Few of the workshop attendees[8] became involved in V-Dem, but the day the conference ended, Gerring and Coppedge continued the discussion in person and via email in the next months as they edited Gerring's paper. As a graduate student, Coppedge had worked as an assistant to Robert Dahl to produce a measure of polyarchy (Coppedge and Reinicke 1990) and had advocated measuring disaggregated components of democracy in order to understand its dimensions (Coppedge 1999, 2007; Coppedge et al. 2008). Almost without knowing it, the conversation shifted from a hypothetical "how would one go about this?" to something they were actually trying to do.

After a slow start refining the conceptual scheme in 2007–9, the project grew quickly. Gerring convened a second workshop at Boston University in May 2009, which included Staffan I. Lindberg and Jan Teorell, who had been part of the planning since fall 2007; and Svend-Erik Skaaning, Allen Hicken, Jeffrey Staton, and Daniel Pemstein – who had since joined the conversation – as well as Gerring and Coppedge.[9] After the second workshop, Gerring, Coppedge, Lindberg, and Teorell constituted themselves as the Principal Investigators[10] and proceeded to invite other researchers to join as "Project Managers," who would bring a combination of thematic and regional expertise to the task of writing questions for an online survey of Country Experts. By the end of 2009, Michael Bernhard, Steven M. Fish, Allen Hicken, Kelly McMann, and Pamela Paxton had become Project Managers, and later David Altman, Adam Glynn, Carl Henrik Knutsen, Daniel Pemstein, Patrick Lindenfors, Steven Wilson, and Brigitte Seim were added.[11] There was a strong feeling

---

[8] The political scientists there were Gerardo Munck, Nicholas van de Walle, Frederick Schaffer, Richard Snyder, and Jack Goldstone, in addition to Gerring and Coppedge.

[9] Other participants in that workshop were Jørgen Elklit, Aníbal Pérez-Liñán, José Antônio Cheibub, Steven Levitsky, Adil Najam, Strom Thacker, and Margaret Sarles.

[10] In early 2016, Svend-Erik Skaaning replaced Jan Teorell as a Principal Investigator. Carl Henrik Knutsen joined the Principal Investigators Board in late 2017, and Jan Teorell rejoined at the same time, bringing the number of Principal Investigators to six.

[11] Four people made contributions as Project Managers before leaving the project: Holli Semetko, Drew Linzer, Megan Reif, and Matthew Kroenig.

that this was an idea whose time had come. This feeling made busy leading scholars surprisingly eager to sign on as Project Managers; and later, helped persuade funders to support the project.

The project took off in mid-2010 with a pilot study generously supported by the Swedish Ministry of Foreign Affairs, which we named "Varieties of Democracy" in March 2011. With a few research assistants, Excel sheets, and lots of time volunteered by the core team of scholars, we managed to collect 450,000 data points covering two countries from six regions of the world. The pilot study results were presented at a workshop at University of Gothenburg on September 30, 2011, and won the first pledges of financial support for a full-scale project from the Canadian International Development Agency, its Danish counterpart DANIDA, the Swedish Ministry of Foreign Affairs, and the European Commission/DEVCO.

By January 2012, the measurement scheme and indicators were finalized, our first regular staff member Natalia Stepanova (now Operations and Outreach Manager) started, and data collection began in earnest. By the fall of 2012, we had set up an organization to collect data from most countries of the world. In fall of 2013, two years after the pilot study, data collection was complete for 100 countries, our database included some 10 million records, and we did our first serious validation exercise. We brought almost all of our Regional Managers (who helped identify Country Experts) from all over the world to Gothenburg for a week, and together with all Principal Investigators, Project Managers, and methodologists including the first two postdocs Eitan Tzelgov and Yi-ting Wang, the team inspected and evaluated these records. This important milestone led to the realization that we needed to incorporate Bayesian IRT modeling to achieve cross-country and over-time comparability. Early results were presented again at a conference on October 25, 2013, at the University of Gothenburg for a mix of donor, government, and international NGO representatives, as well as interested scholars and students. Our effort to bridge academic research and the world of practitioners has thus been an ongoing effort.

On April 14, 2014, data for 68 countries from 1900 to 2012 were released for online graphing and analysis and data for 19 additional countries followed on November 14, 2014. At the end of 2014, we had engaged with 2153 Country Experts from 163 countries. By this time, we had funds to do our first partial update covering 2013–14 for 60 countries, and by March 2015, we released the full data for 120 countries for online graphing and analysis.

We embargoed the first data set for less than a year, following conventional practices and also to give ourselves time to find and correct any mistakes. The team got the first version of the whole data set for internal use (version 3) only in April 2015. After a final year of intensive work, on January 4, 2016, all data for 172 countries (1900–2012) became available for download online, including coder-level data and updates through 2014 for 113 countries (version 5). On March 31, 2016, we released version 6 with updated data through 2015 for 76 countries, and on May 10, 2017, version 7 came out with the first full update and four countries added making a total of 177 countries with coverage from 1900 to 2016 and 16 million data points on democracy.

On April 30, 2018, version 8 was released, adding several new indicators, indices, and countries. One key addition to this version was the integration of "Historical V-Dem" data. With Historical V-Dem covering the years 1789–1920 (extending to 1920 rather than 1900 to ensure 20 years of overlap with "contemporary" V-Dem coding) for up to 91 countries, this implied extending the time series of about 200 V-Dem indicators and numerous indices back into the nineteenth and late eighteenth centuries. Historical V-Dem also added about 70 new indicators, for instance on features of the bureaucracy and the support coalitions of regimes, expanding the total number of V-Dem indicators to about 450. Finally, Historical V-Dem added several currently extinct polities, mainly preunification German and Italian states, thus bringing the total number of countries covered by V-Dem up to 201.

Work on Historical V-Dem had been going on in parallel with the processes described above, starting in 2013 with planning and discussions between Gerring, Knutsen, Skaaning, and Teorell. They soon reached out to scholars outside the current V-Dem team with particular expertise relevant for the historical data collection, namely Agnes Cornell and Daniel Ziblatt, who agreed to take part in the project. The point of departure for the "historical team" was the existing *V-Dem Codebook*, and the team held successive rounds of deliberation in order to identify which questions to omit, adjust in order to fit the historical context, or create for the historical survey. Pilot surveys were conducted on Denmark and Colombia in 2014. After revisions and obtaining funding, the expert coding started in December 2015. Simultaneously, RAs in numerous countries coded factual indicators, and the Historical V-Dem team was expanded with (in sequence) Haakon Gjerløw (PhD candidate), Tore Wig (Postdoc, later Associate Professor), Sirianne Dahlum (Researcher), and Luca J. Uberti (Researcher), all hired at the University of Oslo. Communication and coordination with other members of the V-Dem team at Gothenburg and elsewhere took place from the very beginning, and intensified as the project went along, concerning, for example, adaptation of the survey interface, data cleaning, vignette construction, integration of documentation such as the country units documents, and, adjustment of the measurement model to ensure cross-time comparability.

This collaborative effort culminated in V-Dem version 8, a data set covering 201 countries, 450 indicators, and with some time series extending from the year of the French Revolution to the present. By September 2018, users had downloaded the different versions of the V-Dem data set more than 70,000 times, the website had more than 150,000 unique users, and more than 40,000 users from 208 countries and territories had used the online analysis tools. The demand for V-Dem's new democracy indicators and indices proved to be strong.

1.2 INCLUSION

A second key to the success of the project was a commitment to expand the team to include new leaders who could bring the kinds of expertise that V-Dem needed to do the job well. Most of the added political scientists had already been making important contributions that were relevant for measuring democracy, so the growing collaboration is best seen as the merging of many separate parallel efforts, in which each participant saw an opportunity to accomplish more through their combined efforts than he or she could accomplish alone.

1.2.1 Thematic Expertise

The need for expanded expertise first arose when the Principal Investigators were defining the components of democracy and beginning to write survey questions to measure them. It is impossible for one scholar to master all of the literature on every democratic institution and process. Writing a battery of survey questions on each topic required deep knowledge of specialized literatures. Gerring and Coppedge could claim knowledge of democratic theory in general and parties and elections in particular. Lindberg brought a deeper specialization in elections, clientelism, and regime change, and Teorell had worked on executives, corruption, participation, public administration, and regime change. This was a good start, but they were less familiar with several other crucial areas of democracy. They therefore reached out to Svend-Erik Skaaning, who had recently produced an index of civil liberties (Skaaning 2008); Allen Hicken, a leading authority on political parties in Southeast Asia and co-founder of the Constituency-Level Elections Archive; and Michael Bernhard, known for his work on civil society. Bernhard also shouldered the burden of developing questions on sovereignty, a novel topic in democracy measurement. Pamela Paxton, who had published seminal work in sociology on women's suffrage and democratization and compiled her own data set on suffrage, agreed to cover inclusion and symbolic representation. Jeffrey Staton, who was already busy producing measures of judicial independence, joined the project. An expert on the media in Western Europe, Holli Semetko, helped define the media concepts to measure before Coppedge assumed responsibility for this area. Steven Fish and Matthew Kroenig, who had just published *The Handbook of National Legislatures* (2009), were the obvious choices to work on legislatures. Similarly, Kelly McMann's *Economic Autonomy and Democracy* (2006) included a set of subnational democracy indicators that she developed, which prepared her well to take the lead on subnational government. David Altman's *Direct Democracy Worldwide* (2011) was forthcoming when we belatedly realized the need to include direct democracy. Finally, although several members of the team had experience with measurement methods, the Principal Investigators chose to recruit Daniel Pemstein, who brought cutting-edge methodological expertise in democracy measurement and Bayesian statistics; Adam Glynn, a statistician with expertise on causal inference in political science; Brigitte Seim, with expertise in designing and executing social science experiments; and finally Steven Wilson, a former chief technician in Silicon Valley who switched to earn a doctorate in political science, became responsible for the V-Dem IT infrastructure.[12]

Fortunately, an early sizable research grant from the Swedish Research Council also allowed us to recruit two postdoctoral Research Fellows already in 2013 – Eitan Tzelgov and Yi-ting Wang – with training in Bayesian statistics. They were later followed by other postdocs also at the V-Dem Institute in Gothenburg who continue to be incredibly important for the project's development overall but also in particular areas: Brigitte Seim with experiments and vignettes (2014–15) and also Constanza Petrarca in the same area (2016–18); Kyle Marquardt with Bayesian measurement modeling; Anna Lührmann with policy outreach, autocratization, and the annual Democracy Report (2015–19); Rachel Sigman with new egalitarian and other indices as well as collaborations with the World Bank (2015–17); Steven Wilson on reprogramming the IT infrastructure (2016–17); Sirianne Dahlum with outreach and policy-collaborations (2017–19); and Juraj Medzihorsky, Richard Morgan, Laura Maxwell, and Matthew Wilson, who work on the new subproject *Failing and Successful Sequences of Democracy* (FASDEM).

1.2.2 Geographic Expertise

The project also needed people with expertise on world regions, which was a consideration in the recruitment of Project Managers. The team therefore included experts on Western Europe (Skaaning, Teorell, and Semetko); Eastern Europe, the former Soviet Union, and Central Asia (Fish, Bernhard, Teorell, and McMann); Latin America (Altman, Coppedge, and Staton); Africa (Lindberg); and Asia (Hicken).[13] Area expertise helped ensure that concepts and questions would be meaningful to experts in every part of the world while still capturing the essence of key democratic concepts. Fish also led the recruitment of an International Advisory Board consisting of 21 prominent democracy

---

[12] No separate Project Manager was found to cover either political equality or deliberation, so Gerring and Lindberg collaborated to define them, joined by Coppedge on deliberation. Drew Linzer, the first methodologist recruited, decided to work on other projects.

[13] For more than a year, Megan Reif shared her expertise on the Middle East and North Africa.

advocates from all regions of the world, who were invited to provide input on the *Codebook*.

We had decided that many of our specific questions would be best answered by those who know their own country best. Therefore, we committed to funders that at least 60 percent of the Country Experts would be nationals of, or residents in, the countries they coded; and that we would aim to have five experts per country. This intuition has proven to be well founded. All diagnostics we have run to date give clear evidence that Country Experts who are from the country they code are on average more reliable, higher-quality coders.

During the pilot study in 2011, we realized that the professional networks of the Principal Investigators and Project Managers were not extensive enough to identify and recruit the thousands of Country Experts who would be needed to do the online surveys.[14] We therefore recruited 37 Regional Managers – trusted researchers who had more extensive professional networks in each country in their region – and a Country Coordinator in almost every country to assist the Regional Managers with identification of locally based academic and other experts, and to answer additional questions about relatively objective topics. By fall 2013, it became clear that it would be prudent to complement the standard longitudinal coding of one country over many years with "bridge" coding (experts coding more than one country for the entire period) and "lateral" coding (of several countries in one year only), in order to enhance the cross-national comparability of the ratings. This global team soon grew to more than 3000 Country Experts. Even so, the methods team led us to also adopt the use of anchoring vignettes that all Country Experts are now asked to answer, in order to further secure cross-national comparability on all indicators and indices.

After the first waves of data collection, we needed area experts to validate the data: to compare the trends in the data to the histories of the countries they knew best in order to identify unreliable questions or coders and any problems with the research design. Principal Investigators and Project Managers did a lot of validation, and a critical stage was when we brought most Regional Managers to University of Gothenburg in October 2013 for a full week of validation exercises, and six Regional Managers or Country Coordinators to Santiago in January 2014 to review the Latin American data. Their input based on in-depth regional and local expertise led to several crucial improvements, especially lateral coding and various refinements of the measurement model. Without this, we would never have succeeded to come to where we are today.

---

[14] The Project Coordinators and research assistants at Gothenburg and Notre Dame also did online research to identify thousands of potential Country Experts, but Regional Managers were asked to sort them into three categories of priority to receive invitations.

1.3   COLLECTIVE AND DELIBERATIVE DECISION-MAKING WITH DECENTRALIZATION

Every large project undergoes growing pains, and V-Dem is no exception. At many junctures, project leaders faced pivotal decisions that would affect the quality of the data, and it was not clear how to proceed. The decision-making procedure that evolved was collective and deliberative. In each decision, there were long and sometimes hard-fought debates about what to do, many times involving Project Managers, Research Fellows, administrators, and research assistants. Many important decisions shaping the project were deliberated and decided upon at regular project meetings, starting with APSA meetings in 2009 and 2010, a workshop at the University of Notre Dame in January 2011, and an annual project meeting held at University of Gothenburg since October 2011. The Principal Investigator Board also decided many issues after extensive consultations, eventually supplemented by a larger Steering Committee.[15] Advocates of any side had to persuade three of the four members of the Board. This threshold made it necessary to think through each issue carefully and mount a persuasive case, usually supported by lengthy memos and meticulous data analysis. Whenever possible, these decisions reflected the Principal Investigators' judgments about what was likely to help the project produce the best data, even if it took more time and money. The intensely deliberative nature of the process made it more likely that the best ideas would be adopted.

At the same time, many specific decisions were decentralized, such as issues pertaining to a particular Project Manager's thematic area concerning coding rules, data cleaning and quality control, instructions to coders, usually after consultations with interested team members. In addition, the PI Board encouraged small groups to develop possible innovations for the project, such as designing and testing the measurement model, constructing indices, collecting data on direct democracy and de facto judicial institutions, designing the survey interface and the architecture of the research database, and integrating vignettes into data collection. Time after time, team members volunteered to take responsibility for developing new ideas and then proposed them to the Principal Investigators Board, or after 2015 mainly to the Steering Committee, which deliberated, provided feedback, and eventually approved.

For example, one of the lessons of early data collection was that Country Experts sometimes disagree about even seemingly objective matters such as whether a leader was head of state or head of government, or what the election date was. There was internal debate about whether the data should

---

[15] The PI board was formalized in a December 2013 memorandum of understanding among the four PIs at the time (Coppedge, Gerring, Lindberg, and Teorell), but the procedures had been basically in place since at least 2011. The Steering Committee was formed in 2015 when the V-Dem Institute had become the effective headquarters and made a research infrastructure officially instituted at the university level at Gothenburg.

reflect such disagreements, which would help us assess reliability; or whether the experts should be forced to accept our judgments about these questions. In the end we decided that such information must be centrally coded in advance to ensure that everyone was coding the same actors, institutions, and events; and that the coding interface should never allow Country Experts to change precoded data. This required very large and unplanned spending on research assistants, who had to collect all this data before surveys were made available to coders; on software development; and also a lot of effort to bring already-collected data into line with the precoded data as much as possible. It was the hardest path to take, but the argument that precoding some of the data would improve many other indicators won the day. See Chapter 3 for details.

We also learned that collection of factual data, and the crosschecking of Country Expert ratings needed to be centralized to assure consistency. Initially we divided these tasks among research assistants (RAs) at various universities where team members were based. This resulted in two problems. Most RAs work for professors a semester or two. Constantly retraining people to collect data was not very efficient and made it hard to maintain high quality. In addition, data ended up not being consistent. Slight nuances in interpretation of coding rules and use of sources resulted in incongruences, such as data for legislatures that the elections coding said did not exist, and the reverse. In the end, it turned out to be advantageous to centralize (almost) all coding of factual data at the V-Dem Institute, University of Gothenburg, with the major exceptions of the many indicators of direct democracy produced by Altman in Chile and the indicators of de jure judicial institutions by Staton at Emory University. Another exception was the collection of factual data for Historical V-Dem, where most (though far from all) data collection took place at Aarhus University, Boston University, Lund University, or the University of Oslo, always with close supervision by (at least) one of the Historical V-Dem team members located at these respective institutions.

Another issue was how to combine the scores from multiple Country Experts into a single point estimate for each country-year on each indicator. In very early discussions the team considered a simple mean or median, with a confidence interval. (In fact, the mean is still included in the data set for download.) From mid-2011 to fall 2013, we adopted a "linear opinion pool" formula recommended by Drew Linzer, which was easy to calculate but unable to incorporate any information about the data-generating process other than the raw scores and the confidence of the Country Experts.[16] A face validation exercise of some 6 million data points, spanning almost a week in 2013 and involving 26 of our 37 Regional Managers on site at University of Gothenburg also revealed that the method too frequently provided inaccurate measures. The team invited Daniel Pemstein to develop an appropriate Bayesian IRT-based measurement model for our data. Fortunately, a grant won by Teorell and

---

[16] Linzer was V-Dem's chief methodologist from March 2011 to December 2012.

Lindberg made it possible to recruit the two postdoctoral fellows to execute this task: Eitan Tzelgov and Yi-ting Wang. Both had training in Bayesian statistics and some experience with IRT models. Tzelgov and Wang spent almost all their time during one and a half years working on the model to produce the first version of the data set. In 2015, we then recruited Kyle Marquardt as a research fellow to continue the work, alongside Farhad Miri, a Microfinance MA, as Data Manager. Farhad was followed by a young professional with very impressive programming skills, Joshua Krusell (assisted by Johannes von Römer), who in 2015 reprogrammed the entire data curation process to make it secure and quality controlled and to minimize human error. The model underwent repeated improvements that had to be explained and approved at each stage: incorporating lateral coding, varying coder thresholds, country thresholds, serially dependent errors, confidence ratings, vignettes, and others. There was ample discussion about each of these that led to testing of ideas from various team members – methodologists, Research Fellows, Principal Investigators, and Project Managers. See Chapter 4 for details.

Still, there has been considerable debate within the project about the best way to summarize the measurement model estimates. Eventually we decided that different versions are better for different purposes and that all versions should be made available. Therefore, the data for download by default include four different versions of the expert-coded indicators (means, relative scale, original scale, and ordinalized scores), three of which also have the equivalent of confidence intervals. Both the relative and original scale versions are available for online graphing. See Chapter 4 for details. Ultimately, however, the best version is a sample of 900 posterior estimates for each variable for each country-year. Although there is little precedent for making such a large version of the data set available online, V-Dem arranged to post it in the CurateND archive https://curate.nd.edu as well as at the Swedish National Data archive (https://snd.gu.se/en) along with the complete raw coder-level data. See Chapter 7 for details. Moreover, so that published analyses will always be replicable, all current and previous versions of the data are archived there. We doubt that any scholar acting alone would have decided to go to the trouble of posting so many versions of the data in so many ways, at considerable effort and expense. The consensual nature of the decision-making, however, created incentives to prefer maximum transparency and utility for users.

A third example of deliberative decision-making concerned the anonymity of the Country Experts. Although many of them would like public credit for their role (and many of them claim it on their CVs), those in some countries such as China, Russia, or the Gulf States would risk persecution or intimidation if their identities were known. The Principal Investigators considered publicly crediting experts in some countries but not others, or allowing them to "opt in" to public recognition. In the end the board decided that the only way to protect the anonymity of some coders, and to comply with Swedish and European Union privacy laws and Notre Dame's Institutional Review Board, was to protect the anonymity of all of them. We therefore increased these protections so that all the data in the research database is now anonymized. Identities are only known to a handful of team members with cleared access.[17]

The longest debate within the project concerned formulas for aggregating indicators into indices to measure the most general components and varieties of democracy. Some question whether it should be done at all, as the most disaggregated indicators contain the most fine-grained information, so each successive level of aggregation sacrifices more potentially useful information. (See Chapter 5 on this point.) In the end, the project has produced indices because scholars and the public, including funders, expect it; and because if it has to be done, V-Dem should provide as much guidance as possible. Nevertheless, the theoretical guidance about how to do it is often rather weak. As a result, the more members of the team deliberated about formulas, the more options there were to choose from – actually more possible formulas than participants. The aggregation formulas V-Dem uses are compromises that balance theoretical rationales with face validity and parsimony. The Principal Investigators and Project Managers have modified them before and could modify them again, but the similarities between versions (for example, as measured by correlations between successive versions of the same index) have become greater and greater in each iteration, and the differences are now miniscule. See Chapter 5 for details.

Finally, debates within the team have tended to raise the standards for causal inference. Researchers on the team came to the project with different levels and different kinds of methodological skills. Interacting frequently has exposed all of us to reasoning and techniques that were unfamiliar to some and awakened many of us to unimagined possibilities. Faced with some of the most abundant data in political science, it becomes obvious that it is no longer good enough to report significant associations among variables: there are so many significant relationships that mere statistical significance is now a low bar for drawing conclusions. Making causal claims requires wrestling with all of the problems inherent in panel data – multicollinearity, serial, and spatial autocorrelation, lag structures, and so on – as well as more general threats to inference such as unmeasured confounders or reverse causality. Struggling to make causal claims with observational data is especially important in the wake of the potential outcomes critique of conventional social science. Adam Glynn became a Project Manager specifically to help address this concern, and others such as Brigitte Seim and Kyle Marquardt have since nudged the team in this direction. The collaborative nature of the project has pushed the team toward ever-more

---

[17] The exception is Country Experts for Historical V-Dem, where the above discussed calculus differs due to experts coding a less politically sensitive period of time (e.g., 1789–1920). However, historical Country Experts had the option to be anonymous, although very few chose this option.

rigorous methods; and subsequent analyses learn from and build on the best practices of preceding papers. Chapter 7 elaborates on this point.

1.4 PROFESSIONALIZATION

At the beginning of V-Dem, many of us had run conventional research projects involving some collaborators, a few research assistants, and the creation of data sets. Several had also done field surveys in which one trains and oversees around 20 temporary assistants. But none of us had an idea of what was going to be needed. Handling the recruitment and administration of some 100 Country Experts for the pilot study could be done via our own networks, a couple of dedicated research assistants, some Excel sheets, and a simple database and web interfaces, but scaling up to what became 25,000 potential experts in our database and more than 3000 active Country Experts from more than 180 countries was a much greater challenge.

Fortunately Coppedge, especially in the first phase, could allocate a lot of his time to V-Dem. Support from the Kellogg Institute and other bodies at the University of Notre Dame gave him course reductions in 2010–11 and substantial funding for software development and a research assistant. Critically, this meant that the Center for Computing Research (CRC) at Notre Dame programmed a PostgreSQL database for us, and the initial website and coding interfaces so that we could use a prototype of online coding even during the pilot study. CRC continued to develop and improve these tools on a small budget from early 2011 until spring 2014. However, the software development process was always chaotic. Because V-Dem's requirements were constantly evolving and there was never enough funding or personnel available to accomplish everything that needed to be done, this software was always buggy. As the scale of the project increased, the demands outstripped what CRC could provide. Therefore, in fall 2014 the project contracted a private IT firm in Chicago, Imaginary Landscape, to rework the website and interfaces, fix bugs and security flaws, and make the site run faster. The large grants brought in to the V-Dem Institute at University of Gothenburg by Lindberg at this time, and huge efforts by Natalia Stepanova, made this possible. The streamlined site went live in May 2015. By a strategic recruitment, beginning in fall 2016, a new Postdoctoral Research Fellow, Steven Wilson, who had extensive Silicon Valley experience, joined the V-Dem Institute and began rebuilding all of the software from the ground up. This made an enormous difference and finally our systems were "up to snuff." Regarding tasks that were specific to Historical V-Dem, the efforts and programming skills of Tore Wig and, especially, Haakon Gjerløw at the University of Oslo were critical for automating various tasks related to data cleaning, validation, facilitating communication with historical Country Experts, etc., thus making the enterprise of collecting historical data feasible.

For V-Dem more generally, it was also critical that preparations for actual data collection coincided with Lindberg's arrival at the University of

Gothenburg in May 2010 on an essentially teaching-free position spanning four years, so he could soon work nearly full-time on V-Dem. Lindberg had unusually extensive experience organizing a large music festival, the youth conference Next Stop Soviet in 1989, and a stage manager and producer of plays, television shows, and film.

In 2012, the V-Dem Institute, which is now the headquarters of the larger Varieties of Democracy project, was founded at the University of Gothenburg. Growing funding made it possible to hire Natalia Stepanova (Operations and Outreach Manager) and Josefine Pernes (Program and Financial Manager). They were soon joined by other extremely dedicated young professionals: Vlad Ciobanu, Valeriya Mechkova, Frida Andersson, and, finally, Talib Jabbar, who was based at Lund University with Teorell, followed by Laura Saxer and then Moa Ohlin. In 2015, the Institute hired Anna Lührmann as postdoctoral research fellow, who added to the work on policy analysis and collaboration with practitioners and intergovernmental organizations, who now include UNDP, European Commission, Swedish Ministry of Foreign Affairs, International IDEA, the Community of Democracies, the B-Team, USAID, Article 19, and the Mo Ibrahim Foundation, among others. Rachel Sigman also joined as Postdoctoral Fellow to work on index construction and quality control, as well as the collaborations with the World Bank. In 2017 Sirianne Dahlum joined as postdoctoral research fellow, after having worked as a researcher at the University of Oslo with validation of the Historical V-Dem data, to assist on the work with outreach to the policy-practitioners community and the general public with her background as a journalist. Gradually a team formed to handle the task of sustaining not only the massive data collection effort, but also a larger organization to plan conferences; handle social media; administer grants and contracts; edit working papers, country reports, thematic reports, and briefing papers; produce weekly online graphs; communicate with practitioners and train outside organizations; build specialized indices; among other work.

We soon realized that greater organization was badly needed as the number of potential and actual coders, Regional Managers, and Country Coordinators grew. In 2012, we calculated that just registering new coders, assigning them to surveys, and sending them an initial message with coding instructions was taking 15 minutes per coder, which amounted to almost 16 weeks of full-time work for the then anticipated 2500 coders. What is more, each expert had a unique combination of assignments to specific surveys for individual countries. The staff had to keep track of their progress and the records of communication with each, modify which surveys they could code, provide them with instructions and answer their questions, collect their payment information, obtain tax clearances, and take care of many other small issues. Just for the initial phase this meant more than 30,000 emails as well as uncountable phone and Skype conversations. We therefore worked with a professional company (Premium Systems) in Sweden to develop an administrative database with some 50 custom-designed interfaces that interact smoothly with the administrative database and make it possible to keep identifying information about the coders separate from the research data.

We also had to institutionalize our handling of the "big data." In the first years of data collection, Coppedge was able to do the interactions with the research database that did not require CRC involvement: uploading precoded data, querying the database, extracting data and converting it to Stata files, and correcting errors. However, as the amount of data grew and when the project began using a measurement model, this kind of work became too demanding for a professor with many other responsibilities. V-Dem Institute staff learned to work with the research database from Gothenburg using PGAdmin and FileMakerPro software in order to implement the complex data cleaning and quality control protocols. By fall 2013, Tzelgov and Wang began to help develop and run the measurement model and produce the eventual data sets. Seim joined in 2014 to design and execute the anchoring vignettes project and a series of experiments designed to validate specific aspects of the V-Dem project. By January 2015, Miri and then Joshua Krusell assisted by Johannes von Römer, as Data Managers, began to handle most of the work with the database. Joshua Krusell also came with very advanced programming skills in several languages. This work included extracting the raw data, preparing it, running the measurement model, and creating the different versions of the V-Dem data set. Working with IT specialist and programmer Steven Wilson who joined as a postdoctoral research fellow in 2016 and a Project Manager in 2017, their combined expertise meant that innumerable steps and procedures that had been done manually were automated and reprogrammed. Finally, Marquardt began to work on further developments of the IRT measurement model in August 2015, and Postdoctoral Research Fellow Constanza Petrarca joined in August 2016 to work on the implementation of vignettes and experiments to give us more information about various aspects of Country Expert coding.

This expansion and recruitment of permanent staff to take care of the daily operations – talented and extremely loyal young professionals – was absolutely critical. This team at the V-Dem Institute has also developed and driven the institutionalization of our operations in innumerable ways. They have been, and are critical to V-Dem's development and existence.

I.5 FUNDING

As of the release of version 8 of the data in April 2018, the Varieties of Democracy project has raised $26.88 million in funding, divided between support for building the complex research infrastructure and data collection at $6.0 million, resources for research at $13.3 million, other activities ($1 million) and co-funding from the University of Gothenburg ($6.6 million) and others. Compared to conventional political science research projects, it is expensive, and it cost several times more than we first anticipated. However, considered as a basic research project mobilizing thousands of experts in nearly every country in the world to provide 27 million data points across 450 specific indicators and more than 50 indices that can be used freely across the sciences to investigate innumerable research questions, the costs are understandable. If this project had been carried out by an international organization or a consulting firm, it would have been costlier by orders of magnitude. Just salaries paid to staff and postdocs in an academic setting are several times lower than what professionals typically earn. Critically, most of the research time for professors in the project is already paid for by their universities and is thus not included in the sum above.

By 2010, V-Dem faced a catch-22: potential funders understandably wanted a demonstration of the quality of the data before investing; yet the project could not produce data without funding. The US government has never paid for any of the data collection and, in fact, was tightening NSF funding for political science at the time we sought it.[18] Fortunately, the funding environment for social science was very favorable in Europe, particularly the Nordic countries; and especially Lindberg succeeded in establishing valuable contacts and attracting funding. Table 1.1 itemizes the funding V-Dem has received.

Teorell and Lindberg secured the first grant from the Ministry of Foreign Affairs, Sweden, to run the pilot study. The results were presented to a larger group of mainly European donor organizations, government representatives, and international NGOs at a workshop at University of Gothenburg on September 30, 2011. At the end of the workshop, pledges of financial support for a full-scale project were first made by the Canadian International Development Agency, followed by the Danish development agency DANIDA, the Swedish Ministry of Foreign Affairs, and the European Commission/DEVCO.

By the fall of 2012, additional grants meant we could set up an organization to collect data from most countries of the world. These included funds from the Danish Research Council to Skaaning at Aarhus University, the Quality of Government Institute, a Research Council of Norway funded project run by Håvard Hegre at the University of Oslo, as well as co-funding from University of Notre Dame, and the University of Gothenburg. Riksbankens Jubileumsfond in Sweden also contributed to support the building of our global team of Regional Managers and Country Coordinators by funding a series of workshops around the world to train as many of them as possible face-to-face.

---

[18] Senator Tom Coburn was trying to end National Science Foundation funding for political science at this time, and during protracted interventions in Iraq and Afghanistan, the mood in Washington shifted against projects related to state building or democracy promotion. In the end, the Coburn Amendment failed in cutting off political science funding but succeeded in constraining the topics that were eligible.

TABLE 1.1 *Funding for the Varieties of Democracy project*

Funding source, by recipient institution	Data infrastructure	Research programs	Other/policy consultancy	Co-funding	Year awarded	Principal investigator(s)
V-Dem Institute, University of Gothenburg						
Ministry for Foreign Affairs, Sweden	$229,500				2011	Lindberg & Teorell
Riksbankens Jubileumsfond	$16,065				2011	Lindberg
Riksbankens Jubileumsfond	$43,605				2011	Lindberg
Canadian International Development Agency	$128,221				2012	Lindberg
University of Aarhus/Danish Research Council	$237,303				2012	Skaaning
European Commission/DEVCO	$638,316				2012	Lindberg
Ministry of Foreign Affairs, Denmark	$198,900				2012	Lindberg
Riksbankens Jubileumsfond	$227,205				2012	Lindberg
Quality of Government Institute, University of Gothenburg, Sweden	$32,130				2012	Lindberg
Swedish Research Council		$1,040,400			2012	Lindberg & Teorell
Wallenberg Academy Fellow, Knut & Alice Wallenberg Foundation		$1,147,500			2013	Lindberg
Riksbankens Jubileumsfond	$918,000				2013	Lindberg
Ministry for Foreign Affairs, Sweden		$5,752,800			2013	Lindberg
Swedish Research Council		$2,520,000			2014	Lust & Lindberg

(continued)

Source						Year	PI
International IDEA/Ministry for Foreign Affairs, Sweden	$310,611					2014	Lindberg
University of Aarhus/Danish Research Council	$51,840					2015	Skaaning
European Commission/DEVCO	$571,655					2015	Lindberg
Fundação Francisco Manuel dos Santos, Portugal	$29,988					2015	Fernandes & Lindberg
International IDEA/Ministry for Foreign Affairs, Sweden	$146,458					2015	Lindberg
Marcus & Marianne Wallenberg Foundation	$556,800					2016	Lindberg
Mo Ibrahim Foundation	$219,000					2016	Lindberg
Riksbankens Jubileumsfond	$849,120					2016	Pernes
Swedish Research Council	$432,000					2017	Lindberg
European Research Council (FASDEM)		$2,160,000				2017	Lindberg
Riksbanken Jubileumsfond (V-Aut conference)			$29,700			2017	Lührmann
World Bank I			$14,235			2016	Lindberg
World Bank II			$40,390			2016	Lindberg
World Bank III			$120,590			2017	Lindberg & Sigman
B-Team			$24,800			2017	Lindberg
NORC/USAID			$278,472			2018	Seim
Swedish Research Council			$506,000			2018	Lührmann
University of Gothenburg				$6,558,980	$6,558,980	2011–2018	Lindberg
Subtotal	$58,36,717	$12,620,700	$1,014,187	$6,558,980	$6,558,980		

(continued)

TABLE 1.1 (continued)

Funding source, by recipient institution	Data infrastructure	Research programs	Other/policy consultancy	Co-funding	Year awarded	Principal investigator(s)
University of Notre Dame						
Kellogg Institute		$304,049		$12,000	2012	Coppedge
University of Oslo	$111,183				2012	Hegre & Coppedge
University of Notre Dame	$81,221				2011	Coppedge
Andrónico Luksic Grants Program		$10,000			2013	Coppedge
Pan-American Development Foundation, to Initiative for Global Development, University of Notre Dame		$44,752			2016	Coppedge
Subtotal	$192,404	$358,801		$12,000		
Other						
Nucleus for the Study of Stateness and Democracy in Latin America		$10,000			2013	Altman
National Science Foundation (US), to N. Dakota SU, Boston U, U of Notre Dame		$277,000			2014	Pemstein, Gerring, & Coppedge
Subtotal		$287,000				
Totals by category	$6,029,121	$13,266,501	$10,14,187	$6,570,980		
GRAND TOTAL	$26,880,789					

Note: This overview does not include grants that are specific to Historical V-Dem. Some figures in USD are approximate. Most funding was denominated in SEK or Euro. Exchange rate has been calculated as of the year each grant was awarded, even if many of them extend over several years.

From 2013, we started source funding for annual updates. The University of Gothenburg decided to provide very important direct support at this point; the European Commission/DEVCO gave us a five year grant; the Swedish Ministry of Foreign Affairs renewed their support; agreements with International IDEA, the Marcus & Marianne Wallenberg Foundation, Fundação Francisco Manuel dos Santos in Portugal, and another contract to Skaaning at Aarhus University provided important contributions. The Andrónico Luksic Grants Program and the Nucleus for the Study of Stateness and Democracy in Latin America supported a collaboration between the University of Notre Dame and the Pontifical Catholic University of Chile for a workshop in Santiago. Agreements with the Mo Ibrahim Foundation support data collection in Africa; the World Bank for additional data collection for the World Development Report 2017, and a project on exclusion. Thus total funding for building the complex research infrastructure and collecting data through 2020, including the completed and planned updates, amounts to more than $6 million.

We also received funding for research that supplemented the data collection funds in important ways. Teorell and Lindberg won the first from the Swedish Research Council in 2012 that critically allowed us to hire the first postdocs at the University of Gothenburg and a full-time research assistant at Lund University. The largest grant came from Riksbankens Jubileumsfond providing funds over six years (2014–19) and the basis for our extensive collaborations within the team. This grant also came with substantial co-funding from the University of Gothenburg. At the same time, Lindberg won another personal research grant, the Wallenberg Academy Fellowship (2014–18), making our experiments and vignettes in particular, possible. The University of Gothenburg and the Kellogg Institute again provided co-funding. Finally, a large 10-year grant from the Swedish Research Council brought Ellen Lust to the University of Gothenburg on permanent basis. Part of that grant funds V-Dem's four PhD students: Felix Dwinger, Berker Y. Kavasoglu, Valeriya Mechkova, and Marcus Tannenberg, who as part of their program also assist with policy-practitioner outreach, data curation, and quality control. In terms of research support, we have thus secured over $13 million.

The funding for the Historical V-Dem data collection and related research, e.g., focusing on the effects of various aspects of democracy and other institutions on patterns of economic development, also comes from different sources. The main funding contributions come from two grants won by the two PIs of Historical V-Dem, Knutsen and Teorell, from, respectively, the Norwegian and Swedish Research Councils. However, grants won by Svend-Erik Skaaning and Daniel Ziblatt also contributed to data collection, and additional funding from the University of Oslo financed Haakon Gjerløw's PhD. In total, the funding received for Historical V-Dem data collection and related research amounts to about $2 million.

Finally, we have also started to attract funding to additional research projects that are outgrowths of V-Dem but falls within the umbrella of V-Dem writ large. The European Research Council awarded Lindberg a Consolidator Grant (2017–21) for the *Failing and Successful Sequences of Democratization*-project involving Adam Glynn, Mathew Wilson, Patrik Lindenfors, Richard Morgan, Laura Maxwell, Juraj Medzihorsky, and Joshua Krusell; and other funders have provided seed funding for *Varieties of Autocracy*-project led by Anna Lührmann, as well as the *Varieties of Future* project led by Steven Wilson and Richard Morgan.

Successful fund-raising has rested, directly and indirectly, on vigorous outreach to the policy community. Examples of outreach that has led to collaboration on data collection are listed in Chapter 3. Following is a list of some other significant work with NGOs, international organizations, and development agencies.

- A principal vehicle for us is the annual Policy Dialogue Day held in May every year (and since 2017 in collaboration with the Quality of Government Institute, the Governance and Local Development Program, and the Uppsala Conflict Database Program). This event actively fosters direct dialogue between leading scholars on democracy, governance, development, and conflict, and policy makers and practitioners in these areas. In 2018, the dialogue day had more than 200 participants from more than 50 organizations, such as the World Bank, UNDP, Transparency International, IFES, several ministries of foreign affairs, and development cooperation organizations.
- We are collaborating with Bibliotheca Alexandrina since 2015 on democracy analysis, training, and political stability.
- We are conducting capacity building trainings for NGOs, young researchers and partner organizations. For instance, in cooperation with IDEA in July 2015 we led a workshop in Fiji for a large number of organizations from Melanesia on how to measure democratic progress in the region. We are also conducting statistical training on quantitative research methods and how to use the V-Dem online analysis tools and data; the first one was held in Alexandrina, Egypt in October 2015.
- We have presented V-Dem and our methodology with emerging results at more than 400 workshops, conferences, and talks across the world for international organizations, NGOs, bilateral organizations, and institutes and universities.
- The team has also had direct interaction and often substantial exchange with, for example: Article 19, European Partnership for Democracy (EPD), OECD/DAC, Fordi, UN Democracy Fund, USAID, the European Endowment for Democracy, Transparency International, Global Integrity, the Foundation for International Relations and Foreign Dialogue (Fride), Carnegie Endowment for International Peace,

United Nations Research Institute for Social Development (UNRISD), the Netherlands Institute for Multiparty Democracy (NIMD), the African Institute for Economic Development and Planning (IDEP), the World Bank Collaboration on International ICT Policy in East and Southern Africa (CIPESA), the National Endowment for Democracy (NED), the United Nations Capital Development Fund (UNCDF), the Department of Foreign Affairs and Trade/Australian Aid, Zambia National Women's Lobby, Foundation for Democratic Process/Zambia, Swiss Peace Foundation, the International Forum for Democratic Studies, German Development Institute, GIZ, CARE/DK, IBIS/DK, ONE, and many more.

Because most of the funding has been awarded to Lindberg as the Principal Investigator and administered by the University of Gothenburg, the V-Dem Institute there became the dominant institutional home for V-Dem and eventually turned into its headquarters, where also the annual academic V-Dem conference as well as the annual Policy Dialogue Day are held.

1.6 PLAN OF THE BOOK

Chapter 2 provides the conceptual rationale for the project. Although there were already many democracy measures, they oversimplified this complex concept. Our approach recognizes several competing visions of what democracy is and holds that the only way to measure them well is to break them down into much more specific components. This chapter therefore situates our project within democratic theory and begins to connect conceptualization to measurement.

Chapter 3 describes how the project collects data, emphasizing the kinds of expertise it has relied on and the practical lessons learned about managing the first "big data" democracy project.

Chapter 4 explains the intricate process that translates the 15 million coder-level ratings into the country-date ratings that most users are downloading or graphing online. Central to this process is a sophisticated Bayesian latent variable measurement model that utilizes several innovations. We strongly recommend that users of the data read this chapter to get a sound understanding of how the data were generated.

After generating point estimates for the disaggregated indicators, however, we reaggregate them into more general components and indices of the different V-Dem. Chapter 5 provides the rationale for each of the most general indices, contrasts them, and discusses the trade-off between having a small number of general indices and having a large number of specific measures.

Chapter 6 reveals the substantive similarities and difference between V-Dem measures and more familiar measures, including more Polity and Freedom House. Our many fine-grained measures shed light on which attributes of democracy these alternatives capture well and which they tend to overlook. The chapter also highlights the consequences of these measurement choices for research on the causes and consequences of democracy.

Chapter 7, the final chapter, offers advice on how users can get the most out of V-Dem data. Many researchers are familiar with some of the specification and estimation issues that can arise with panel data, but the magnitude of our data set – the hundreds of variables, the large number of countries, and the long time series – makes it imperative to deal with all these issues responsibly. This chapter will help researchers avoid common mistakes. It also makes users aware of the opportunity to incorporate measurement uncertainty into their models – a degree of rigor that is not possible with other democracy data sets.

2

Conceptual Scheme[*]

Conceptualization stands prior to quantification, Sartori (1970) advises. This requires us to define what we mean by democracy before we try to measure it.

We begin with the term itself, which might seem trivial. However, the two most frequently used empirical measures of democracy, the Polity2 Index (from the Polity IV project) and the Political Rights and Civil Liberties indices (from Freedom House), are meant to capture authority structures and human rights, respectively.[1] Strictly speaking, they are not indices of democracy at all, even though they are commonly regarded as such.

The Varieties of Democracy project has been oriented around the key word *democracy* from the very beginning. Accordingly, before developing the indicators for this project we spent a good deal of time considering how this term should be understood. Defined in a very general way, democracy means *rule by the people*. This common understanding has a heritage stretching back to the classical age (Dunn 2005; Held 2006). Beyond this core element there is great debate, however. The debate concerns both descriptive and normative aspects of the concept, i.e., what political regimes are and what they ought to be. Within the sphere of social science, democracy is perhaps the archetypal "contested concept" (Gallie 1956: 169; Collier et al. 2006).

While freedom and equality are generally regarded as the primary values associated with democracy – both in antiquity and in modernity (Hansen 1989; Kelsen 1930; Munck 2016) – these concepts are themselves contested. At a lower level of abstraction, a wide variety of attributes are associated with the concept of democracy. A short list would include elections, civil society engagement, public deliberation, checks and balances, majority rule, economic

---

[*] The lead authors of this chapter are John Gerring and Svend-Erik Skaaning, with contributions from David Altman, Michael Bernhard, Michael Coppedge, Carl-Henrik Knutsen, Staffan I. Lindberg, Kelly McMann, and Jan Teorell.

[1] On the conceptual origins of the Polity project, see Eckstein and Gurr (1975).

equality, and individual rights. Some of these features tend to go hand in hand, while others do not and may even stand in direct contrast to each other. Consequently, it matters a great deal which elements are chosen for inclusion in an index that purports to measure democracy.

As an initial example, let us consider the well-traveled Polity2 Index. Polity2 rates the US as fully democratic (by common interpretation) throughout the twentieth century and much of the nineteenth century. This is a fair conclusion if one's definition of democracy focuses solely on electoral contestation (and checks on executive power, which Polity2 weighs heavily). However, Polity2 disregards the composition of the electorate – from which women, most blacks, and many poor people were excluded (Keyssar 2000; Paxton 2000). If one considers the history of suffrage to be a key element of democracy, the US does not appear highly democratic until the last third of the twentieth century, after the passage of the Nineteenth Amendment (the extension of suffrage to women) in 1920 and the Voting Rights Act of 1965 (assuring suffrage rights to African Americans in the South).[2]

Evidently, any attempt to measure democracy is dependent upon an author's understanding of "democracy." Since there are multiple ways of conceiving democracy – all of which resonate in some fashion with the core meaning of *rule by the people* (Cunningham 2002; Held 2006; Møller and Skaaning 2013) – there is no apparent way to resolve this definitional conundrum to everyone's satisfaction. Naturally, one can always impose a particular definition, insist that *this* is democracy, and then proceed blithely to the task of measurement. But this is unlikely to convince anyone not predisposed to the author's point of view.

V-Dem embraces multiple meanings of democracy. This is our fundamental point of departure and, at a conceptual level, what distinguishes the project from others. At the same time, we recognize that the number of meanings associated with the concept of democracy is not infinite. Our reading of the voluminous literature on the subject suggests the existence of seven traditions centered on distinct values – *electoral, liberal, majoritarian, consensual, participatory, deliberative,* and *egalitarian.* These principles, summarized in Table 2.1, define seven "varieties of democracy." Together, they offer a fairly comprehensive accounting of the concept of democracy as used in the world today.

We begin this chapter by laying out the seven principles. These principles constitute the foundation for our thinking about democracy and, accordingly, for our measures of democracy. Next, we show how this seven-part framework fits into our overall thinking about democracy, including multiple levels of disaggregation – to components, subcomponents, and indicators. The final

---

[2] Similar challenges could be levied against other indices that focus narrowly on the electoral properties of democracy without adequate attention to suffrage. For example, the democracy-dictatorship index developed by Alvarez et al. (1996) does not take it into account at all, and Vanhanen (1997) uses turnout rates to proxy the extension of suffrage.

TABLE 2.1 *Principles of democracy*

I. Electoral	V. Participatory
• *Question*: Are important government offices filled by free and fair multiparty elections before a broad electorate? • *Core Values*: Contestation/competition. • *Attributes*: Inclusive suffrage, clean elections, elected officials, freedom of association, freedom of expression, and alternative information.	• *Question*: Do citizens participate in political decision-making? • *Core Values*: Direct, active participation in decision-making by the people. • *Attributes*: High turnout, mechanisms of direct democracy, civil society activism, local democracy.
II. Liberal	**VI. Deliberative**
• *Question*: Is power constrained and are individual rights guaranteed? • *Core Values*: Individual liberty, checks and balances, constitutionalism. • *Attributes*: Civil liberties, judicial independence, legislative independence.	• *Question*: Are political decisions the product of public deliberation based on reasoned and rational justification? • *Core Values*: Reasoned debate and rational arguments, consultation. • *Attributes*: Public debate, respectful, open-minded discussions, reasoned justification with reference to the public good, consultative institutions.
III. Majoritarian	**VII. Egalitarian**
• *Question*: Does the majority rule via one party, and does it dominate policy making? • *Core Values*: Majority rule, power concentration, efficient decision-making, responsible party government. • *Attributes*: Power-concentrating institutions, power-centralizing institutions, simple majority decision-making.	• *Question*: Are all citizens equally capable to use their political rights? • *Core Values*: Equal political capabilities. • *Attributes*: Equal protection of rights and freedoms, equal distribution of politically relevant resources equal access to power.

IV. Consensual

• *Question*: Do numerous, independent, and diverse groups and institutions participate in policy making?
• *Core Values*: Voice and representation of all groups, power dispersion, power sharing.
• *Attributes*: Power-dispersing institutions, power decentralizing institutions, supermajority decision-making.

section of the chapter discusses several important caveats and clarifications pertaining to this ambitious taxonomic exercise.

2.1   THE ELECTORAL PRINCIPLE

The *electoral* principle of democracy focuses on the role of elections as a mechanism for making rulers responsive (and/or accountable) to citizens.[3] In the V-Dem conceptual scheme, this principle is captured by Robert A. Dahl's (1971, 1989, 1998) concept of "polyarchy."[4] Dahl (1971: 3) originally conceived eight requirements or institutional guarantees. In later work, these were whittled down to seven (Dahl 1989: 221) and eventually to six (Dahl 1998: 85–86): elected officials; free, fair, and frequent elections; and, to ensure that elections are free and fair, freedom of expression, access to alternative sources of information, associational autonomy, and inclusive citizenship.[5] Since freedom of expression and alternative sources of information are virtually indistinguishable we collapse these features into five core attributes, as follows:[6]

1 *Elected officials*. Legislation and government power is vested in officials elected by citizens.
2 *Clean elections*. Elected officials are chosen in frequent and fairly conducted elections in which coercion is comparatively uncommon.
3 *Freedom of expression and alternative sources of information*. Citizens have a right to express themselves without danger of severe punishment on political matters broadly defined, including criticism of officials, the government, the regime, the socioeconomic order, and the prevailing ideology. Furthermore, citizens have a right to seek out alternative and independent

---

[3] Although elections of representatives played no part in the original democracy of ancient Athens (which selected most officials by drawing lots), they have been an essential practice in practically all democratic and proto-democratic polities larger than small towns since the Roman Republic, with increasing extensions of the suffrage.

[4] Dahl (1971: 9) distinguished between democracy and polyarchy because he wanted to reserve the former concept for an ideal, unachievable fulfilling all of his demanding criteria for a democratic process and the latter for the institutional arrangements that can be considered an imperfect approximation of the ideal. Note, furthermore, that following Dahl (1971: 10–14), our conception of electoral democracy/polyarchy is only concerned with political institutions at national levels and does not take into consideration the degree of regional or local level democracy.

[5] The two requirements included in the first conception but missing in the last (compare Dahl 1971 and Dahl 1998) are "Eligibility for public office" and "Institutions for making government policies depend on votes and other expressions of preference." We agree with Dahl that these could be omitted, the first on the one hand because eligibility and suffrage tend to go hand in hand (see Coppedge and Reinicke 1990: 53), and on the other because several of the aspects of "Freedom of organization," such as freedom to organize political parties and for them to run in elections, capture much of the eligibility criteria. The second can be dropped because it is more of a summary proxy for all the other institutional requirements taken together, and not the least by the mechanism of free, fair, and regular multiparty elections.

[6] Note that we have kept some of Dahl's formulations in the specification of attributes.

sources of information from other citizens, experts, newspapers, magazines, books, telecommunications, and the like. Moreover, alternative sources of information actually exist that are not under the control of the government or any other single political group attempting to influence public political briefs and attitudes.

4 *Freedom of association.* To achieve their various rights, including those required for the effective operation of democratic political institutions, citizens also have a right to form relatively independent associations or organizations, including independent political parties and interest groups.

5 *Inclusive suffrage.* No adult citizens residing in the country and subject to its laws can be denied voting rights in the election of political representatives.

Dahl's concept of polyarchy builds on Joseph Schumpeter's influential "minimal" definition. Schumpeter (1942: 269) claimed that "the democratic method is that institutional arrangement for arriving at political decisions in which individuals acquire the power to decide by means of a competitive struggle for the people's vote." However, Schumpeter makes no reference to political liberties or to the extent of participatory rights. Indeed, he states explicitly that "disqualifications on grounds of economic status, religion and sex [are] compatible with democracy" (Schumpeter 1942: 244–45; see also Møller and Skaaning 2010: 268–69). Schumpeter thus stresses competition or contestation at the expense of inclusiveness or participation, and is therefore considerably narrower than Dahl's vision of polyarchy.

Of course, defenders of Schumpeter might argue that an electoral conception of democracy *should* be centered on elections, excluding features that do not relate directly to that core feature. Our view is that ancillary factors such as freedom of expression cannot be ignored because they determine the degree to which electoral contestation is likely to flourish. As Larry Diamond (2002: 21) writes, "democracy requires not only free, fair, and competitive elections, but also the freedoms that make them truly *meaningful* (such as freedom of organization and freedom of expression, alternative sources of information, and institutions to ensure that government policies depend on the votes and preferences of citizens)" (italics added). To avoid the "fallacy of electoralism" (Karl 1986), even election-centered notions of democracy need to take into account some nonelectoral aspects – most importantly freedom of organization and expression – in order to ascertain whether elections are free and fair.

Although additional factors might also enhance electoral contestation (e.g., additional civil liberties and an independent judiciary), we consider these factors to be of secondary importance (see Dahl 1956; Przeworski et al. 2000; Schumpeter 1950). They are therefore classified with other principles of democracy, as described below.

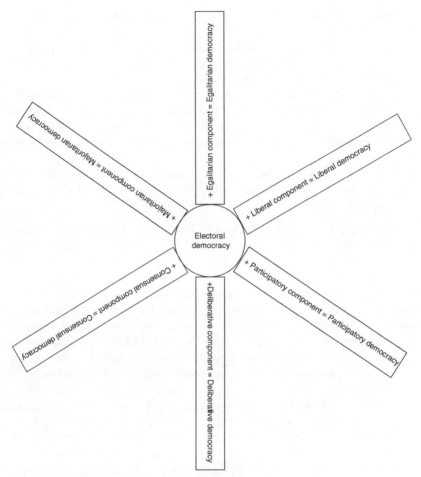

FIGURE 2.1 Principles and components of democracy.

The electoral principle has a special status in the V-Dem conceptual scheme as the *sine qua non* of democracy (see Figure 2.1). We would not want to call a political regime without multiparty elections "democratic." Here is where we push back against the dictator Rafael Trujillo, who spoke of the Dominican Republic as a *neodemocracy*; Hitler, who envisaged a Germanic *Führerdemokratie*; Franco, who articulated his rule as *organic democracy*; and communist regimes in Eastern Europe, which referred to themselves as *people's democracies*. These regimes were not democracies because they did not allow free elections.

Having adopted a broad view of electoral democracy it is important nonetheless to stress the limitations of this principle. We do not claim that it encompasses all the meanings of democracy. There is more to democracy than elections.[7] Additional principles of democracy, laid out below, thus function as extensions of the narrow, *electoral* approach to the topic.

2.2 THE LIBERAL PRINCIPLE

The *liberal* principle of democracy stresses the value of protecting individual rights against state oppression and unrestricted majoritarian rule ("tyranny of the majority"). This perspective is rooted in the classical liberal tradition, which evolved in Europe during the Age of Enlightenment as a reaction to absolutist rule, aristocratic privileges, and clerical dogmas. Key values include reason, tolerance, pluralism, freedom of religion, and freedom of choice (Held 2006: 59). Insofar as rule by the people entails individual liberty, the liberal principle may be considered central to the concept of democracy.

From a liberal perspective, the state is a double-edged sword: political institutions are necessary in order to safeguard individual freedoms but they also pose a direct threat to those freedoms (Holmes 1995: 270).[8] Accordingly, the power of rulers should be limited by fundamental law, enshrined in a constitution grounded in the protection of individual rights and an implied social contract. Government authority must be derived from, and limited by, law (Holmes 1995; O'Donnell 2007; Ross 1952; Sartori 1987; Vile 1998). Constitutional rules should emphasize the protection of civil liberties, constraints on the executive, and protection of minority rights (Gordon 1999).

One of the distinguishing features of the liberal principle is the idea of checks on government (Locke 1963; Montesquieu 1989; Hamilton et al. 1992). Since the executive is the branch of government most prone to abuse, we regard the judicial and legislative branches as providing checks against arbitrary and excessive executive authority. Independent courts also serve the function of adjudicating among citizens and between citizens and public authorities.

Another key feature of the liberal component is a catalog of fundamental rights. In addition to freedom of expression and freedom of association, already included in the principle of electoral democracy,[9] the liberal principle embraces associated rights such as freedom from torture, political killings, and serfdom or slavery; freedom of movement; freedom of religion; property rights; and

---

[7] By contrast, most influential indices – including Polity2, Freedom House's Political Rights, and Democracy-Dictatorship (Przeworski et al. 2000, Boix et al. 2013) – focus on electoral activity in their coding of regimes. This, by itself, would not be a problem if they were understood narrowly as indices of electoral democracy. Unfortunately, they are commonly interpreted as measuring democracy *at large*.

[8] Held (2006) identifies two strands of liberalism: a protective version and a developmental version. Here we focus on the former, which probably represents what most scholars have in mind when referring to the liberal component of democracy (see, e.g., Diamond 1999; Fukuyama 2014; Møller and Skaaning 2011; Zakaria 2003).

[9] Note that from the liberal perspective, these are defining features of democracy – not simply aids to political competition.

equality before the law. All of these rights may be grouped together under the rubric of *civil liberties*.

Taken together, civil liberties, judicial independence, and legislative independence fulfill the liberal ideal insofar as all three impose constraints on the executive, forcing that individual (or body) to abide by the rule of law and helping to secure fundamental rights for citizens. Note that the liberal model generally takes a negative view of the concentration of political power insofar as it judges the quality of democracy by the limits placed on government and the enjoyment of an extended set of individual rights and liberties.

2.3   THE MAJORITARIAN PRINCIPLE

The *majoritarian* principle of democracy captures the idea that the will of the majority of the people should be sovereign. Accordingly, democracy is enhanced if political institutions ensure that the many prevail over the few. To facilitate this, political institutions should centralize and concentrate power (within the context of competitive elections), rather than dispersing it, generating an efficient mechanism of decision-making and implementation. This does not entail an *illiberal* political order, however. Majority rule is consonant with the liberal principle, introduced above, insofar as constitutional limitations are respected.

The intellectual lineage of majority rule may be traced back to Walter Bagehot (1867/1963: 219–22), who contrasted the developing Westminster polity with the highly decentralized American polity: "The English Constitution," he wrote, "is framed on the principle of choosing a single sovereign, and making it good; the American, upon the principle of having many sovereign authorities, and hoping that their multitude may atone for their inferiority." For eighteenth- and nineteenth-century Liberals and reform-minded Tories – such as Bagehot, Edmund Burke, Robert Peel, Benjamin Disraeli, and William Gladstone – strong government serves as a mechanism to restrain corruption and allow the educated middle classes to rule. A somewhat different motivation for centralized power may be found among social liberals such as Thomas Hill Green, Leonard Trelawny Hobhouse, Graham Wallas, and Sidney and Beatrice Webb (Freeden 1978). For Fabians, strong government was a vehicle for social progress – strong enough to deal with the complexities of a turbulent, industrializing society and to overcome the resistance of corporations, privileged classes, and other special interests.

In the majoritarian model of democracy, rule by the people is achieved through the mechanism of electoral accountability – and in this respect may be viewed as an extension or refinement of the electoral principle. Note that the precept of power concentration has the effect of enhancing vertical accountability (Schumpeter 1942). Since power is centralized in the hands of an executive and his/her party, who control all the elective levers of power while in office, they alone may be held responsible for any accomplishments or failures on their watch. There can be no passing the buck, no finger-pointing, no excuses. By contrast, when power is divided it is difficult for citizens to determine whom to reward, or blame, for the state of the nation. Elections lose their capacity to serve as mechanisms of (vertical) accountability.

Likewise, in between elections one might argue that majoritarian systems are more efficient in that the government is empowered to pass whatever legislation it deems appropriate in order to fulfill its electoral mandate. It enjoys considerable autonomy to manage the policy agenda, within the scope of the country's constitutional framework. Out-parties are reduced to the role of critics, which means that the risk of policy gridlock is small.[10]

To fulfill the majoritarian ideal political institutions should be power concentrating. They should centralize power, typically in the hands of a single party with the backing of a majority of voters, thus limiting the number of "veto points" and the ability of different minority groups to block the majority will. A majoritarian constitution is unitary rather than federal. Likewise, legislatures should be unicameral rather than bicameral – or, if bicameral, the two houses should have asymmetric powers (where one chamber, usually the lower chamber, is dominant) or symmetric composition (where the same parties are in charge). In most circumstances, majoritarian rule is facilitated by parliamentarism – where the executive is chosen by, and responsible to, an elected legislature, rather than chosen directly by the electorate as in presidential systems.[11]

It is often difficult to anticipate whether a set of electoral rules will have a centralizing or decentralizing effect on political power. This depends, among other things, on the geographical concentration or dispersion of particular blocks of voters. For example, single-member districts with plurality rules may help to winnow competition down to two or three parties, as in the US and the UK. Or it may serve to entrench highly fragmented party systems, as in India and Papua New Guinea (Gerring 2005). Thus, although the Westminster system is commonly regarded as "majoritarian," we reserve judgment about which electoral rules are most likely to concentrate power in the hands of a single political party or coalition.

Before quitting this subject we must take note of a fundamental ambiguity in the principle of majority rule. This has to do with how "majority" is defined. By

---

[10] This way of thinking about democracy is closely tied to the tradition known as Responsible Party Government, which in turn builds on Bagehot and many others (Ford 1898/1967; Goodnow 1900; Lowell 1889; Ranney 1962; Schattschneider 1942, 1960; Wilson 1879/1965, 1885/1956). One may also discern a majoritarian flavor in studies that champion the virtues of political parties and decry the power of interest groups (Lowi 1969; McConnell 1966).

[11] In situations where the legislature is weak and divided, the president may represent a centralizing force. Likewise, where the constitutional powers of the president overshadow the legislature to such an extent that power is centralized despite a formally divided constitutional system (see O'Donnell 1994), we may regard a directly elected president as a majoritarian institution. Much depends upon the interaction of the executive and legislature in a particular historical context.

one understanding, majority refers to a majority of the electorate, i.e., those citizens entitled to vote. However, in most polities many citizens do not vote, meaning that elections are decided by a smaller set of voters who show up at the polls. Additionally, there is always some slippage between votes cast and seats received by a party. This means that the *effective* majority often constitutes a relatively small part of the total electorate. Under the circumstances, the practice of majority rule often looks more like plurality rule.[12]

2.4 THE CONSENSUAL PRINCIPLE

The *consensual* principle of democracy may be understood as the mirror image of the majoritarian principle. Accordingly, in order to realize popular rule political power should be widely dispersed and formal political institutions should encourage the inclusion of as many political perspectives as possible in the decision-making process. All voices, or at least all voices with a stake in a particular policy area, should be heard. Inclusionary measures should prevent "tyranny of the majority," preserving minority interests even when opposed by the governing party. Institutions should also be conducive to the formation of a broader political consensus, since supermajorities will be needed in order to change the status quo (Dixon 1968; Hamilton et al. 1992; Lijphart 1999; Powell 1982). From a consensual perspective, this is the best way to achieve the core goal of democracy, rule by the people.

Because policies build on a broad base of support, and because (once adopted) they are difficult to change, we may expect considerable policy continuity in a polity with consensual institutions (Finer 1975; Tsebelis 2000). This, in turn, may enhance the credibility of government commitments into the future (North 1993).

Consensual institutions evidently run contrary to majoritarian institutions (while sharing a commitment to electoral democracy). Executive powers should be fairly weak, the constitution should be federal (rather than unitary), the legislature should be bicameral with equal powers and different constituencies rather than unicameral, and considerable power should be delegated to independent bodies at national and subnational levels. Decision-making at various levels should be by supermajority rather than simple majority or plurality. In addition, there may be institutions designed explicitly to facilitate power sharing such as oversized coalition governments, an executive that represents all parties (as in Switzerland), and supermajority agreements with

---

[12] Of course, those who choose not to vote, or who vote for losing parties, may still be represented in a more diffuse sense within a majoritarian system. We should not suppose that their views and interests are entirely ignored, especially as the system is grounded in electoral democracy and vertical accountability. There will be another election, and the threat of that upcoming election may be sufficient to provide effective representation for groups that did not bother to vote or were unsuccessful in electing "their" people to office. Nonetheless, the fact that the key concept of a majority is ambiguous should give one pause.

respect to specific policies. Since the role of electoral rules is often ambiguous – for reasons already discussed – we leave aside these institutions in our consideration of consensual democracy.

2.5 THE PARTICIPATORY PRINCIPLE

The *participatory* principle of democracy embraces the values of direct rule and active participation by citizens in politics. It is rooted in the tradition of direct democracy as practiced in ancient Greece and (much later) envisaged by Jean-Jacques Rousseau (Hansen 1991; Ober 1989; Rousseau 1762/1984).

The benefits claimed for active participation are several-fold. First, active participation develops public awareness and the capacities of citizens, improving their sense of membership in the community. This may be especially important for minority groups and those that face discrimination in society. Second, citizens gain a sense of ownership over the political process, which increases its legitimacy. Third, decision-making is enhanced, along with the implementation of policies, improving the quality of governance (Putnam 1994).

Over the past several decades, the participatory model of democracy has received renewed attention from scholars and activists due to widespread dissatisfaction with the working of electoral or liberal democracy (Barber 1988; Macpherson 1977; Pateman 1976; Mansbridge 1983). This should not be taken to imply that participation and representation are in conflict with one another. It does mean, however, that representative democracy and the institutions associated with electoral and liberal democracy (as described above) are not sufficient to achieve the participatory ideal. Rather than looking solely at formal rights to suffrage, as defined in the constitution or electoral law, one must examine rates of turnout (actual voting). This addresses the problem that sometimes formal rights do not translate into de facto practices. In addition to voting, the polity should provide other mechanisms of citizen participation – also in between elections – such as direct democracy (initiatives and referenda), party primaries, a strong and engaged civil society (including demonstrations, protests, and strikes), and subnational (local and regional) elective bodies with significant policy-making power.

2.6 THE DELIBERATIVE PRINCIPLE

The *deliberative* principle of democracy enshrines the idea that political decisions in pursuit of the public good should be informed by respectful and reason-based dialogue rather than by emotional appeals, solidary attachments, parochial interests, or coercion.

This idea is relatively new. Although it is inspired by the ideal of participation found in ancient Greece and in republicanism (Pocock 1975), the term *deliberative democracy* was formulated as an explicit theoretical framework in the 1980s (Bressette 1980; Habermas 1987), largely due to dissatisfactions with perceived pathologies of contemporary democracy, e.g., the personalization of politics, disrespect for alternative views, pork-barrel legislation, affective appeal to base interests, and an unreflective pursuit of preferences.

The deliberative principle suggests that a legitimate political order is one that is justifiable to all members of a polity. "The key objective," writes Held (2006: 237), "is the transformation of private preferences via a process of deliberation into positions that can withstand public scrutiny and test." To achieve this, attention should be directed to the prevoting processes of opinion formation (Habermas 1996; Elster 1998; Gutmann and Thompson 1998; Bohman 1998). Democracy requires more than an aggregation of preferences.

Likewise, process matters a great deal to the quality of democracy. A deliberative process is one in which public reasoning focused on the common good motivates political decisions. This implies "debate and discussion aimed at producing reasonable, well-informed opinions in which participants are willing to revise preferences in light of discussion, new information, and claims made by fellow participants." (Chambers 2003: 309). Respectful dialogue should exist at all stages – from preference formation to final decision – among informed and competent participants who are open to persuasion (Dryzek 2010: 1). Rational political deliberation should be "'fact-regarding' (as opposed to ignorant or doctrinaire), 'future-regarding' (as opposed to myopic) and 'other-regarding' (as opposed to selfish)" (Offe and Preuss 1991: 157).

Most proponents of deliberative democracy view deliberation as a feature of – rather than a replacement for – representative democracy (Chambers 2003: 308; Fishkin 1991). What is distinctive about deliberative democracy is the criteria of public deliberation, respectful discussion, and reasoned justification with reference to the public good.

2.7   THE EGALITARIAN PRINCIPLE

The *egalitarian* principle highlights the goal of political equality (Beitz 1990).[13] To be fully democratic, a polity must ensure that all citizens possess equal capacity to influence policy decisions. This means that whatever factors enhance political power – e.g., the enjoyment of rights, access to decision makers, access to resources that might affect political outcomes, organizational capacity, the ability to hold public office, and levels of electoral participation – should be spread equally among the citizenry. Individuals may choose to be more or less involved in politics. But social groups, as defined by ethnicity, language, race, gender, sexuality, or other salient characteristics, should be equally advantaged.

---

[13] An elaboration on the egalitarian principle can be found in Sigman and Lindberg (2018).

The egalitarian perspective on democracy grows out of a critique of electoral democracy from the left. Writers in the Marxist tradition sometimes view free and fair elections as a democratic façade whose purpose is to ensure class rule (of the bourgeoisie) but not rule by all (e.g., Marx 1933; Luxembourg 2006). Other writers in the social democratic tradition offer a hopeful prognosis in which socialist policies are integrated into electoral democracy (Bernstein 1899/ 1961; Heller 1930). But even Robert Dahl, whom many consider the icon of liberal theories of democracy, explicitly emphasized the fundamental importance of equality for the realization of pluralistic and liberal forms of democracy (Dahl 1989, 1998).

Of particular importance are inequalities of income, health, and education, which may translate into political inequalities (Sinclair 1962; Dahl 2006). For example, if citizens are denied health care in a way that leads to sickness or even death, they are effectively prohibited from exercising the right to vote or express themselves. Consequently, in order to achieve political equality it may be necessary to ensure that the entire population enjoys basic necessities – e.g., basic income protection, education, and health care. Rule *by* the people implies a degree of equality *among* the people. An egalitarian perspective on democracy also pays close attention to the de facto distribution of power, which may be at variance with de jure constitutional or statutory rights. Real power, not formal power, is the essence of rule by the people.

Accordingly, besides ordinary electoral democracy, the egalitarian principle of democracy requires that rights and freedoms of individuals are protected equally across all social groups. Moreover, resources – which might be translated into political power – must be distributed equally across all social groups.

2.8 FROM CONCEPTUALIZATION TO MEASUREMENT

Having introduced the core concept of democracy and outlining seven principles of democracy, we now clarify how this conceptual framework lays the groundwork for the empirical aspects of this project. To do so, we recognize five tiers (levels of aggregation/disaggregation) in the conceptualization and measurement of democracy:

- Democracy, the core concept
  - Democracy Indices
    - Democracy Components
      - Subcomponents and related concepts
        - Indicators

Below the core concept are *democracy indices,* understood to represent different conceptions of democracy. Because we regard electoral democracy as foundational, the other democracy indices incorporate electoral democracy into their respective indices. Following the conceptual logic presented in Figure 2.1, electoral democracy is at the core and other indices are characterized by combinations of the electoral principle with other components. For example, liberal democracy is formed from the combination of electoral democracy and the liberal component of democracy. (Note that we have not constructed empirical indices for the majoritarian and consensual principles, so these will not be found in the current V-Dem data set.)

Components may be regarded as "thin" concepts that form the basis for a set of more specific indices that we call *component indices* to distinguish them from the general *democracy indices*. The construction of democracy indices and component indices is described in greater detail in Chapter 5. Because the component indices ignore the quality of electoral democracy we do *not* regard these component indices as measuring democracy per se. Nonetheless, they provide useful descriptions of a polity and are helpful empirically insofar as they are defined in a mutually exclusive fashion. While democracy indices overlap, component indices are distinct.

Component indices may be further disaggregated into meso-level indices of concepts such as rule of law, corruption, freedom of association, clean elections, equality before the law, or civil society strength. We refer to these as *mid-level indices*.

Some of these mid-level indices, such as those for political corruption, female empowerment, and party institutionalization, do not fit neatly into our higher-level indices. For example, political corruption is, in line with the academic literature, usually defined as the use of public office for private gain. Its four attributes refer to different kinds of public officeholders: members of the executive, members of the legislature, public sector employees, and members of the judiciary (see McMann et al. 2016). Clearly, none of the presented principles approve of corruption in the making, adjudication, and implementation of political decisions. Nonetheless, the issue is typically not mentioned explicitly in connection to conceptualizations of democracy (but see, e.g., Inglehart and Welzel 2005). We measure these mid-level concepts because they are implicitly relevant for comprehensive or holistic ways of thinking about democracy that encroach on other general concepts such as the rule of law or good government.

The final step in disaggregation is the identification of low-level *indicators*. In identifying indicators we look for features that (a) are related to at least one property of democracy; (b) bring the political process into closer alignment with the core meaning of democracy (rule by the people); and (c) are measurable across polities and time.

Some indicators refer to de jure aspects of a polity – rules that statute or constitutional law (including the unwritten constitution of states like the UK) stipulate. Others refer to de facto aspects of a polity – the way things are in practice. There are some 350 unique democracy indicators in the V-Dem data set. Each is listed in the *V-Dem Codebook*.

2.9 CAVEATS AND CLARIFICATIONS

Having laid out our conceptual scheme, we must now introduce several caveats and clarifications.

First, our quest to conceptualize and measure democracy should not be confused with the quest to conceptualize and measure *governance*.[14] Of course, there is overlap between these two concepts: attributes of democracy may also be considered attributes of good governance, and vice versa. Much depends upon how one chooses to define these diffuse concepts. Arguably, "rule by the people" refers not only to decision-making but also to the implementation of policies, once decided upon. The people are not truly sovereign if their decisions are subverted by corruption, waste, and the inefficacy of public servants. As such, virtually every aspect of governance could be considered a subject of democracy. We do not make any claims on this point. Nonetheless, the V-Dem project does measure quite a number of features traditionally associated with the concept of governance, including corruption, rule of law, and sovereignty.

Second, we do not attempt to incorporate the *causes* of democracy (except insofar as some attributes of this far-flung concept might affect other attributes). Regime types may be affected by economic development (Lipset 1960; Boix 2003), colonial experiences (Bernhard et al. 2004), or attitudes and political cultures (Almond and Verba 1963/1989; Hadenius and Teorell 2005; Welzel 2007). However, we do not regard these attributes as *constitutive* of democracy.

Third, aspects of democracy sometimes conflict with one another, an issue raised at the outset of this chapter. At the level of principles, there is an obvious conflict between majoritarian and consensual norms, which adopt contrary perspectives on most institutional components. The majoritarian principle can also be hard to unite with liberal ideals of constraints on majority rule such as individual rights and checks and balances. Likewise, strong civil society organizations can have the effect of pressuring government to restrict the civil liberties enjoyed by marginal groups. Furthermore, the same institution may be differently viewed according to different principles of democracy. Such contradictions are implicit in democracy's multidimensional character. No wide-ranging empirical investigation can avoid conflicts among democracy's diverse attributes. However, with separate indicators representing these different facets of democracy it should be possible to examine potential trade-offs empirically.

Fourth, the seven principles introduced in this chapter, while much easier to define than *democracy* (at large), are still resistant to authoritative conceptualization. Our objective has been to identify the most essential and distinctive attributes associated with these concepts. Even so, we are keenly aware that others might make different choices, and that different tasks require

---

[14] See Rose-Ackerman (1999) and Thomas (2010).

different choices. The goal of the proposed conceptual framework is to provide guidance, not to legislate in an authoritative fashion. The schema demonstrates how the various elements of V-Dem hang together. We expect that other writers will assemble and dis-assemble these parts in whatever fashion suits their needs and objectives. In this respect, V-Dem has the modular qualities of a LEGO set. Those who disagree with our conceptualizations may utilize a vast array of indicators with which they can build different measures of our varieties or different conceptualizations of democracy altogether.

Fifth, and relatedly, the most important aspect of the V-Dem project may be its disaggregated quality. While the world may never agree on whether the level of democracy in a particular country can be summarized as a "4" or "5" (on some scale), we may be able to reach agreement on more specific properties – for example, the mid-level indices described in the previous section. Generally speaking, concepts become more tractable at lower levels of abstraction. Lower-level concepts also provide more empirical traction. While holistic measures of democracy float hazily over the surface, the indicators and indices of a disaggregated data set are comparatively specific and precise. Contrasts and comparisons become correspondingly acute, and our ability to understand the world – both descriptively and causally – improves.

Finally, the proposed set of democratic principles, while fairly comprehensive, is by no means exhaustive. The protean nature of *democracy* resists closure. There are always new properties or combinations of properties, from one perspective or another, that may be associated with this essentially contested term. Note that our goal is to encompass extant work on the subject. As this tradition of intellectual work evolves, we anticipate that the relevant categories will also evolve. This is not a feature to decry. Indeed, empirical progress on a topic is rarely possible if conceptual categories are maintained in a rigid, unyielding fashion.

3

Data Collection[*]

The V-Dem team set out to measure democracy in a historical, multidimensional, disaggregated, and transparent way (Coppedge and Gerring 2011: 247). Our multidimensional understanding of the nature of democracy requires leadership by multiple researchers who have expertise in a wide range of institutions and practices. Our commitment to disaggregation, as explained in Chapter 2, requires breaking general conceptions of democracy into hundreds of more specific, and therefore more easily measured, attributes. Because no small group of scholars possesses sufficient expertise to rate hundreds of attributes of democracy in a large number of countries over more than two centuries of history, V-Dem requires a collaboration among a very large number of Country Experts. The most efficient way to tap their expertise is an online survey, which requires a custom-designed research database and web interfaces. Other web interfaces serve to share the data and full information about the project transparently. V-Dem also requires research assistants who can efficiently gather the most objective and publicly available data. Finally, managing all these people and processes requires the staff of the V-Dem Institute to recruit and manage Country Experts, oversee central data collection, clean and process data, evaluate its reliability, develop software, write and update documentation, submit grant applications, administer finances, organize conferences, and publicize the project on social media.

This chapter describes all of these dimensions of the Varieties of Democracy project. It covers (1) the definition of the countries that we code, (2) the types of data that we produce, (3) the different types of coding, (4) the databases and software for data collection and project management, (5) the online surveys, (6) additional data collection for cross-national comparability, (7) data cleaning,

[*] The principal authors of this chapter were Staffan I. Lindberg, Valeriya Mechkova, Natalia Stepanova, Jan Teorell, Michael Coppedge, and Carl Henrik Knutsen.

(8) personnel, (9) phases of data collection, and (10) V-Dem's international collaborations.

3.1 COUNTRIES

Our principal concern for the data collection process is with political institutions that exist in fairly well defined political units, which can claim a sovereign or semisovereign existence (i.e., they enjoy a degree of autonomy at least with respect to domestic affairs) and serve as the operational unit of governance. We refer to these units as "countries" even if they are not fully sovereign. This means, for example, that V-Dem provides a continuous time series for Eritrea coded as an Italian colony (1900–1941), a province of Italian East Africa (1936–41), a British holding administered under the terms of a UN mandate (1941–51), a federation with Ethiopia (1952–62), a territory within Ethiopia (1962–93), and an independent state (1993 to the present). For some former colonies, Historical V-Dem data allows us to extend coding even further back than 1900, examples being Brazil (from 1789), India (1789), Indonesia (1800), and Singapore (1867).

Originally, we collected data on countries from 1900, or the first year of their existence (if later), to the most recent year of their existence. With Historical V-Dem, integrated from version 8 of the data set, we extend coding further back in time, often all the way back to 1789, for 91 countries on a large number of indicators. Therefore, for example, the coding of countries such as the US, China, and Ethiopia begins in 1789, coding for Greece begins in 1822 (before which it is included in the Ottoman Empire/Turkey), coding for Panama begins in 1903 (before which it is included in Colombia), and coding of the post-Soviet states such as Ukraine and Uzbekistan begins in 1991 (before which they were included in the Soviet Union, although for Uzbekistan we code what we consider the historical predecessor polity of Bukhara from 1789–1920). Similarly, coding of Bavaria ends in 1871, South Vietnam ends in 1975, East Germany ends in 1990, and so on. For further details, see *V-Dem Country Coding Units*, which is available at https://v-dem.net/.

3.2 DATA FORMATS

V-Dem provides time series ratings that reflect historical changes as precisely as possible. Election-specific indicators are coded as events occurring on the date of the election. We code other indicators continuously, with an option (which some coders utilize) to specify exact dates (day/month/year) corresponding to changes in an institution. The V-Dem "standard" data set is in the country-year format, where date-specific changes are aggregated at the year level. However, we also provide a separate country-date data set for users who want greater precision. All data sets with point estimates based on aggregation of multiple expert ratings also provide confidence intervals (highest posterior densities) from the Bayesian IRT model. In the data archive, which is accessible via the data download page on our website, we also provide the raw Country Expert coder-level data. This allows users to inspect the data directly or use it for alternate analyses. Finally, in the same archive we also provide the posterior distributions from the Bayesian IRT model for each variable to facilitate their direct use in analyses.

3.3 CODING TYPES

The about 450 V-Dem specific indicators listed in *V-Dem Codebook* fall into four main types: (A) factual (i.e., relatively objective) indicators coded by members of the V-Dem team, (B) factual indicators coded by Country Coordinators, (C) evaluative indicators based on multiple ratings provided by Country Experts, and (D) composite indices. The extended version of the data set also provides some extant (E) data (both factual and evaluative) including other democracy measures and background or explanatory factors. In addition, V-Dem data sets include several alternative forms of the C-indicators that reflect different levels of measurement (interval, ordinal, and a hybrid) and upper and lower confidence bounds for each of these and the V-Dem indices. (Chapter 4 describes all of these in detail.) Consequently, the most complete versions of the data set actually contain several thousand variables.

We gather Type (A) data from extant sources, e.g., other data sets or secondary sources, as listed in the *Codebook*. These data are largely factual in nature, although some coder judgment may be required. Principal Investigators and Project Managers supervise the collection of these data, which the Data team at the V-Dem Institute and assistants connected to the project carry out using multiple sources. For some variables such as election dates, names of head of state and head of government, we have also used input from V-Dem's Country Coordinators. For the historical (pre-1900) data, most of the A indicators were coded by different RAs, located at various institutions and under supervision by members of the Historical V-Dem team, although several measures were taken to ensure consistency in the time series.[1]

Country Coordinators, under the supervision of Regional Managers, gather Type (B) data from country-specific sources. As with Type (A) data, this sort of coding is largely factual in nature. Type (B) coding is not conducted for the pre-1900 period.

Type (C) data requires a greater degree of judgment about the state of affairs in a particular country at a particular point in time. Country Experts (CEs) code these data. Generally, for the post-1900 period, each CE codes only a selection

---

[1] For instance, for several of these variables, data for overlapping years, typically 1900–20, were collected independently by both contemporary and historical RAs. Thereafter, these RAs (and other team members) would go through "mismatches" (if any) to ensure consistency in interpretation and identify and correct potential errors.

of indicators for one or two specific countries following their particular background and expertise (e.g., the survey on the legislature in Indonesia). For reasons outlined in Sections 3.5 and 3.8, we pursued a different strategy for the pre-1900 expert recruitment and data collection, with historical Country Experts coding all surveys for their country.

Type (D) data consists of indices constructed from (A), (B), or (C) variables. They include cumulative indicators such as "number of presidential elections coding start" as well as more highly aggregated variables such as the main democracy indices.

Type (E) data fall into three categories. First, there ordinal and typological versions of the V-Dem indices that are used by some members of the V-Dem team (Lindberg 2015; Lührmann et al. 2018). Second, there are alternative indices and indicators of democracy and related concepts drawn from Freedom House, Polity, and 21 other sources, as described in the *Codebook*. They are included to facilitate comparisons and contrasts with V-Dem indices and indicators. Third, E-indicators also include more than 80 outside measures of education, geography, economics, socioeconomic status, natural resources, infrastructure, demography, and conflict that are often needed in quantitative research on democracy.

3.4 DATABASES AND SOFTWARE

The V-Dem Institute at University of Gothenburg is led by its Director, Professor Staffan I. Lindberg, assisted since 2018 by Deputy Director and Assistant Professor Anna Lührmann. It is now in practice the headquarters of the V-Dem research infrastructure and research programs with executive management responsibilities for most aspects of the project: data collection and processing, management of the research program, international collaborations, training, and capacity building for partners, regional centers, policy analysis, and outreach. (See Chapter 1 on the role of the Kellogg Institute at the University of Notre Dame in the development of the project.)

V-Dem's data collection relies heavily on a research database, an administrative database, and a suite of web interfaces. We discuss each in turn.

3.4.1 The Research Database

The research database is a relational database programmed in the PostgreSQL language.[2] It contains 54 tables – each one the equivalent of a regular

---

[2] The website, survey interfaces, and research database were originally designed, following our guidance, by the Center for Research Computing (CRC) at the University of Notre Dame in 2010–14. They were subsequently overhauled and refined by the Chicago firm Imaginary Landscape in a process directed by Natalia Stepanova at the V-Dem Institute. By 2017, a new Project Manager for Computational Infrastructure, Steven L. Wilson, assumed responsibility for

rectangular data set – linked together by key variables. These interlocking relationships make it possible to extract and tabulate many different sources and types of data and documentation.

The largest table in the V-Dem research database is the ratings table. This contains all the democracy ratings provided by the more than 3000 Country Experts for the 201 countries and 228 years of history, amounting to a total of 19 million data points.[3] This is also the table where we upload centrally coded factual data. Due to the nature of the data collection process, programming issues, and the complex nature of the data submissions, the data in this table need systematic quality control and cleaning after each new round of data collection.[4]

There are also tables in the research database for many other purposes, including a special set of tables used for uploading processed data to be publicly available for online graphing. (See more on the online tools below.) These are interconnected tables containing the aggregated data at the country-year level; the name, type, and hierarchy of variables and indices; and countries and their timespans, to name just a few. Adjustments and revisions to relationships between variables, the construction of indices, and uploading of data require an intricate set of coordinated operations in which data must be revised concurrently and consistently for the online set of tools to work properly. The research database code also includes routines that enable it to communicate with the administrative database, the web-based coding and administrative interfaces, the website, and the online tools.

3.4.2   Web-Based Coding and Administrative Interfaces

The web-based coding and administrative interfaces are directly connected with the research database. The administrative interfaces consist of a series of interlinked functions where we can manage country names, assign coders, check progress reports, and construct and adjust survey questions, the composition of surveys, and related issues. Many surveys need to be

---

its design, and as a consequence, many parts of it have been reprogrammed. Administration, cleaning, extraction, and other management of data used to be handled using specialized programs like PGAdmin using SQL-scripts, but each operation was delicate, creating the risk that data could be corrupted or deleted. This type of work is best handled by a qualified, permanent data manager rather than by temporary research assistants or busy professors. Senior Data Manager Joshua Krusell automated most of these operations so that they can run quickly between the updating of data by Country Experts in January and the release of the new version of the data set in the spring of each year.

[3] Information is based on statistics as of October 2018.

[4] We first developed a series of protocols for these exercises handled in a series of steps, using both complex scripts to be executed in a particular order and a series of crosschecks and visual inspection techniques, for the result to be a perfectly ordered and cleaned data set. This was a central element of the everyday work of the data team and assistants. These administrative tasks became redundant with automation and the professionalization of workflow.

customized to accommodate different starting and ending years, different election dates, and whether Country Experts in the updates were new or returning. Up until 2017, we were managing more than 3000 customized versions of the original 11 surveys. Currently, the system allows to work only with the original 11 V-Dem surveys, as well as 10 surveys for the historical (pre-1900) coding. The customization is managed at the back end and happens automatically based on the selected criteria and country cases. This type of programming and automation minimizes mistakes and errors.

Most of the functions have been integrated into the administrative database and its administrative tools since the administrative processing times are at least 20 times faster there, but question and survey construction, in particular, were still managed using the web interfaces until 2018.

Figure 3.1 is an example of the basic online coding interface, which is designed to make it possible for coders to efficiently rate one country at a time on one question for many years. It consists of a series of web-based functions that in combination allow Country Experts and Country Coordinators to log in to the system using their individual, randomized username and self-assigned, secret password; access the series of surveys assigned to them for a particular country (or set of countries); and submit ratings for each question in each survey over long series of years. The coding interfaces combine features such as allowing for many types of questions (binominal, ordinal, multiple selection, etc.), country-specific and question-specific year masks (for example to allow coding of elections only in years they occurred), question-specific instructions and clarifications, and the assignment of self-assessed confidence levels for each rating in every country-year.

3.4.3   The Administrative Database and Tools

The administrative database, which uses FileMakerPro software, is connected to the research database and the web-based coding interfaces. It pulls together almost all of the functions needed for data updates, progress tracking, and management of experts.[5] It contains a relational database with dozens of interlinked tables to manage some 25,000 potential experts and more than 3000 actual Country Experts using information on qualifications, country expertise, surveys, affiliation, emails sent and received, coding progress, forms and informational material sent, dates logged in and coding conducted, payments made, and much other information. Unlike the research database, however, the FileMakerPro software provides tools that make it possible to merge this information with correspondence templates. The Program Managers can therefore easily send out a personalized invitation to a potential Country Expert, in the right language, and with all associated materials automatically

---

[5] Josefine Pernes developed the management software at the V-Dem Institute in collaboration with a consultant agency, Premium System AB.

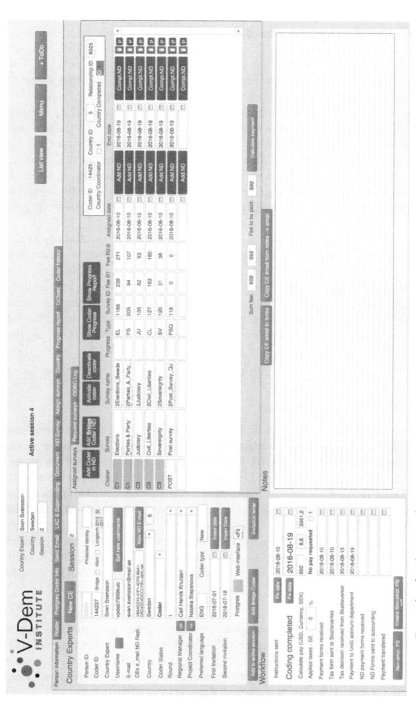

FIGURE 3.1 Example of coding interface.

inserting names and titles and other information such as suggested surveys, deadline, and remuneration offered.

When a potential Country Expert accepts an invitation, the Program Managers can easily assign a coder to one or more countries. The administrative database then automatically communicates with the research database and the coding interfaces, creates a coder ID and sends commands to these other parts of the infrastructure to create the same coder ID in relevant tables and interface, generates a user ID to be used in the coding interfaces and sends an email to the new coder with the username and instructions for how to log in and create a password. From that point, the administrative database communicates automatically with the research database and reads off each coder ID's progress on coding for each of the indicators that the coder is assigned to, and reports to the project staff on the coder management tool pages.

The coder management tool is just one out of more than 20 tools in the administrative software. There are tools for management of countries, surveys and questions, Country Coordinators, Regional Managers, for logging activities, and for analyzing progress on recruitment, coding, planning, and general management. Connected to the administrative database is also a secure web-interface portal that makes it possible for Regional Managers to securely upload Country Expert rosters to the administrative database, without having to share confidential information via email.

3.4.4 Website for Public Access

The V-Dem website is the public face of the project (https://v-dem.net/). It consists of a series of pages with informational material about the project, the leadership, advisory board, managers, and staff, as well as news, reference documents, and all V-Dem publications. A critical component of the website is the provision to freely download the different versions of the V-Dem data set (country-year, country-date, coder-level data). The documents describing the project rationale, methodology, country selection, and the comprehensive *Codebook* with details of all variables and indices are also available on the website. One section of the website hosts eight custom-designed online tools for analysis, which can be used to explore the V-Dem data.

Featured Tools:

- *Country Graph*: For displaying user-selected series of variables and/or indices for one country over time, allowing for several design features such as varying time period, as well as "drilling down" into the components of indices. The online graphs can be downloaded in several formats, including a new feature of exporting the graph data to a csv file.

- *Variable Graph*: As above but with the ability to compare multiple countries for one index or one variable at a time.
- *Interactive Maps*: This tool visualizes data by creating a color-coded map to view the distribution of scores for one indicator in one year around the world.
- *Motion Chart*: Allows for bivariate graphical modeling over time of two variables with bubble sizes and colors to represent two other variables, using software adapted from that originally developed by the Gapminder initiative.

Chart Tools:

- *Country Radar Chart*: Allows the user to view the "profile" of a country across several variables to compare scores for two different years.
- *Variable Radar Chart*: This tool displays multiple countries for one variable over time in a radar chart.
- *Scatter Chart*: This tool displays one indicator/index in a form of a scatter plot.
- *Heat Map*: This tool displays one indicator/index on a heat map – a graphical representation of data where values are represented by colors.

We illustrate these online analysis tools with one picture taken of the Variable Graph tool in Figure 3.2, comparing trajectories of the Electoral Democracy Index in Brazil, Hungary, India, Turkey, and the US from 1900 to 2017.

As of October 2018, the website had more than 190,000 unique users from 203 countries and territories in the world. More than 100,000 unique users have used the online tools and created 500,000 graphs. Since the release to the public of the V-Dem data set on January 4, 2016, versions of the data set have been downloaded more than 70,000 times. The 79 V-Dem working papers published so far have been downloaded more than 46,000 times, V-Dem Democracy Reports downloaded more than 7000 times and country and policy briefs produced by the team record more than 5000 downloads. Facebook and Twitter messages from V-Dem sometimes reach more than 20,000 followers and others, and more than 8000 individuals have signed up to receive the monthly V-Dem newsletter. In short, the demand for V-Dem is massive.

3.5   THE SURVEYS AND THE EXPERT CODING PROCESS

Because of the special significance of the coding process involving the Country Experts, we detail it below. We start by describing the process for the post-1900 coding: Drawing from rosters of potential Country Experts as prioritized by Regional Managers, Program Managers issue invitations until the quota of five coders is obtained, using the priority list of coders in each area of coding per

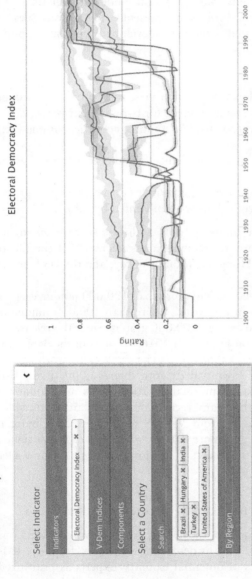

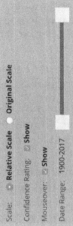

FIGURE 3.2 Example of online tool for analysis.

country in order to secure participation by the most qualified coders.[6] They often recruit six or seven coders for countries based on experience that one or two of them typically fail to complete the assignment. Coders receive a modest honorarium for their work that is proportional to the number of surveys they have completed. When a potential Country Expert accepts an invitation, the Program Managers mark their acceptance, the areas of coding, and assign them as coders for one or more countries using the interfaces described above, and then manage their participation.

The C-indicators that Country Experts code are organized into four clusters and 11 surveys:[7]

1 Elections
  Political parties/electoral systems
2 Executive
  Legislature
  Deliberation
3 Judiciary
  Civil liberty
  Sovereignty
4 Civil society organizations
  Media
  Political equality

We suggest (but do not require) that each Country Expert code at least one cluster; many do two of them. In practice, this means that a dozen or more Country Experts provide ratings for each country across all surveys.[8] All Country Experts carry out their coding using the specially designed online coding interface described above: to (1) log in to the system using their individual, randomized username and self-assigned, secret password; (2) access the series of surveys assigned to them for a particular country (or set of

---

[6] From the beginning of data collection, Pernes and Stepanova at the V-Dem Institute have been the Program Managers issuing the bulk of the invitations. Before July 2014, there was a third Program Manager at the Kellogg Institute who managed Country Experts in Latin America and a few in the Middle East and North Africa.

[7] For the pre-1900 coding, there are 10 surveys, as the deliberation survey is omitted (a few remaining questions from this survey are instead distributed among other surveys). Furthermore, the Sovereignty survey is renamed the State survey, due to the inclusion of several extra questions on features of the bureaucracy, military, and other state institutions.

[8] The historical (pre-1900) coding is an exception, where we, for reasons outlined below, ask the selected historical experts to code all questions for the ten historical surveys. But, also in some rare cases for the post-1900 coding – mainly for small and understudied countries – we ask individual experts to code the whole set of surveys simply because experts on the various specific parts of the survey are not available. Similarly, it is also not always possible to reach the goal of having five Country Experts code each indicator for these countries. Starting with v7.0, the data sets include a variable with the number of Country Experts providing ratings for each country-year-variable combination to provide full transparency.

countries); and (3) submit ratings for each question over a selected series of years. The interface also requires that, for each rating, experts assign a level of confidence, indicating how certain they are that their rating is correct (on a scale of 1–100, where each 10-percent interval has a substantive anchor point), providing another instrument for measuring uncertainty associated with the V-Dem data. Later, we incorporate this confidence estimation into the measurement model. (See Chapter 4 for details.) Country Experts also have an opportunity to register uncertainty in the "Remarks" field that lies at the end of each section of the survey.

In order to ensure wide recruitment of potential experts, and guarantee that we measure the same concepts across different regions and settings, we have translated all type-C questions, as well as coder-instructions and documentation for them, and the website coding into five other languages: Arabic, French, Portuguese, Russian, and Spanish. Approximately 15 percent of the experts code using a non-English version.

To assure informed consent and conform to standards of ethics, the online survey provides full information about the project and the use of the data, and coders certify that they accept the terms of the agreement. Any data we release to the public excludes information that might be used to identify coders.

Once the data collection is complete for a group of countries, Regional Managers and other members of the V-Dem team look closely at the point estimates in an attempt to determine whether systematic bias may exist. We also perform a series of automated validity checks comparing new estimates to earlier versions to prevent mistakes from undermining the integrity of the data.

For the historical part of the time series, the expert coding process is somewhat different. First, there are relatively fewer true experts on eighteenth- and nineteenth-century politics, particularly for smaller countries.[9] Thus, rather than dividing up the 10 historical surveys for a particular country, we aimed to recruit experts with general knowledge of the history of the country's political system – mainly political historians or political scientists doing historical work. These historical experts were given much longer time frames (and higher remuneration) for finalizing the coding, and they were expected to, e.g., take the time to go through source material.

3.6 CROSS-NATIONAL COMPARABILITY: BRIDGE, LATERAL, AND VIGNETTE CODING

In addition to regular ratings by multiple Country Experts for C-type indicators, we encourage Country Experts with the requisite expertise to conduct bridge coding: coding of more than one country through time; and lateral coding:

---

[9] Due to the fewer true historical experts, we also decided that the two-thirds nationals and/or residents criterion needed to be relaxed for this part of the coding.

coding for a number of countries limited to a single year – 2012.[10] See Chapter 4 for details. The purpose of this additional coding is to assure cross-country equivalence by forcing coders to make explicit comparisons across countries. This helps the Bayesian IRT measurement model to estimate, and correct for, systematic biases across coders and across countries that may result if Country Experts employ varying standards in their understanding of a question, e.g., about what a "high" level of repression might consist of (see further details in Chapter 4).

Bridge coding typically covers 1900 to the present. Bridge coding is most useful when the chosen countries have different regime histories. This generates variance across a Country Expert's ratings, which in turn provides information about the coder's judgments that can be used to inform the Bayesian IRT measurement model. In order to maximize variance, and therefore gain as much information as possible about each expert's thresholds and reliability, we encourage Country Experts to select – from among countries they are familiar with – those that have the most distinctive historical trajectories. As of March 2018, we have more than 450 bridge coders – over 15 percent of all experts. On average, these experts have coded 6.1 surveys for 2.1 countries.

For a couple of years we encouraged Country Experts and a number of well-known comparativists in political science to perform a simpler type of cross-country comparison called *lateral* coding. That is, they code a number of countries for a single point in time – January 1, 2012 – focusing on the same set of questions. More than 350 experts (about 12 percent) have performed lateral coding, covering on average of 5.5 countries and 6.3 surveys.

V-Dem's three-pronged approach using IRT models, recruiting bridge and lateral coders, and employing empirical priors helped to produce a data set that stands up well to tests of validity. Nonetheless, we have also included anchoring vignettes. IRT models allow for the possibility that coders have different thresholds for their ratings (e.g., one coder's *somewhat* might fall above another coder's *almost* on the latent scale), estimate those thresholds from patterns in the data, and adjust latent trait estimates accordingly. Therefore, they allow us to correct for this potentially serious source of bias, known as differential item functioning (DIF).

Anchoring vignettes are descriptions of hypothetical cases that provide information necessary to answer a given survey question. Vignettes provide bridging data that requires no specific case knowledge, enabling us to obtain bridging information across raters who are not qualified to code the same set of real-world cases. They also ensure that coders are considering the same information when evaluating cases, helping us to isolate the effect of DIF on experts' codes. Given the relatively fewer coders per country, and the fewer

---

[10] About one-third of historical experts also conducted lateral coding, coding the first year with an election after the year 1900 for three additional countries, picked from a set of six countries (USA, UK, France, Mexico, China, and Russia).

opportunities for ensuring cross-country comparability through bridge coding, we deemed anchoring vignettes to be critical for the Historical V-Dem coding.[11] Thus, for *all* historical experts, the vast majority of questions (i.e., all questions where vignettes were considered relevant by the team) in the historical surveys were prefaced by a set of anchoring vignettes. For the post-1900 coding, we fielded our first (pilot) wave of vignettes during the 2015–16 update, presenting 116 vignettes for 31 V-Dem questions to 599 coders from 94 countries. We did the first full round of vignettes during the 2016–17 update, presenting 224 vignettes for 66 V-Dem questions to 1400 coders from 174 countries. Coders were not required to complete vignettes, but were requested to do so. For the last update, we rewrote the 20 percent of the worst-performing vignettes and asked all experts to code vignettes again: a randomized selection of vignettes for all questions they answered. Thus, our efforts to build in vignettes as a standard feature is now fully operational.

As a result of these efforts, we feel much more confident in the cross-national comparability of estimates from version 6 of the data set. As a result of bridge, lateral, and vignette coding there are linkages equivalent to more than 1100 "fully covered" countries – in other words, countries that have been "cross-coded" by lateral or bridge coding across all indicators in the data set, and for which the Bayesian IRT model also uses the vignettes data to further adjust for coder-specific differences in threshold to achieve what we believe is a very high degree of cross-national (and over time) comparability.

3.7 DATA CLEANING

With *factual* questions (A + B-type indicators), we correct problems whenever the Principal Investigators, in consultation with the relevant Project Managers, become convinced that a better (i.e., more correct) answer is available. On a day-to-day basis, this work is carried out by staff at the V-Dem Institute. Based on analysis of submitted data by Country Coordinators, certain variables are designated as "B + A." Using the original B-data as a point of departure and crosschecking with external resources, we designed and implemented a coding scheme to recode these indicators, as the *Codebook* describes. Indicators affected include all indicators from the direct democracy survey, four indicators on the executive, four on elections, and nine on legislatures. The decision to reassign these indicators was also due to the interaction between question formulation and coder interpretation. For example, in some instances the meaning of "plebiscite" was interpreted in a different way than what the Project Manager envisaged, leading to discrepancies in coding.

---

[11] Another relevant and vital feature of the data collection is that the historical coding is linked with the contemporary coding through the historical and contemporary experts coding 20 over-lapping years (typically 1900–1920).

We handle problems with *evaluative* questions (C-type indicators) with restraint. We know that any question requiring judgment will elicit a range of answers, even when all coders are highly knowledgeable about a subject. A key element of the V-Dem project – setting it apart from most other indices that rely on expert coding – is coder independence: each coder does her work in isolation from other coders and members of the V-Dem team (apart from clarifying questions about the process). The distribution of responses across questions, countries, and years thus provides vital insight into the relative certainty of each data point. Since a principal goal of the V-Dem project is to produce informative estimates of uncertainty we do not wish to tamper with evidence that contributes to those estimates. Arguably, the noise in the data is as informative as the signal. Moreover, wayward coders (i.e., coders who diverge from other coders) are unlikely to have a strong influence on the point estimates that result from the measurement model's aggregation across five or more coders. This is especially the case if the wayward coders are consistently off (across all their ratings).

That said, there have been instances when we have altered C-data. A few questions were largely of factual nature (e.g., number of legislative chambers; if a local government exists, which offices were elected in a particular election). Since we later acquired enough funding to have assistants conduct the factual coding based on systematic consultation of credible sources, we discharged the data submitted by Country Experts for these particular questions and any data dependent on them.

For example, if a Country Expert indicated that there were two chambers in the legislature for a particular year, s/he then coded "downstream" in the questionnaire a series of questions regarding both the lower and upper chamber. If our research established that an upper chamber did not, in fact, exist in that particular year, we removed from the data set the records of data provided by the expert for the upper chamber. This cleaning affected 19 percent of all executive data submitted for those downstream variables, 7.7 percent of the data in the election survey and 11 percent in the legislative survey. These numbers reflect places where coders unnecessarily coded due either to (1) technical bug creating a problem with the skipping function in the online surveys, (2) coders' ability to change the precoded, factual data in the initial years of the project, or (3) an initial decision, subsequently reversed, to have Country Experts answer some of the A-coded (more factual) questions.

In a final case, we removed original coding by some Country Experts because of a factual misunderstanding (or misunderstanding about response-categories) about the existence of the internet in eras prior to its invention. In all these situations, we maintain the original coder-level data in archived files that may be retrieved by special request of the Principal Investigators.

We also purge the raw data of duplicate ratings. The way the research database and coding interfaces were constructed (now changed), data was recorded as a unique new entry each time a Country Expert pressed "submit" in the online coding system. This often resulted in several duplicate ratings (sometimes with a different value) for a particular coder-country-variable-year combination. Assuming that the last submitted score reflects the coder's final call, we decided to use the unique rating IDs (equivalent to time stamps) to delete the duplicate ratings and keep the last one only.

3.8 PERSONNEL

For the post-1900 coding, V-Dem relies on a network of 30 respected scholars who serve as Regional Managers. Regional Managers are typically prominent scholars in the region in question who have democracy expertise. In some cases, Regional Managers are located outside of the region, if they are currently active in well-respected international think tanks or similar institutions. The "regions" in the V-Dem world are unorthodox and determined by expertise in order to ensure that Regional Managers are comfortable with the countries they handle. When a person agrees to be a Regional Manager, we work with him or her to identify suitable candidates to be Country Coordinators. Country Coordinators are almost always nationals and residents of the country to be coded. They are also typically scholars, although more junior than Regional Managers. All Country Coordinators are vetted by a Regional Manager and at least one Principal Investigator and one program manager, sometimes with input from a Project Manager with expertise in that area of the world.

Once a Regional Manager and a Country Coordinator are recruited for a country, the search for potential Country Experts begins. Since we endeavor to find a minimum of five Country Experts to code each country-year for every indicator, and since few Country Experts code more than a few surveys out of the 11, we often end up recruiting 15 to 20 Country Experts per country. Since the coding by Country Experts involves evaluative judgments on the part of the coder, we take a number of precautions to ensure that coders are qualified in order to minimize error and noise in the data. Consequently, we pay a great deal of care and attention to the recruitment of these scholars, following a strict protocol.

First, we identify a list of potential coders for a country (typically 100–200 names per country). Regional Managers, in consultation with Country Coordinators, use their detailed knowledge of the country to identify the bulk of the experts on this list. Staff at the V-Dem Institute, and sometimes Principal Investigators and Project Managers, also supply names of external experts, using readily available information drawn from the internet, professional associations, and recommendations from their colleagues.

We have institutionalized a protocol with five criteria for potential Country Experts. The most important selection criterion is an individual's expertise in the country or countries and surveys they may be assigned to code. This expertise is usually signified by an advanced degree in the social sciences, law, or history; a record of publications; or positions outside political society that establish their expertise in the chosen area (e.g., a well-known and respected senior media editor; a respected former high court judge). Regional Managers and Country Coordinators are also asked to indicate for which surveys a potential coder has expertise. Naturally, coders are drawn to areas of the survey that they are most familiar with, and are unlikely to agree to code topics they know little about. As a result, self-selection also works to achieve our primary goal of matching questions in the survey with coder expertise.

The second criterion is connection to the country to be coded. By design, at least three out of five of the Country Experts recruited to code a particular country survey should be nationals or permanent residents of that country. Exceptions are made for a small number of countries where it is difficult to find in-country coders who are both qualified and independent of the governing regime, or where in-country coders might be placed at risk.

The third criterion is the prospective coder's seriousness of purpose, i.e., her or his willingness to devote time to the project and to deliberate carefully over the questions asked in the survey. Sometimes, personal acquaintance is enough to convince the Regional Manager and Country Coordinator that a person is fit, or unfit, for the task. Sometimes, this feature becomes apparent in communications with Program Managers that precede the offer to work on V-Dem. This communication is quite intensive, with an average of 13 interactions before coding is concluded, and it involves requiring the potential coder to read and work with several lengthy, detailed documents. This process tends to flag potential coders who are not serious enough.

The fourth criterion is impartiality. V-Dem aims to recruit coders who will answer survey questions in an impartial manner. We therefore avoid those individuals who might be beholden to powerful actors – by reason of coercive threats or material incentives – or who serve as spokespersons for a political party or ideological tendency. Close association (current or past) with political parties, senior government officials, politically affiliated think tanks or institutes, are grounds for disqualification. In the few cases where finding impartial coders is difficult (such as present-day Venezuela), we aim to include a variety of coders who collectively represent a range of views and political perspectives on the country in question.

The final criterion is obtaining diversity in professional background among the coders chosen for a particular country. For certain areas (e.g., the media, judiciary, and civil society surveys), such diversity entails a mixture of academics and professionals who study these topics. It also means finding experts who are located at a variety of institutions, universities, and research institutes since people in institutions sometimes develop a particular collective perspective.

We compile basic information on each Country Expert using short biographical sketches, publications, website information, or similar material, including their country of origin, current location, highest educational degree, current position, and area of documented expertise to make sure we adhere to the five recruitment criteria.

After weighing these five criteria, Regional Managers and Country Coordinators suggest a priority from "1" to "3" for all the 100–200 potential experts on the list of candidates for each country, indicating the order of priority we give to recruiting an expert. The Program Managers and one of the Principal Investigators review these choices and make adjustments if necessary.

Using this process, we have recruited more than 3000 scholars and experts from more than 170 countries selected from our database of potential experts containing some 25,000 names. Over 30 percent of the Country Experts are women[12] and more than 80 percent have PhDs or MAs and are affiliated with research institutions, think tanks, or similar organizations. Because attrition is unavoidable, we have had to recruit replacements. Replacement Country Experts recruited after the initial round of coding, which covered 1900 to 2012, are asked to code a short period starting in 2005. This avoids forcing recoding of a long period that has already been covered with sufficient number of Country Experts, and also ensures sufficient coding of overlapping years to allow the Bayesian IRT model to compare new Country Experts to preexisting ones. In the update for 2017, 75 of the Country Experts were returning coders.

Except for the second and fifth criteria, listed above, for recruiting experts to the post-1900 coding, the same criteria were applied for recruiting historical experts. (We note that the fourth criterion was of little practical relevance for the lists of experts considered for the historical coding). Yet, given the relative scarcity of historical experts, and the differences in design discussed above, the weighting of the criteria is slightly different, and the first, and most important, criterion on expertise is adjusted.

Since Historical V-Dem originally remunerated one expert for taking on the task of coding all C questions,[13] the first criterion (expertise) suggested that we should prioritize recruiting academics with a broad knowledge of the political system in the 1789–1920 time span (or, at least, large parts of it). Political historians having written renowned monographs on "The Political History of Country X," were often considered to be the preferred expert.

The "seriousness of purpose" criterion was also key when deciding between potential experts. Team members – typically RAs in Oslo or Lund and/or Knutsen and Teorell – engaged in email and sometimes Skype conversations with potential experts. This helped ensure that prospective experts were properly motivated and they understood and were comfortable with the

---

[12] The number of women among the ranks of our Country Experts is lower than we would have liked, despite our strenuous efforts to recruit women. However, it reflects gender inequalities with regard to education and university careers in the world.

[13] Later on, several historical time series have been coded by a second expert.

coding task. (Not all historians, for example, are comfortable with assigning "crude" scores on ordinal scales to complex phenomena).[14]

In sum, ideal historical experts would have a long academic record working on the political history of "their" country, and experts with identifiable competencies in a broad specter of relevant political institutions and processes were prioritized. Secondly, evaluations on "seriousness of purpose" were weighted whenever dealing with about equally qualified experts. Next, everything else equal, experts with comparative knowledge of other countries were prioritized over other experts.

Given the difficulty of identifying and replacing historical experts, the process for recruiting and following them up was also different. Team members, including specifically assigned RAs, conducted thorough searches for potential experts, employing scholarly networks (especially within communities of historians) as well as web and literature searches. Suggestions were compiled and evaluated with the aim to rank-order the best possible experts for each country. Selected team members or RAs constructed initial rankings, with written justifications. These evaluations were thereafter debated by the two PIs (Knutsen and Teorell), who would either make a decision on the final ranking or go back to the team member making the suggestion for further clarification and discussion. Next, we contacted the first-priority expert. (Whenever there were two or more about equally qualified experts, we would contact them simultaneously.) If the highest priority expert(s) declined, we continued with the next priority, and so on. Whenever we received new information, especially suggestions for alternative experts from prioritized experts who declined, we updated the list and reevaluated the prioritized order. Some experts, with comprehensive knowledge of different polities, were asked and agreed to code more than one polity (for instance, the Baden expert also coded Würtemberg).

3.8.1 Confidentiality

In order to preserve confidentiality, V-Dem has adopted a policy of neither confirming nor denying the identities of Country Experts. At present, only the two Program Managers (and the Institute's Director, who has supervisory authority over the process) are actively involved in the final stage of recruitment and have access to the identities of the actual Country Experts. The Program Managers also handle all correspondence with Country Experts so that we do not inadvertently reveal this confidential information through communication with third parties.

---

[14] During such communication, experts would also often provide feedback on the proposed country definitions and engage in discussions about the meaningfulness of responding to particular questions and how to interpret core concepts, e.g., on the understanding of "civil society" and "political parties" in the nineteenth-century context. Historical experts were also recommended, continuously throughout the coding process, to bring up such issues and were in close contact with a researcher on the team, Haakon Gjerløw at the University of Oslo, in this regard.

Thus, while we publicize the identity of other members of the V-Dem endeavor on our web site, we preserve the confidentiality of Country Experts. Several reasons motivate this practice. First, there are a number of countries in the world where authorities might sanction Country Experts, or their families or friends, for their involvement in the project. Second, there is no way to predict which country may in the future become repressive, such as happened in Turkey over the last few years. Third, we anticipate that V-Dem data may become used in evaluations and assessments internationally in ways that could affect a country's status. These assessments create incentives for certain governments to try to influence Country Experts. Fourth, although many Country Experts are not subject to such pressures, revealing their identities would make it easier to identify other by process of elimination. The Principal Investigators therefore decided that the best way to protect the anonymity of some participants is to protect the anonymity of all of them.

Given the lower political sensitivity of coding the pre-1900 period than the present-day situation, the above-described risks to coders, generally, do not apply. Hence, the historical coders had the option to be named as the historical expert for their country (and be listed on the V-Dem webpage) or remain anonymous. Only a small handful of the historical experts have so far preferred to be anonymous.

3.8.2 Staff

The V-Dem research infrastructure includes human capital built during several years. We have had many temporary research assistants in Gothenburg and, at American universities, many doctoral students who worked on the project during the development phase for 6–24 months but no longer work with V-Dem. However, the V-Dem Institute now has dedicated and qualified staff who are relatively permanent. While some alternation is unavoidable, they are mostly permanent employees and postdocs who have been trained over an extended period, and to a large extent come to contribute directly to the development of the research infrastructure in many critical ways. Taken together, they are today responsible for all aforementioned tasks, as well as for overall management, financial management and administration, communication and outreach, and participation in fund-raising and policy-related activities. Their continuity and accumulated experience are crucial for the maintenance and improvement of the V-Dem infrastructure, the timely annual data updates, and for preserving the high standard of work.

3.9 PHASES OF DATA COLLECTION

In the first phase of data collection (from 2012 to 2014), we asked Country Experts to code their surveys for a single country from 1900 (or the relevant first year for a particular country) to the end of 2012. Over almost three years,

Program Managers worked in overlapping "waves" where different sets of countries were coded until eventually the initial 173 countries (out of which 168 still existed in 2012) were covered.

Now we have moved to an annual update cycle that roughly looks like this:

- *August to December* is the preparations phase, including recruitment of returning and new Country Experts with assistance of Regional Managers and Country Coordinators based on predicted needs from the last round of coding. During this phase we review and test the coding interface and related functions to ensure full functionality; collect and upload precoded factual data (election dates, number and names of legislative chambers, titles and names of head of state and head of government); analyze the missingness of data from previous rounds; prepare country-surveys for the next upcoming update and test and review them; restructure and test the remaining systems, data coding interface, data storage system, and cleaning and quality control protocols; improve the user-friendliness of online tools and the performance of the website, as well as adding or improving necessary functionality to the research database, the administrative database, and the coding interfaces, when funds allow.
- *January*: Country Coordinators and Country Experts code the year(s) to be updated across all surveys; Program Managers attend to bug fixes, questions, coding progress, and reminders.
- *February–March*: We execute quality control and cleaning protocols; run measurement model to aggregate data from coder to country-years; aggregate indicators to indices; finalize A-data update collection and crosschecks; run data diagnostics and crosschecks; create all versions of the V-Dem data set; upload new data sets into tables for online graphing; update the *Codebook*, methodology, countries, and organization and management documents; and handle the payments of coders.
- *April*: We publish the data and V-Dem's annual Democracy Report, and hold public events and talks.
- *May–June*: There is an annual V-Dem conference in Gothenburg in May. We also do financial evaluation and reporting; systems checks, evaluation of protocols and procedures, planning of adjustments; and make a detailed plan for next year's data update cycle.

From fall 2014 to spring 2015 we started this annual cycle and conducted the first update. It covered 54 countries – bringing their data up to end-2014 – and also added six new countries (with data from 1900 to 2014) for which we had funding. When they coded for 2013 and 2014, returning Country Experts saw their previously submitted ratings for the years from 2010 to 2012, so as to encourage consistency in ratings over time, although we did not allow them to alter those ratings. We asked the new replacement Country Experts to code 10 years (2005–14) so as to ensure that their scores overlap by a number of years with returning Country Experts' ratings.

The second round of annual updates was 2014–15. We had funding for 76 countries, 22 of which were also covered in the first update. Hence, v6.0 of the V-Dem data set released in March 2016 includes data for all 173 countries up to 2012, and up to 2014 or 2015 for 114 countries. Returning coders saw their prior ratings as in the first update, and were this time able to revise them if they wished to. New Country Experts coded the years 2005–15. Finally, we implemented the first trial series of anchoring vignettes for each survey to give us additional leverage on measurement error.

The third update took place during 2016–17, with the release of data in May 2017. This was the first full update covering all the 173 countries plus adding four new countries: Oman, Singapore, Equatorial Guinea, and Kuwait. We also implemented vignettes for all questions and all Country Experts for the first time. All Country Experts were asked to answer a random sample of vignettes for each survey, with randomization being engineered to ensure all vignettes also reached a sample quota to guarantee enough data for the measurement model.

The fourth update was concluded in April 2018. We added four more countries (Bahrain, United Arab Emirates, Luxembourg, and Hong Kong) to make the total number 181 and fielded the two first pilot questions for a project aiming at prediction: *Varieties of Future Democracy*. A major addition in this update was the merger of Historical V-Dem's data with the existing data, for the first release of the full version 8 data set covering 1789–2017.

Going forward it is our ambition to continue with annual updates of all countries in the V-Dem data set, and if possible, add a few more countries. At the time of writing, we have secured funding to guarantee this will happen in 2019 and 2020.

3.10   INTERNATIONAL COLLABORATIONS TO PRODUCE DATA

V-Dem data is not only relevant for the academic world: we are also striving to reach out to policy makers, democracy practitioners, students, journalists, civil society activists, and citizens interested in democracy development. In order to bridge the academic-practitioners-policy worlds, we have engaged in many collaborations and participated in different types of policy forums and dialogues. Some of these efforts have led us to branch out into data collection and index creation for partner organizations. These collaborations include:

- V-Dem and International IDEA collaborated from 2014 to 2017. This has generated funding via NORAD-Norway and the Ministry for Foreign Affairs-Sweden for updating data for 40 countries as well as a series of country reports. We have also assisted IDEA with the creation of its own Global State of Democracy indices, which follow IDEA's conceptual frame-work but make extensive use of V-Dem data. Svend-Erik Skanning spear-headed this project.

- For the World Bank, we designed and conducted a special expert survey on elite bargaining over power and authored a background paper for the 2017 World Development Report on sequencing of accountability mechanisms using V-Dem data. The WDR report also include analyses using V-Dem data.
- The World Bank Governance Indicators are now starting to use V-Dem data as a source.
- V-Dem has been involved in UNDP's work on how to measure Sustainable Development Goal 16 since 2014. We presented the V-Dem data and achievements in the UNDP Headquarters in New York, have been active in the Virtual Network expert group, and participated in a series of high-level conferences and meetings. The report resulting from the work of the network includes 60 V-Dem indicators. This work continues today in a collaboration coordinated by the Community of Democracies for UNDP.
- With the Community of Democracies, we have also engaged in several activities and have developed a measurement scheme for them to have their own democracy measure based on the 19 founding principles of the Warsaw Declaration.
- We have developed an index on political participation, based on V-Dem data, for the Council of Europe.
- The Mo Ibrahim Foundation have decided to use several V-Dem indicators and indices in their Ibrahim Index of African Governance. We continue to consult IIAG on measurement, data, and index construction.
- Transparency International has decided to include some of our corruption measures in their compilation of the Corruption Perceptions Index.

4

The Measurement Model and Reliability[*]

V-Dem relies on Country Experts who code a host of ordinal variables, providing subjective ratings of latent – that is, not directly observable – regime characteristics over time. Sets of around five experts rate each case (country-year observation), and each of these raters works independently. Since raters may diverge in their coding because of either differences of opinion or mistakes, we require systematic tools with which to model these patterns of disagreement. These tools allow us to aggregate ratings into point estimates of latent concepts and quantify our uncertainty around these point estimates. This chapter provides an introduction to the statistical tools that V-Dem uses to aggregate experts' ratings into country-year scores, and to estimate measurement uncertainty. Specifically, we describe item response theory models that can account and adjust for differential item functioning (i.e., differences in how experts apply ordinal scales to cases) and variation in rater reliability (i.e., random error). We also discuss key challenges specific to applying item response theory to expert-coded cross-national panel data, explain the approaches that we use to address these challenges, highlight potential problems with our current framework, and describe long-term plans for improving our models and estimates. Finally, we provide an overview of the different forms in which we present model output.

The V-Dem data set contains a variety of measures, ranging from objective – and directly observable – indicators that research assistants

[*] The lead author of this chapter was Daniel Pemstein, with contributions by Kyle Marquardt, Brigitte Seim, Eitan Tzelgov, Yi-ting Wang, and Farhad Miri. This chapter is largely based on the 3rd edition of V-Dem Working Paper 21. Readers may wish to consult the current version of the working paper, which stays current with V-Dem's measurement strategy.

Question: Is there freedom from political killings?

Clarification: Political killings are killings by the state or its agents without due process of law for the purpose of eliminating political opponents. These killings are the result of deliberate use of lethal force by the police, security forces, prison officials, or other agents of the state (including paramilitary groups).

Responses:

  0 Not respected by public authorities. Political killings are practiced systematically and they are typically incited and approved by top leaders of government.

  1 Weakly respected by public authorities. Political killings are practiced frequently and top leaders of government are not actively working to prevent them.

  2 Somewhat respected by public authorities. Political killings are practiced occasionally but they are typically not incited and approved by top leaders of government.

  3 Mostly respected by public authorities. Political killings are practiced in a few isolated cases but they are not incited or approved by top leaders of government.

  4 Fully respected by public authorities. Political killings are nonexistent.

FIGURE 4.1 V-Dem question *v2clkill*, freedom from political killings.

coded, to subjective – or latent – items rated by multiple experts. Our focus in this chapter is on the latter set of measures, which are subjective ordinal items that a number – typically five – of raters[1] code for each country-year. Figure 4.1 provides an example of one such measure, which assesses the degree to which citizens of a state were free from political killings in a given year, using a scale from zero to four. This question includes a substantial subjective component: raters cannot simply look up the answer to this question and answer it objectively. Indeed, many states take active measures to obfuscate the extent to which they rely on extrajudicial killing to maintain power. Furthermore, not only is the evaluation of the latent trait subjective, but raters may have varying understandings of the ordinal options that we provide to them: Mary's "somewhat" may be Bob's "mostly." Finally, because this question is not easy to answer, raters may make mistakes or approach the question using different sources of information on the topic, some more reliable than others.

---

[1] V-Dem documentation refers to "raters" as "Country Experts," "Expert Coders," or "Coders."

Here we describe the statistical tools that we use to model the latent scores that underlie different coders' estimates. These tools take into account the subjective aspect of the rating problem, the potential for raters to inconsistently apply the same ordinal scales to cases (generally country-year observations), and rater error. We also identify key potential problems with our current methods and describe ongoing work to improve how we measure these items. Finally, we discuss the different forms in which we present the output from our models.

4.1 BASIC NOTATION

To more formally describe our data, we introduce notation to describe the V-Dem data set, which contains ratings of a vast number of indicators that vary both geographically and temporally. Moreover, more than one rater codes each indicator. As a result, there are

- $i \in I$ indicator variables,
- $r \in R$ raters,
- $c \in C$ countries,
- and $t \in T = \{1, \ldots, \bar{t}\}$ time periods.

I is the set of indicator variables while i represents one element from that set, and so forth. Each of the $|R|$ raters provides ratings of one or more of each of the $|I|$ indicators in some subset of the available $n = |C| \times |T|$ country-years[2] covered by the data set. Each country enters the data set at time $\underline{t}_c$ and exits at time $\bar{t}_c + 1$. We refer to rater r's set of observed ratings/judgments J_r. Each element of each of these judgment sets is an i, c, t triple. Similarly, the set of raters that rated country-year c, t is R_{ct}. Finally, we denote a rater's primary country of expertise c_r. In this chapter we focus on models for a single indicator, and therefore drop the i indices from our notation. For a given indicator we observe a sparse[3] $|C| \times |T| \times |R|$ array, y, of ordinal ratings.

4.2 MODELING EXPERT RATINGS

The concepts that the V-Dem project asks raters to measure – such as access to justice, electoral corruption, and freedom from government-sponsored violence – are inherently unobservable, or latent. There is no obvious way to objectively quantify the extent to which a given case

---

[2] Some variables in the V-Dem data set do not follow the country-year format. For example, elections occur with different patterns of regularity cross-nationally. The V-Dem coding software also allows coders to add additional dates within years, if something changed significantly at a particular date. However, for the purpose of simplicity, we refer to the data as being country-year unless otherwise specified.

[3] The majority of raters provide ratings for only one country, as we discuss in more detail below.

"embodies" each of these concepts. Raters instead observe manifestations of these latent traits. Several brief examples illustrate this point. First, in assessing the concept of equal access to justice based on gender, a rater might take into consideration whether or not women and men have equal rates of success when suing for damages in a divorce case. Second, to determine whether or not a country has free and fair elections, a rater may consider whether or not election officials have been caught taking bribes. Third, in assessing whether or not a government respects its citizens' right to live, a rater might take into account whether or not political opposition members have disappeared.

As different raters observe different manifestations of these latent traits, and assign different weights to these manifestations, we ask experts to place the latent values for different cases on a rough scale from low to high, with thresholds defined in plain language. (Again, Figure 4.1 provides an illustration.) However, we assume that these judgments are realizations of latent concepts that exist on a continuous scale. Furthermore, we allow for the possibility that coders will make nonsystematic mistakes, either because they overlook relevant information, put credence in faulty observations, or otherwise misperceive the true latent level of a variable in a given case. In particular, we assume that each rater first perceives latent values with error, such that

$$\tilde{y}_{ctr} = z_{ct} + e_{ctr}, \tag{4.1}$$

where z_{ct} is the "true" latent value of the given concept in country c at time t, $\tilde{y}_{ctr}$ is rater r's perception of z_{ct}, and e_{ctr} is the error in rater r's perception for the country-year observation. The cumulative distribution function for the rating errors is

$$e_{ctr} \sim F(e_{ctr}/\sigma_r). \tag{4.2}$$

Having made these assumptions about the underlying latent distribution of country-year scores, it is necessary to determine how these latent scores map onto the ordinal scales which we present to raters.

4.2.1 Differential Item Functioning

The error term in Eq. (4.1) allows us to model random errors. However, raters also answer survey questions and assess regime characteristics in systematically different ways. This problem is known as differential item functioning (DIF). In our context, individual experts may idiosyncratically perceive latent regime characteristics, and therefore map those perceptions onto the ordinal scales described by the *V-Dem Codebook* (Coppedge et al. 2016a) differently from one another. Consider again Figure 4.1, which depicts *v2clkill*, Freedom from political killings. While it might seem easy to define what it means for political killings to be "nonexistent,"[4] descriptions of freedom from political killings like "mostly respected" and "weakly respected" are open to interpretation: raters may be more or less strict in their applications of these thresholds. Indeed, the fact that five different coders rate a particular observation the same on this scale – e.g., they all give it a "3" or "Mostly respected" – does not mean that they wholly agree on the extent to which the relevant public authorities respect citizens' freedom from political killing. These differences in item functioning may manifest across countries, or between raters within the same country; they may be the result of observable rater characteristics (e.g., nationality or educational background), or unobservable individual differences. Many expert rating projects with multiple raters per case report average rater responses as point estimates, but this approach is inappropriate in the face of strong evidence of DIF (King and Wand 2007).[5] We therefore require tools that will model, and adjust for, DIF when producing point estimates and measures of confidence.

To address DIF, we allow for the possibility that raters apply different thresholds when mapping their perceptions of latent traits – each $\tilde{y}_{ctr}$ – into the ordinal ratings that they provide to the project. Formally, for the cases that she judges (J_r), rater r places a country-year in category k if $\tau_{r,k-1} < \tilde{y}_{ctr} \leq \tau_{r,k}$, where each τ represents a rater threshold on the underlying latent scale. The vector $\boldsymbol{\tau}_r = (\tau_{r,1}, \ldots, \tau_{r,K-1})$ is the vector of unobserved ranking cutoffs for rater r on the latent scale. We fix each $\tau_{r,0} = -\infty$ and $\tau_{r,K} = \infty$, where K is the number of ordinal categories raters use to judge the indicator.

4.2.2 A Probability Model for Rater Behavior

When combined, the assumptions described by the preceding sections imply that our model must take differences in (1) rater reliability and (2) rater thresholds into account in order to yield reasonable estimates of the latent concepts in which we are interested. As a result, we model the data as following this data-generating process:

---

[4] Even when raters know of no evidence that political killings occurred in a given country-year, public authorities might not fully respect freedom from such violence: even descriptions that might seem clear-cut at first glance are potentially open to interpretation. In such situations, two raters with identical information about observable implications for a case might apply different standards when rating a regime's respect for personal right to life.

[5] Reporting rater means and standard deviations, without adjusting for DIF, remains the standard operating procedure in expert rating projects within political science. However, practices are beginning to change. For example, see Bakker et al. (2014), which applies anchoring vignettes (King and Wand 2007) to an expert survey of European party positions. Lindstadt et al. (2015) offer a detailed critique of the standard practice and propose a bootstrapping procedure as an alternative approach.

$$\Pr(y_{ctr} = k) = \Pr(\tilde{y}_{ctr} > \tau_{r,k-1} \wedge \tilde{y}_{ctr} \leq \tau_{r,k})$$

$$= \Pr(e_{ctr} > \tau_{r,k-1} - z_{ct} \wedge e_{ctr} \leq \tau_{r,k} - z_{ct})$$

$$= F\left(\frac{\tau_{r,k} - z_{ct}}{\sigma_r}\right) - F\left(\frac{\tau_{r,k-1} - z_{ct}}{\sigma_r}\right) \tag{4.3}$$

$$= F(\gamma_{r,k} - z_{ct}\beta_r) - F(\gamma_{r,k-1} - z_{ct}\beta_r).$$

The last two lines of Eq. (4.3) reflect two common parameterizations of this model. The first parameterization is typically called multirater ordinal probit (MROP) (Johnson and Albert 1999; Pemstein et al. 2010),[6] while the latter is an ordinal item response theory (O-IRT) setup (Clinton and Lewis 2008; Treier and Jackman 2008). Note that $\beta_r = \frac{1}{\sigma_r}$ and $\gamma_{r,k} = \frac{\tau_{r,k}}{\sigma_r}$.[7] The parameter σ_r is a measure of rater r's reliability when judging the indicator; specifically, it represents the size of r's typical errors. Raters with small σ_r parameters are better, on average, at judging indicator i than are raters with large σ_r parameters. In the IRT literature, β_r is known as the discrimination parameter, while each γ is a difficulty parameter. The discrimination parameter is a measure of precision. For example, a rater characterized by an item discrimination parameter close to zero will be largely unresponsive to true indicator values when making judgments, i.e., her coding is essentially noise. In contrast, a rater with a discrimination parameter far from zero will be very "discriminating": her judgments closely map to the "true" value of a concept in a given case. The γ and τ parameters are thresholds that control how raters map their perceptions on the latent interval scale into ordinal classifications.[8]

As discussed previously, we allow these parameters to vary by rater to account for DIF.

4.2.3 Temporal Dependence and Observation Granularity

V-Dem experts may enter codes at the country-day level, although many provide country-year ratings in practice. Yet, as Melton et al. (2014) argue, it is often unwise to assume that the codes that experts provide for regime characteristics are independent across time, even after conditioning on the true value of the latent trait.

Note that temporal dependence in the latent traits – the fact that regime characteristics at time t and $t + 1$ are not independent – causes no appreciable problem for our modeling approach. This fact may not seem obvious at first, but note that (4.1) – (4.3) make no assumptions about temporal (in)dependence across each z_{ct}. While we do make prior assumptions about the distribution of

---

[6] If we assume $F(\cdot)$ is standard normal.

[7] This equivalency breaks down if we allow for β_r parameters less than 0. Thus, the O-IRT model is potentially more general than MROP.

[8] The term "difficulty parameter" stems from applications in educational testing where the latent variable is ability and observed ratings are binary (in)correct answers to test questions.

each z_{ct}, the approach we describe in Section 2.4 will tend to capture the temporal dependence in regime traits; our priors are also vague and allow the data to speak for themselves. In fact, as Melton et al. (2014) argue, "dynamic" IRT models (Martin and Quinn 2002; Schnakenberg and Fariss 2014; Linzer and Staton 2015) are more restrictive than standard models with vague priors, because their tight prior variances assume that latent traits at time t equal those at $t - 1$. While these dynamic models can be helpful in shrinking posterior uncertainty by incorporating often-accurate prior information about regimes' tendency toward stasis, they can over-smooth abrupt transitions (Melton et al. 2014). They are also inherently optimistic about model uncertainty. We prefer a more pessimistic approach.[9]

Importantly, temporal dependence in rater errors violates the assumption described by Eq. (4.2).[10] The mismatch between actual rating granularity and the standard practice of treating expert codes as yearly – or even finer-grained – observations, is perhaps the key driver of temporal dependence in rater errors, in our context. Crucially, when, in practice, experts code stable periods, rather than years, their yearly errors will be perfectly correlated within those periods. It is difficult to discern the temporal specificity of the ratings that our experts

---

[9] Analyses we conducted over the course of developing the model bore out our pessimism. We attempted to model the complete time series of the V-Dem data using two main strategies. The first strategy involved assuming that all years following the initial coding year are a function of the previous year (i.e., $Z_{c,t} \sim N(Z_{c,t-1}, 1)$). The second strategy modeled country-year data as a function of a prior radiating from the year in which the country had the best bridging, which itself had either a vague or empirical prior. As expected, both of these methods and their subsets substantially smoothed country-year estimates for countries with substantial, and abrupt, temporal variation. For example, in the case of political killings in Germany, this smoothing meant that the years of the Holocaust obtained scores substantially higher than is either accurate or what the raters intended: these years clearly belong to the lowest category, and raters universally coded them as such. However, Germany's high scores in the postwar era pulled Holocaust-period estimates upward, albeit with great uncertainty about the estimate. We were able to ameliorate this problem somewhat by divorcing country-years with sharp shifts in codes from the overall country time trends. For example, we assigned a vague prior to country-years with a change in average raw scores greater than one or allowed the prior variance to vary by the change in the size of the shift in raw scores. However, both of these approaches are problematically arbitrary in terms of assigning variance or cutoffs for a "large" shift; they also reduce bridging in the data. Finally, our attempts to add temporal trends to the data also yielded unforeseen problems. Most noticeably, in years with constant coding (i.e., no temporal variation in rater scores), scores would trend either upward or downward in a manner inconsistent with both the rater-level data and our knowledge of the cases. Attempts to remedy this issue by reducing prior variance for years with constant coding again faces the issue of being arbitrary, and also only served to reduce the scale of the problem, not the trends themselves. Additionally, temporal modeling of the data with radiating priors leads to "death spirals" in countries with generally low scores and few coders: years in the lowest categories yielded strong and very low priors for preceding years, which the data were not able to overcome. As a result, the priors essentially locked these countries in the lowest category for years preceding events in the lowest category, even if rater-level data indicated that these preceding years should not be in the lowest category.

[10] Note that dynamic IRT models do not address this issue; rather, they model stickiness in the latent traits.

provide, but it is self-evident that experts judge chunks of time as whole units, rather than independently evaluating single years. Indeed, the V-Dem coding interface even includes a "click and drag" feature that allows raters to quickly and easily apply a single code to an extended swath of time.[11] Typically, expert ratings reported at fine granularity may actually provide ratings spanning "regimes," or periods of institutional stasis, rather than years or days. As a result, treating these data as yearly – or, worse, daily – would likely have pernicious side-effects; most notably it could cause the model to produce estimates of uncertainty that are too liberal (too certain), given actual observation granularity.

While we cannot completely address the potential for serially correlated rating errors,[12] we have adopted a conservative approach to the problem of observation granularity. Specifically, we treat any stretch of time, within a country c, in which no expert provides two differing ratings, or estimates of confidence,[13] as a single observation. As a result, each time period t represents a "regime," rather than a single year or day,[14] and time units are irregular.[15] This is a conservative approach because it produces the smallest number of observations consistent with the pattern of variation in the data. In turn, treating the data as observed at this level of granularity yields the largest possible estimates of uncertainty, given patterns of rater agreement. For example, for many measures, numerous northern European states sport constant, and consistently high, codes across all raters in the postwar period. If we were to treat these observations as yearly, we would infer that our raters are remarkably reliable, based on repeated intercoder agreement. These reliability estimates would, in turn, yield tight credible intervals around point estimates. Using our approach, such periods count as only a single observation, providing substantially less assurance that our raters are reliable. This approach is probably too conservative – experts might be providing nominally

---

[11] Unfortunately, our web-based coding platform does not record when experts make use of this feature.

[12] Rating errors may exhibit intertemporal dependence even across periods of regime stasis, an issue that the literature on comparative regime trait measurement has yet to adequately address, and an issue we hope to remedy in future work.

[13] As we note in Section 4.2.4, the V-Dem interface allows raters to provide an estimate, on a scale from zero to 100, of their relative confidence in each score that they provide.

[14] Regimes start and end on days, not years, although the V-Dem data are released at both daily and yearly granularity.

[15] For cases in which one or more raters reported a change in a variable value over the course of a year (i.e., they report more than one value for a single year), we interpolated the scores of the other coders to that date (i.e., we assumed that they would have coded that date as being the same as the rest of the year, as their coding suggests) and then estimated the latent value for that date within the framework of the overall model. These estimates are available in the country-date data set. The country-year data set represents the day-weighted average of all scores in a given country-year.

independent ratings of time chunks, such as decades – but we have chosen to err on the side of caution with respect to estimates of uncertainty.

It is important to note that we are relying on the roughly five Country Experts, who generally rate the whole time period for each country, to delineate "regimes." As we note in Section 2.4, we have obtained lateral codes from numerous raters, asking them to rate a single year within a country – other than their primary country of expertise – about which they feel qualified to provide data. When these ratings fall within a multiyear "regime," our data-collapsing approach will treat their single-year rating as an evaluation of the whole span. This provides substantial dividends with respect to obtaining cross-national scale identification,[16] but it entails a strong assumption. Namely, we are assuming that our lateral coders would not have changed their ratings across periods of stasis identified by Country Experts. Thus, while our data reduction approach is generally a conservative decision, it does, in a sense, impute observations for lateral coders. We argue that this assumption is reasonable because experts should be qualified to identify periods of stasis within their countries of focus, but we hope to avoid making this assumption when more data are available, as we describe in Section 4.6.

4.2.4 Prior Assumptions and Cross-National Comparability

Cross-national surveys such as V-Dem face a scale identification problem that is driven by the fact that the γ and τ parameters may – and perhaps are even likely to – vary across raters hailing from different cultural and educational backgrounds. While we have many overlapping observations – typically the whole time span of more than 100 years – for experts within countries, relatively few observations allow us to compare the behavior of experts across countries. While the measurement model that we describe above therefore has little trouble estimating relative thresholds (e.g., γ) for raters within countries, it can have difficulty estimating the relative threshold placement of raters across countries. For that reason, we have collected a substantial number of bridge – where a Country Expert rates a second country for an extended time period – and lateral – where a Country Expert rates multiple additional countries for a short period, typically one year – coders to help alleviate this problem. Nonetheless, few experts have the ability to rate more than a few countries, and many justifiably do not feel comfortable providing judgments for countries other than their own. As a result, we currently lack the necessary overlapping observations to completely identify the scale of the latent trait cross-nationally (Pemstein et al. 2015). While we are developing techniques and collecting further data to overcome this issue, we currently adopt an explicitly Bayesian

---

[16] Although, as we note in Section 4.2.4, we currently lack sufficient bridge and lateral coding to obtain strong cross-national scale identification.

approach and make substantial use of prior information to obtain estimates that exhibit strong face validity, both within and across countries.[17]

Completing the model specification described in Section 4.2.2 requires adopting prior distributions for the model parameters. We focus on the O-IRT parameterization here. First, we assume $\beta_r \sim \mathcal{N}(1,1)$, truncated so that it never has a value less than zero. The assumption of truncation at zero equates to assuming that raters correctly observe the sign of the latent trait and do not assign progressively higher ordinal ratings to progressively lower latent values. In other words, we assume that all of our experts are well informed enough to know which direction is up, an assumption that is reasonable in our context. Second, we adopt hierarchical priors for the rater threshold vector, γ. Specifically, we assume

$$\gamma_{r,k} \sim \mathcal{N}(\gamma_k^{c_r}, 0.2),$$

$$\gamma_k^c \sim \mathcal{N}(\gamma_k^\mu, 0.2), \quad \text{and}$$

$$\gamma_k^\mu \sim U(-2, 2), \tag{4.4}$$

subject to the threshold ordering constraint described in Section 4.2.1. In other words, each individual threshold $\gamma_{r,k}$ is clustered around a country-level threshold γ_k^c – the average k-threshold for experts from country c – and each country-level threshold is clustered around a world-average k-threshold, γ_k^μ. While it is traditional to set vague uniform priors for the elements in γ, as we do with γ^μ, we adopt more informative priors for the remaining γ parameters. More precisely, we assume that DIF is not especially large relative to the standard normal scale, while allowing DIF across countries to be substantially larger than DIF within countries. These assumptions help the model effectively leverage the information provided by bridge and lateral coders. This assumption is especially helpful for countries with few experts who participate in bridge or lateral coding because it magnifies the information acquired through the few coders who do participate in this exercise. It also assures that the model is weakly identified when a country is completely unconnected from the rest of the rating network.[18] This approach represents a compromise between allowing DIF to exist at any magnitude, and the standard approach for expert rating projects, which is to assume that DIF is zero.[19]

---

[17] A large team of experts within V-Dem has evaluated the face validity of the resulting estimates. A number of papers (Coppedge et al. 2015; McMann et al. 2016) also systematically evaluate the validity of the V-Dem measures, using a variety of criteria.

[18] Such data isolation is rare in the data set. Future updates will include further lateral and bridge coding to ameliorate and eventually eliminate this concern.

[19] While somewhat arbitrary, the variance parameters were set at 0.2 after substantial experimentation and based on an extensive discussion about reasonable DIF magnitudes. We hope to relax this assumption in future work, leveraging new data, particularly anchoring vignettes, to better estimate DIF.

Finally, we require a prior for the vector z. Typically, one a priori sets each $z_{ct} \sim \mathcal{N}(0, 1)$. This assumption arbitrarily sets the overall scale of the estimated latent traits to a roughly standard normal distribution, which the literature generally refers to as a "vague" or "weakly informative" prior. When one has sufficient data to fully identify relative scale across observations and to estimate rater thresholds with high precision, then this assumption is sufficient to identify the model when combined with our priors for β and γ. In standard IRT domains with a dense rating matrix, such as educational testing, scale identification is rarely a problem. However, because we lack substantial cross-national rating data, the problem is potentially severe in our context (Pemstein et al. 2015). While there is no statistical test to certify that one has obtained scale identification, a lack of such identification can be easy to diagnose. In the case of our data, analyses we conducted using the traditional mean-zero prior indicate that, in cases where we lack sufficient bridge or lateral coding to anchor a country to the overall scale, the case's average will shrink toward zero. This phenomenon is readily apparent in face validity checks, especially with regard to countries that have little internal variation and modest coding overlap with the rest of the data set. For example, numerous northern European countries exhibit little or no variation in ratings for many indicators – they obtain perfect scores from the raters – in the postwar period, yet the ratings for these countries sometimes shrink toward the middle of the distribution. However, we know a priori with reasonable confidence that such shrinkage should not occur. While placing hierarchical priors on the γ vector, as we describe above, mitigates this problem, it does not eliminate it.

To address this issue without losing many of the advantages of the IRT framework, we adopt informative priors for the vector, z, of latent traits. Specifically, we adopt the prior

$$z_{ct} \sim N(\bar{\bar{y}}_{ct}, 1), \tag{4.5}$$

where

$$\bar{\bar{y}}_{ct} = \frac{\hat{y}_{ct} - \bar{\bar{y}}}{s},$$

$$\hat{y}_{ct} = \frac{\sum_{r \in R_{ct}} \omega_{ctr} y_{ctr}}{\sum_{r \in R_{ct}} \omega_{ctr}}, \tag{4.6}$$

$$\bar{\bar{y}} = \frac{\sum_{\{c,t\} \in CT} \hat{y}_{ct}}{|C \times T|}.$$

In these equations, s represents the standard deviation of $\hat{y}_{ct}$ across all cases, and ω_{ctr} a confidence self-assessment – on a scale from zero to 100 – that coder r

provides for her rating of observation ct.[20] Note first that we retain a constant prior variance across cases and that prior variance is on par with the variation in the prior means, which are normalized to have variance one. Thus, the prior remains vague and allows the data to speak where possible; we do not translate high rater agreement into prior confidence. The empirically informed prior means $(\bar{\bar{y}}_{ct})$ help the model to place cases relative to another in a reasonable way when the model lacks the necessary information (i.e., it lacks sufficient bridge and lateral coding) to situate a case relative to the rest of the cases. One way to think about this prior is that we are assuming the distribution of values that a traditional expert survey would provide based on average coder ratings. We then allow the model to adjust these estimates where it has the information to do so. Another interpretation is that we start from a prior assumption of zero DIF and allow the model to relax that assumption where the data clearly indicates violations. Of course, this approach will not identify or adjust for DIF where bridging information is sparse. This lack of DIF identification in certain cases is a weakness of the current analysis. Nonetheless, our approach represents a practical approach in light of data limitations and provides numerous advantages over simply reporting means and standard deviations.

Figure 4.2 graphically illustrates the advantage of our approach, presenting different methods of modeling data from the Netherlands over the V-Dem coding period.[21] Specifically, Figure 4.2a illustrates the raw mean and standard deviation of the coder data across time, with horizontal lines representing the different ordinal categories. Figure 4.2b presents the output from a model with the traditional $N\,(0, 1)$ prior, and Figure 4.2c a model with the $N\,(\bar{\bar{y}}_{ct}, 1)$ empirical prior; in these graphics, the horizontal lines represent the overall thresholds (γ^{μ}). All models show essentially the same trends over time: relatively high scores both preceding and following the Nazi occupation, with relatively low scores during the Nazi occupation. However, intercoder variance makes the mean and 95 percent confidence interval (CI) approach overly noisy: CIs from all periods substantially overlap. Moreover, the high variation during the period 1960–2012 is problematic from a substantive standpoint: while there may be debate about whether or not political killings were isolated or nonexistent, most scholars would agree that political killings were definitely in one of these two categories during this time.

Both models that incorporate our latent variable modeling strategy yield more reasonable estimates of confidence, with estimates from during the Nazi occupation falling clearly below those for other periods. However, there are substantively important differences between the model with a vague prior and

---

[20] In plain English, $\hat{y}_{ct}$ is the average ordinal rating for case ct, across the raters of the case weighted by self-assessed coder confidence; $\bar{\hat{y}}$ is the average $\hat{y}_{ct}$, across all cases. Therefore, $\bar{\bar{y}}_{ct}$ is the normalized weighted average rating for case ct.

[21] This analysis is based on V-Dem version 5.

(a) Raw mean and 95 percent CI

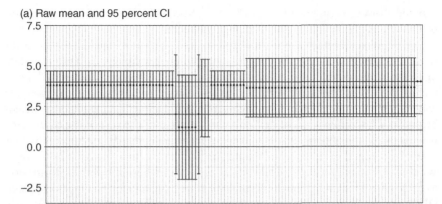

(b) Posterior median and 95 percent HPD interval, model with vague prior

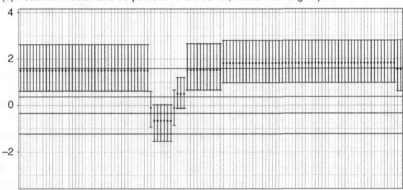

(c) Posterior median and 95 percent HPD interval, model with empirical prior

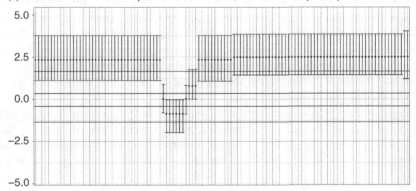

FIGURE 4.2 Longitudinal trends in freedom from political killings in the Netherlands, 1900–2014.

that with an empirical prior. Specifically, for regimes outside of the period of Nazi occupation, the model with a vague prior consistently pulls the estimates toward the center of the distribution,[22] contrary to the general rater scores. Perhaps most disconcertingly, the estimate for the period 2013–14 drops relative to the pre-2013 period, when in fact it was the only period in which all raters agreed that the Netherlands was free from political killings. In contrast, the model with the empirical prior consistently ranks these regimes as having high values, with the period of 2013–14 having the highest estimates of freedom from political killing of any regime, though uncertainty increases because of coder attrition.

4.2.5 Model Overview

At its heart, this model does three things. First, it takes ordinal observations and maps raters' thresholds onto a single interval-valued latent variable.[23] In other words, it provides a reasoned way to deal with a relatively large class of differences in how individual respondents interpret Likert scales. Second, it allows raters to vary in how reliably they make judgments but largely assumes away the potential for systematic rater biases that are not covered by varying thresholds.[24] This latter point is clearest in the MROP version of the model. Specifically, in a standard MROP, one assumes $F(\cdot)$ is standard normal, such that $e_{ctr} = \mathcal{N}(0, \sigma_r^2)$. In other words, raters get things right on average, but they make stochastic mistakes where the typical magnitude of mistakes that rater r makes on indicator i is σ_r^2. So, if $\sigma_r^2 < \sigma_{r'}^2$ then rater r provides more reliable judgments about z than r' because she makes smaller mistakes on average. Finally, taking differences in rater thresholds and precisions into account, the model produces interval-valued estimates of latent traits – each z_{ct} – accompanied by estimates of measurement error that reflect both the level of disagreement between coders on the case in question, and the estimated precision of the coders who rated the case. Specifically, the conditional posterior distribution of each latent trait is

$$z_{ct} \sim \mathcal{N}\left(\frac{a_{ct}}{b_{ct}}, \frac{1}{b_{ct}}\right),$$

(4.7)

---

[22] This is really a problem of cross-national comparability, which Figure 4.2 fails to highlight.

[23] V-Dem data also include dichotomous variables, which we estimated in a similar fashion with modifications to reflect the fact that, instead of multiple thresholds, dichotomous variables have a unique intercept. Specifically, we hierarchically estimated a rater-specific intercept for each variable as opposed to rater-specific thresholds.

[24] For instance, the model cannot account for a rater who applies one set of thresholds to one country and a different set to another. Nor does this model capture the possibility that rater precisions or thresholds might vary over space and time, although the model might be expanded to handle such issues (see Fariss 2014).

where

$$a_{ct} = \overline{\overline{y}}_{ct} + \sum_{r \in R_{ct}} \beta_r \widetilde{y}_{ctr} \text{ and } b_{ct} = 1 + \sum_{r \in R_{ct}} \beta_r. \tag{4.8}$$

Interpreting (4.7) and (4.8), we see that the conditional posterior mean of each z_{ct} is the average of the (latent) rater perceptions, weighted by raters' discrimination parameters.[25] The conditional posterior variance is also a function of the rater discrimination parameters; posterior variance decreases as raters become more discriminating.

4.3 ESTIMATION AND COMPUTATION

We estimate the model using Markov chain Monte Carlo methods; Figure 4.3 provides our implementation of the IRT model using the Stan probabilistic programming language (Stan Development Team 2015). We simulate four Markov chains for each variable in the V-Dem data set for a sufficient number of iterations, using Gelman and Rubin's (1992) diagnostic to assess convergence. This process follows a standardized procedure in which we first run each variable for 5000 iterations, with a 500 draw burn-in. We then thin the draws from the algorithm such that we saved every tenth draw. As a result, we achieve a 450-draw posterior distribution for each of the four chains (1800 draws total). If more than 5 percent of the latent scores fail Gelman and Rubin's (1992) test for convergence (as defined by $\hat{r} \geq 1.1$), we rerun the model with a greater number of iterations, beginning with 10,000 iterations and continuing with 20,000, 40,000, and, in rare cases, 80,000 iterations.[26] We increase the burn-in to cover to the first 10 percent of draws from each model (e.g., 1000 iterations for a simulation with 10,000 iterations total), and also set the thinning interval so that we would have 450 draws from each of the four chains, regardless of the number of iterations. These models require anywhere from a couple of hours to multiple days to run. Moreover, we fit these models to around 170 variables, necessitating the use of cluster computing environments.

4.4 PRODUCTS

We provide three sets of point estimates and measures of uncertainty to allow scholars and policymakers to choose a version which best fits their objectives. The first set consists of data taken directly from the measurement model

---

[25] The thresholds enter the equation through the conditional distributions of the latent perceptions, each $\widetilde{y}_{ctr}$. See Johnson and Albert (1999), especially their chapters 5 and 6, for a full discussion of how these models work.

[26] Given the sheer number of parameters in these models, we expect some tests to fail by chance, hence the 5 percent threshold.

```
data {
  int<lower=2> K; // categories
  int<lower=0> J ; // Coders
  int<lower=0> N; // N
  int<lower=0> C; // countries
  int<lower=-1,upper=K> wdata [N, J ] ; // data
  int<lower=1,upper=C> cdata [J] ; // j country indices
  real gsigmasq ; // rater-level gamma variance around country-level gammas
  real gsigmasqc ; // country-level gamma variance around world gammas
  vector [N] mc ; // prior means
}

parameters {
  vector [N] Z ;
  ordered        [K-1] gamma [ J ] ;
  vector [K-1] gamma_mu ; // world-level cutpoints
  matrix [C, (K-1)] gamma_c ; // country-level cuts , rows are countries
  real<lower=0> beta [ J ] ; // reliability score
}

model {
  vector [K] p ;
  real left ;
  real right ;
  for (i in 1:N) {
   Z [ i ] ~ normal (mc [ i ] , 1 );
  }
  gamma mu ~ uniform(-2 , 2 );
  for ( c in 1:C) {
   gamma_c [ c ] ~ normal (gamma_mu, gsigmasqc ) ; // row-access of gamma-c
  }
  for ( j in 1:J ) {
   gamma [ j ] ~ normal (gamma_c [ cdata [ j ] ] , gsigmasq ) ; // note row-access
   beta [ j ] ~ normal ( 1 , 1 )T[ 0 , ] ;
   for ( i in 1:N) if (wdata [ i , j ] != -1) {
    left <- 0;
    for (k in 1: (K-1)) {
     right <- left ;
     left <-Phi_approx(gamma [ j , k ] - Z [ i ] * beta [ j ] ) ;
     p [ k ] <- left - right ;
    }
    p [K] <- 1.0 - left ;
    wdata [ i , j ] ~ categorical (p ) ;
   }
  }
}
```

FIGURE 4.3 Stan code.

(interval-level trait estimates), while the other two sets are transformations of this output: they present the output on an ordinal scale and linearized ordinal scale. Finally, we also provide estimates of the difficulty and discrimination parameters to enable scholars to develop a better sense of the V-Dem data.

4.4.1   Interval-Level Latent Trait Estimates

The primary quantities of the interest generated by our measurement framework are interval-level estimates of the latent score vectors, z, for each indicator. Our estimation procedure simulates 1800 draws from the posterior distributions of these scores. We use the medians of these sets of posterior distribution draws as point estimates of the latent traits and can use the distributions to calculate credible intervals, highest posterior density (HPD) regions, and other measures of measurement uncertainty. These estimates are described as "Relative Scale" – Measurement Model Output in the *V-Dem Codebook*, and the release data set provides point estimates (the posterior median), the posterior standard deviation, as well as upper and lower bounds of the 70 percent HPD intervals. Full posterior samples are available in the V-Dem archive on the CurateND (http://curate.nd.edu) website.

4.4.2   Difficulty and Discrimination Parameters

The MCMC algorithm also produces simulations from the posterior distributions of rater difficulty – including the hierarchical components described in Eq. (4.4) – and discrimination parameters. The difficulty parameters are useful for mapping latent trait estimates back onto the *Codebook* scale, either at the rater, country, or data set level. Analysts can rely on these threshold estimates to interpret how the typical coder would describe ranges on the latent scale, providing an important aid to qualitative interpretation of the model's estimates. Plotting point estimates of these thresholds as horizontal lines on latent trait plots, for instance, helps to ground the latent scale to real-world descriptions of regime characteristics.

The discrimination parameters (β_r) describe the inverse reliability of the raters. While their primary role is to allow the model to weight estimates and calculate measures of confidence, as we describe in Section 4.2.5, they can also be a useful diagnostic tool. In particular, analysts can use these estimates to examine where the V-Dem raters are most and least reliable, and to model potential sources of modeling error.

We do not bundle difficulty and discrimination parameter estimates with the core V-Dem data set because they are measured at the coder level, but full posterior samples of both the difficulty and discrimination parameters are available in the V-Dem archive on the CurateND website.

4.4.3 Ordinal-Scale Estimates

We can use the difficulty parameters to generate latent trait estimates on the original ordinal scale described for each indicator in the *V-Dem Codebook*. Specifically, for each indicator, we generate samples from the posterior distributions of the classifications a typical rater would give to each case on the original *Codebook* scale. Consider a single country-year case, *ct*. For each sample, *s*, drawn from the simulated posterior distribution, we assign the ordinal score of zero to the draw if $z_{ct}^{(s)} \leq \gamma^{\mu(s)}_1$, a score of one if $\gamma^{\mu(s)}_1 < z_{ct}^{(s)} \leq \gamma^{\mu(s)}_2$ and so on. The estimates are part of the V-Dem data set; the *Codebook* refers to them as "ordinal scale" – Measurement Model Estimates of Original Scale Value. The core V-Dem data set includes both a point estimate (the integerized median score across posterior draws) and integerized ordinal 70 percent HPD intervals. Users can find full posterior samples in the V-Dem archive on the CurateND website.

4.4.4 Linearized Ordinal-Scale Posterior Predictions

While the ordinal-scale estimates that we describe above are useful for situating our measurement model output within a qualitative frame, they can be somewhat awkward to visualize, especially with associated HPD regions, because they are purely ordinal. Therefore, to provide users with a convenient heuristic tool for interpreting model output on the original *Codebook* scale, we linearly translate the latent trait estimates to the ordinal *Codebook* scale as an interval-level measure. First, for each posterior draw, we calculate the posterior predicted probability that a typical coder would assign each possible ordinal score to a given case. As an example, consider an indicator with ordinal levels ranging from zero to three. Then,

$$
\begin{aligned}
p^{(s)}_{ct,0} &= \phi\left(\gamma^{\mu(s)}_1 - z_{ct}^{(s)}\right), \\
p^{(s)}_{ct,1} &= \phi\left(\gamma^{\mu(s)}_2 - z_{ct}^{(s)}\right) - \phi\left(\gamma^{\mu(s)}_1 - z_{ct}^{(s)}\right), \\
p^{(s)}_{ct,2} &= \phi\left(\gamma^{\mu(s)}_2 - z_{ct}^{(s)}\right) - \phi\left(\gamma^{\mu(s)}_2 - z_{ct}^{(s)}\right), \\
p^{(s)}_{ct,3} &= 1 - \phi\left(\gamma^{\mu(s)}_3 - z_{ct}^{(s)}\right).
\end{aligned}
\tag{4.9}
$$

Next, we linearly map these predicted probabilities onto the indicator's *Codebook* scale:

$$
o^{(s)}_{ct} = 0 \times p^{(s)}_{ct,0} + 1 \times p^{(s)}_{ct,1} + 2 \times p^{(s)}_{ct,2} + 3 \times p^{(s)}_{ct,3}.
\tag{4.10}
$$

The V-Dem data set provides median estimates, posterior standard deviations and 70 percent HPD bounds for each o_{ct} for each indicator; the *Codebook* refers to them as *"Original Scale" – Linearized Original Scale Posterior Prediction* estimates. It is important to note that there are two potential issues in interpreting this output. First, this transformation can distort the distance between point estimates: the distance between 1.0 and 1.5 on this scale is not necessarily the same as the distance between a 1.5 and 2.0. Second, the estimates are not uniquely identified: different combinations of weighted posterior predictions could yield the same linearized posterior prediction score.

4.5   GRAPHICAL ILLUSTRATION OF THE V-DEM DATA

To illustrate both the utility of our latent variable estimation strategy and the different ways in which we present the output from the measurement model, we present visualizations of V-Dem data, focusing on freedom from political killings for three countries. Figure 4.4 shows data from the US, a country with which most readers will be familiar; Figure 4.5 depicts Germany, a case with a generally large number of raters and great variation in freedom from political killings; and Cambodia (Figure 4.6) is a substantively important case with fewer raters. For each country, we present (1) the raw mean and standard deviation of rater codings (for countries in which raters were in perfect agreement, the standard deviation is set at zero), (2) the interval-level median estimate and 95 percent HPD interval, (3) the linearized original scale median estimate and its 95 percent HPD interval, and (4) the integerized median ordinal-scale estimate and its 95 percent HPD interval. For ease of interpretation, each graphic also contains horizontal lines denoting quantities of substantive importance. In the case of the raw mean, original-scale and ordinal-scale graphics, these lines represent the scale items with which raters were presented. More specifically, an estimate close to zero indicates that raters believe the country-year to have systematic political killings, a one a country year in which political killings are frequent, a two a country-year with occasional political killings, a three a country that is largely free from political killings, and a four a country that is free from political killing. In the case of the interval-scale estimates, the line represents the world-average thresholds for the scale items (γ^{μ}): a score above the highest horizontal line indicates that a country-year's estimate falls in the typical rater's fourth category (free from political killings); a score below the lowest line indicates a country-year in which the average rater perceived that political killings were systematic.

For example, Figure 4.4 presents four graphics representing temporal trends in freedom from political killings in the US between 1900 and 2012. Figure 4.4a illustrates the raw mean and standard deviation of rater scores. Figure 4.4a clearly shows that coders generally believe the US to be between the third and the fourth category, i.e., having either isolated or no political killings, though there is disagreement about this ranking, especially in the first half of the twentieth century. Figure 4.4b presents the output of the measurement model, which coincides with the raw mean and standard deviation in that estimates are generally between the third and fourth categories. However, the measurement model output diverges from the raw estimates by systematically discounting

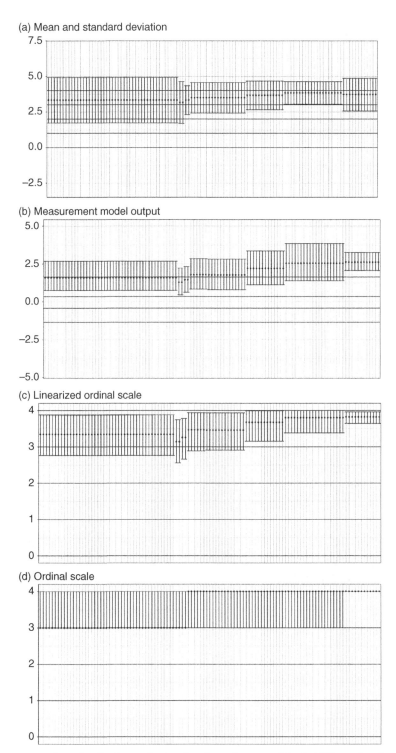

FIGURE 4.4 Longitudinal trends in freedom from political killings in the US, 1900–2012.

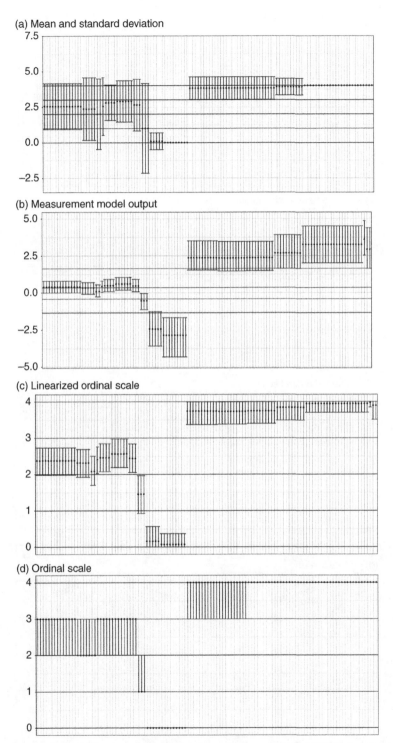

(a) Mean and standard deviation

(b) Measurement model output

(c) Linearized ordinal scale

(d) Ordinal scale

FIGURE 4.5 Longitudinal trends in freedom from political killings in Germany, 1900–2014.

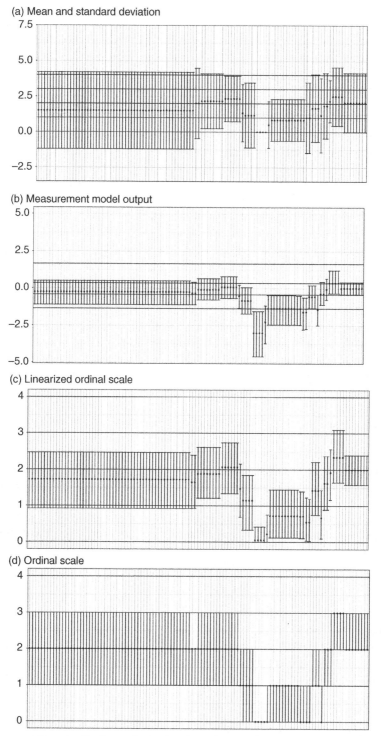

FIGURE 4.6 Longitudinal trends in freedom from political killings in Cambodia, 1900–2012.

unreliable coders and incorporating different coder thresholds. As a result, the model generally estimates the US to be between the third and fourth thresholds until the twenty-first century, at which point is estimated to be almost certainly in the highest category. The linearized original scale (Figure 4.4c) unsurprisingly yields estimates that are in line with the measurement model, though in a perhaps more easily interpretable fashion: estimates are clearly generally between the third and fourth categories. Finally, the ordinal-scale output provides the most succinct analysis of the data, showing that our best guess for the US rating is generally either the third or fourth category; only in the twenty-first century are we almost fully confident that it was free from political killings.

Figure 4.5 provides similar illustrations, but regarding freedom from political killings in Germany. As with the data from the US, the data from the beginning of the twentieth century is very noisy for the raw mean estimates, making interpretation difficult. However, during certain regimes (i.e., the Holocaust, the late twentieth century, and early twenty-first century) raters are in perfect agreement regarding Germany's scores. Data from the measurement model reflect those periods of perfect agreement by indicating that during the Holocaust Germany was well below the lowest threshold and has been above the highest threshold for the last several decades. The model also significantly tightens confidence toward the beginning of the twentieth century, indicating that some of the variance may have been due to unreliable coders or different thresholds. The linearized original-scale and ordinal-scale output reflect these trends.

Data from Cambodia, illustrated in Figure 4.6, evinces greater variation at the rater level than that from either Germany or the US, save for the period of the Cambodian Genocide during which raters were in universal agreement that Cambodia belonged in the lowest category. All output reflects this variation: whereas scores for Germany and the US generally vary fall between two categories, in Cambodia they often include three. However, through coder-specific thresholds and reliability measures, the model does reduce the variance significantly, and captures the observations for which the coders are in full agreement.

4.6   DISCUSSION AND FUTURE PLANS

This chapter describes the latent variable model that we use to generate point estimates and measures of confidence for those ordinal V-Dem measures that multiple experts subjectively coded. This model provides a number of advantages over the standard practice – common among expert surveys within political science – of releasing rating means and standard deviations as point and confidence estimates, respectively. It builds upon a specific probability model, long used in the psychometric literature, to estimate rater reliability and to model a large class of DIF issues, allowing the model to adjust for variations in how raters conceptualize and apply ordinal scales to observations. The traditional approach to analyzing expert-coded data with means and standard deviations may provide quite misleading point estimates, and measures of uncertainty, when reliability varies across experts and when items function differentially. Our approach adjusts estimates to account for both of these issues. Of course, our data present specific challenges that complicate our measurement efforts and we see the modeling framework described here as only a first step in an iterative measurement process.

Most notably, we lack sufficient data to fully model DIF cross-nationally, weakening the cross-national comparability of the V-Dem measures. While our method should produce measures that are at least as cross-nationally comparable as the mean/standard deviation approach, and often dramatically outperform the standard procedure, our reliance on informative prior assumptions to handle DIF in situations where data are sparse means that we cannot altogether rule out cross-national comparability problems. We are currently working to solve these issues. First, we are developing tests for evaluating global scale identification and creating methods for efficiently selecting bridge and lateral coders to most efficiently obtain cross-national comparability (Pemstein et al. 2015). We have also developed a large battery of anchoring vignettes (King and Wand 2007) for the V-Dem survey, and are conducting a pilot study to evaluate their quality and the extent to which they allow us to relax modeling assumptions. These vignettes will serve as bridge cases that all V-Dem experts will rate,[27] providing a wealth of information that the model can use to estimate cross-national variation in rater difficulty parameters.

Second, our current approach to dealing with temporal dependence and unclear observation granularity is somewhat ad hoc and liable to produce estimates of uncertainty that are too conservative. We hope to deploy new methods for modeling stickiness in rater errors in IRT models as those methods evolve (Melton et al. 2014).

Finally, while we provide large samples simulated from the posterior distributions of all the parameters in our model on CurateND, few political scientists have the background to make effective use of these posterior draws. We have developed a tutorial on best practices for incorporating the estimates of measurement uncertainty that we provide when conducting substantive analyses using the V-Dem data (Bizzarro et al. 2016). In the longer term, we are developing software that will facilitate this process in commonly used statistical packages like R and Stata.

---

[27] Technically, many, given coder attrition. Resource constraints made it impossible to develop and deploy anchoring vignettes in tandem with the original waves of the survey.

5

Dimensions and Components of Democracy*

In this chapter we focus on the measurement of five key principles, or traditions, that offer distinct approaches to defining democracy – electoral, liberal, participatory, deliberative, and egalitarian. For each principle, we discuss (1) the theoretical rationale for the selected indicators, (2) whether these indicators are correlated strongly enough to warrant being collapsed into an index (drawing on Bayesian factor analysis, where relevant), and (3) the justification of aggregation rules for moving from indicators to components and from components to higher-level indices. Throughout, we consider alternative aggregation formulas and conduct analyses of how sensitive the resulting indices are to the choice of particular aggregation rules. In each section we also (4) highlight the top- and bottom-five countries on each principle of democracy in early (1812 or 1912) and late (2012) years of our sample period,[1] as well as the aggregate trend over the whole time period 1789–2017 (where applicable).

Our approach to aggregation and index construction follows from some common points of departure. The first is mutual exclusiveness: we never use the same indicator to measure more than one concept (at any level of aggregation), in order to retain the distinctiveness of the concepts and preserve the possibility of studying relationships between them. Second, to facilitate comparison we scale all indices to range from 0 to 1. Third, depending on the concept to be measured, we need to make a distinction

---

* The lead author of this chapter was Jan Teorell. Portions of this chapter were previously published as Coppedge at al. (2016b) and Teorell et al. (2019).
[1] The choice of "late" year (2012) simply reflects the end year of the initial V-Dem data collection, covering 173 polities in the world at any time point. The choice of "early" year (1912) was made to cover a 100-year period and to maximize the number of sovereign countries in the sample (which increases from 31 to 49 in 1900–12).

between *reflective* and *formative* indicators. Reflective indicators are effects or "symptoms" of the concept being measured, and are typically estimated by factor analysis, which treats each indicator as the result of one or more common factors and a unique error component trait (Treier and Jackman 2008). Formative indicators reverse the equation, treating indicators as determinants of the concept being measured (Goertz 2006). Reflective indicators should be correlated, as they are all held to be effects of a common cause. There is no such expectation for formative indicators (Bollen 1989).[2] When indicators are reflective, we base the aggregation on factor scores (weighted averages). When they are formative, depending on theoretical demands, the aggregation rule could be taking the maximum or simple average (when each indicator or component is a substitute or near-substitute), or through multiplication (when each indicator or component is a necessary condition), or some combination of different rules.

We will devote one section each to the five democratic principles. The sixth and final section looks at how the different principles are intercorrelated, and tries to assess the trade-offs involved between the conceptual parsimony achieved by aggregating to a few general concepts and the retention of useful variation permitted by aggregating less.

5.1 THE ELECTORAL PRINCIPLE: POLYARCHY

Dahl (1971: 2) famously defined democracy as "a political system one of the characteristics of which is the quality of being completely or almost completely responsive to all its citizens." He reserved "democracy" for an ideal system while his theory proposes a set of realistic empirical requirements for "polyarchies." As pointed out in Chapter 2, these "institutional guarantees," originally eight, can for measurement purposes and following Dahl (1989, 1998) be narrowed down to five attributes, or components (see Figure 2.1). In this section, we first discuss these five components and the indicators used to measure them. We then present the aggregation rules for combining them and the resulting index of electoral democracy (polyarchy) in the next section.

---

[2] Bollen (2011) distinguishes between two types of formative indicators: cause indicators and composite indicators. In both, the concept to measure is on the left-hand side of the equation and the indicators are on the right. The difference is that the equation for cause indicators has an error term, while that for composite indicators does not. In our view, however, the virtue of Goertz's (2006: chapter 2) approach, which is what Bollen calls "composite," is to highlight the fact that the relationship is theoretical or conceptual, not empirical. A composite measure, lacking an error term, is not an estimate from a regression, but simply a calculation. Any error in the components is passed along to the composite measure. Henceforth, we will refer to what Bollen terms "composite" indicators simply as formative indicators.

5.1.1   Measuring the Parts: Five Components of Polyarchy

A   *Elected Officials Index*: This index measures whether the chief executive is elected – directly through popular elections or indirectly
through a popularly elected legislature appointing the executive.
This is sometimes referred to as the "effectiveness" (Hadenius
1992: 49) or "decisiveness" (O'Donnell 2001: 13) of elections. A
"popular election" is thus minimally defined and includes sham elections with limited suffrage and no competition. "Appointment" by
the legislature only implies selection and/or approval, not the power
to dismiss.[3]

The logic behind the construct is schematically portrayed in Figure 5.1. Unlike
the other four component indices of polyarchy, this index is thus based on a set
of formative indicators that define the construct on purely theoretical grounds.

There are six links of appointment/selection to account for, all scaled to vary
from 0 to 1. First and second, whether the head of state (a_1) and/or head of
government (a_2) is directly elected (1) or not (0). Third, the extent to which the
legislature is popularly elected (b) measured as the proportion of legislators who
are directly or indirectly elected (if the legislature is unicameral), or, if the
legislature is bicameral *and* the upper house is involved in the appointment of
the chief executive, a weighted average of the proportion elected for each
house.[4] Fourth and fifth, whether the head of state (c_1) and/or head of
government (c_2) is appointed by the legislature (1), or the approval of the

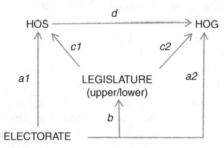

FIGURE 5.1 The logical structure of the Elected Officials Index.

---

[3] The rationale is that counting dismissal powers would introduce "bias" in favor of parliamentary
systems, which rely on institutionalized powers of dismissal. In presidential systems, there
typically is no recall vote at the national level and in the assembly-independent (albeit very
unusual) Swiss system, the legislature lacks power to dismiss the cabinet.

[4] The share of directly and indirectly elected legislators are coded separately and then added as a
weighted sum. The weights are defined as $1/s$, where s is the number of stages in the election
process. Due to data limitations, we have decided to exclude indirect electoral systems with more
than two stages, hence the weight for directly elected legislators is $1/1 = 1$, and for indirectly
elected legislators $1/2$.

legislature is necessary for the appointment of the head of state (1), or not (0). Sixth, whether the head of government is appointed by the head of state ($d=1$) or not ($d=0$).

In polities with unified executives (head of state is also head of government; Elgie 1998; Siaroff 2003), the complexity of this conceptual scheme reduces to the links a_1 and $b * c$. Since these are considered perfect substitutes (*either* a directly elected president *or* a president elected by a directly elected parliament suffices), the index value is achieved at by taking the maximum value of the two. In dual systems, where there is both a head of state and a separate head of government, the chief executive is determined by comparing the two executives' power over the appointment and dismissal of cabinet ministers. If the head of state and head of government share equal powers over the appointment and dismissal of cabinet ministers, the index averages across the degree to which they are directly or indirectly elected.

In a second step, the extent to which the legislature is elected (b) is also independently taken into account in order to penalize presidential systems with unelected legislatures, or legislatures with a large share of presidential appointees, for example. Assuming that the extent to which the chief executive and the legislature are elected are partially substitutable, we average the two. The resulting index (called *v2x_elecoff*) has a bimodal distribution with mostly 0s or 1s. The rare values falling between 0 and 1 are mostly bicameral systems where the upper house is not directly elected, but also include cases such as Burma/Myanmar that (currently) has a unified executive with a president elected by a parliament in which only 75 percent of the seats are directly elected.[5]

B *Clean Elections Index*: The second component, which Dahl (1998: 85) calls "free, fair, and frequent" elections, is designed to capture the level of integrity of elections measured as the absence of manipulation and bias in the administration of elections (e.g., Schedler 2002; Lehoucq 2003; Birch 2011; Kelley 2013; van Ham and Lindberg 2015). Disregarding the "frequency" aspect, since that builds an unnecessary temporal aspect into the concept of polyarchy, this component thus in essence taps into whether an election could be considered free from manipulation ("clean").

The V-Dem data set includes six indicators pertaining to this latent trait measuring for each election the extent of (1) registration irregularities, (2) vote buying, (3) ballot fraud and intentional irregularities, (4) government-induced intimidation of opposition candidates, (5) other types of election violence (not

---

[5] One potential limitation of the index is that the extent to which nonelected "accountability groups" (such as the military) may affect dismissal of the executive, or can veto important domestic policy proposals, is not taken into account. Although there are V-Dem indicators of such veto and dismissal powers (see Teorell and Lindberg, 2019), we have found no nonarbitrary way of computing the size of the penalty these should incur.

instigated by the government or ruling party), and (6) an overall assessment of whether the election overall was "free and fair."[6] Finally, two indicators are measured on annual basis: the (7) autonomy and (8) capacity of the election administration body (EMB) to conduct well-run elections.

The aggregated country-year data on these eight indicators are arguably reflective indicators caused by the latent trait "clean elections." To test this proposition, we ran a Bayesian factor analysis (BFA) model and the results are reported in Table 5.1. Vote buying and election violence (not conducted by the government) indicators have somewhat weaker loadings and a larger share of their variance unaccounted for (uniqueness), but the fit to a unidimensional model is adequate.

The index of clean elections consists of point estimates from the BFA, accompanied by measures of uncertainty.[7] Since this index is observed only for election years, however, we simply repeat the index values from the last election until either another election occurs or there is an "electoral interruption," defined as either (1) the dissolution, shut-down, replacement or in any sense termination of the elected body (such as after coups or violent takeovers of the government), or (2) an elected body which, while still intact or in place, is no longer appointed through (direct) elections (such as after an autogolpe).[8] Taking such interruptions into account also partially addresses Dahl's criterion of "frequent" elections.

A thornier issue concerns the value to assign to the index during nonelectoral periods (i.e., prior to the first election or after an electoral interruption). Scores from the item response theory measurement model have no natural zero point and a theoretically defined minimum cannot be identified. Our solution is first (this step pertains to all V-Dem indices composed using BFAs) to convert the

---

[6] If legislative and presidential elections were held concurrently, the measures pertain to both of them. If multiple elections (or rounds of elections) were held in the same year, each election is measured separately. For present purposes, the estimates have been averaged across multiple elections within a year to arrive at country election-year estimates.

[7] We randomly select 100 draws from each variable's posterior distribution, run a unidimensional BFA sequentially for each randomly selected draw in each grouping of variables, and combine the posterior distributions of the latent factor scores in each variable group to yield the latent factor scores. By this procedure, we take full advantage of the estimates of uncertainty at the indicator level to provide realistic (not overly narrow) estimates of uncertainty for the index.

[8] The V-Dem data set's indicator for capturing electoral interruptions is *v2x_elecreg*. Basically, *v2x_elecreg* is coded 0 until the first observed executive or legislative election, then 1, if the election was not aborted, until there was an electoral interruption (otherwise continuously 1). Aborted elections are operationalized as elections that did not result in a newly elected executive or legislature within 12 months after the election. We capture the second aspect of an "electoral interruption" (whether the elected body, while still intact or in place, is no longer appointed through elections) by looking at interruptions (or aborted elections) in the other branch: we thus code a legislative shutdown as a signal that the executive (while still "elected") will not be subject to election anymore either, and we code an executive coup as a signal that the legislature (while still "elected") will not be subject to election anymore – until (nonaborted) elections to the branch in question are being held again.

TABLE 5.1 *Measuring clean elections (BFA estimates)*

Indicator	Loadings (Λ)	Uniqueness (Ψ)
Proper voter registry (*v2elrgstry*)	0.732	0.467
Vote buying (*v2elvotbuy*)	0.619	0.619
Ballot fraud/vote irregularity (*v2elirreg*)	0.794	0.372
Government intimidation (*v2elintim*)	0.772	0.406
Other electoral violence (*v2elpeace*)	0.584	0.661
Overall judgment "free & fair" (*v2elfrfair*)	0.812	0.341
EMB autonomy (*v2elembaut*)	0.783	0.387
EMB capacity (*v2elembcap*)	0.723	0.477

Note: Entries are factor loadings and uniqueness from a normal theory Bayesian factor analysis model; n = 4427 election years.

index score to a probability (0–1) score by using the normal cumulative distribution function (*cdf*). This transformed index score could thus be interpreted as the probability of observing the corresponding BFA point estimate score or lower. (A BFA score of –1.65 thus corresponds to a probability of 0.05, a score of 0 to a probability of 0.5, and so on.) Second, we substitute all values during periods of electoral interruption with zero. While this transformed 0–1 index (called *v2xel_frefair*) slightly compresses the original BFA estimates at the higher and lower ends, we argue this is a price worth paying for getting the index properly scaled.[9] The resulting index of clean elections is bimodally distributed but with a heavy skew toward observations with no elections.

C *Freedom of Association Index*: The two component indices above do not take into account the degree of pluralism. They could at least in theory reach relatively high values even in a totalitarian, single-party state. This is why we need a separate index capturing the degree of what Dahl (1998: 85) calls "associational autonomy," or freedom of association. As a component of polyarchy, the core of this construct is party-centered: are political parties free to form, operate autonomously from the ruling regime, and field candidates in national elections? In addition, associational autonomy in the political sphere also requires that there be no state repression of, or barriers to the entry and exit of, a wider set of civil society organizations providing alternative means for voice and political activity that make policy depend on votes and preferences. Following this

---

[9] We also see no preferable alternative ways of achieving this normalization. Drawing on empirical maxima and minima, for example, would make the scale completely sample-dependent and highly sensitive to extreme values (also incurring a scaling change every time a new max or min was observed).

TABLE 5.2 *Measuring freedom of association (BFA estimates)*

Indicator	Loadings (Λ)	Uniqueness (Ψ)
Party ban (*v2psparban*)	0.823	0.323
Barriers to parties (*v2psbars*)	0.862	0.257
Opposition parties autonomy (*v2psoppaut*)	0.862	0.257
Elections multiparty (*v2elmulpar*)	0.711	0.406
CSO entry and exit (*v2cseeorgs*)	0.792	0.370
CSO repression (*v2csreprss*)	0.768	0.411

Note: Entries are factor loadings and uniqueness scores from a normal theory Bayesian factor analysis model; $n = 24,184$ country-years.

theoretical guidance from Dahl, we have thus opted for the set of reflective indicators of freedom of association indicated in Table 5.2. They clearly load on a single underlying dimension.[10] The resulting index (called *v2x_frassoc*), rescaled to 0–1 through the normal cdf, is bimodally distributed.

D *Suffrage Index*: Dahl's (1971, 1989, 1998) component called "inclusive citizenship" in effect amounts to the extension of the suffrage. This is not an index but a centrally coded single V-Dem indicator based on an estimate of the proportion of adult citizens eligible to vote, measured for all country units since 1789. The resulting 0–1 indicator (called *v2x_suffr*) is bimodally distributed.

E *Freedom of Expression and Alternative Sources of Information Index*: Finally, Dahl's concept of polyarchy includes a conspicuously nonelectoral aspect: freedom of expression. Staying true to his widely accepted concept thus necessitates employing a core set of indicators capturing overall media freedom (Behmer 2009), such as active state censorship of print/ broadcast media, media self-censorship, and harassment of journalists. In addition, polyarchy requires freedom of discussion in society at large, for both men and women (Skaaning 2009). It also includes four indicators of media content to capture Dahl's (1971) "alternative sources of information": whether the media is biased against opposition parties and candidates, whether major print and broadcast outlets routinely criticize the government, and whether they represent a wide range of political perspectives, as well as general repression of cultural and academic expressions of political dissent.

---

[10] Since the multiparty elections indicator is observed only in election years, we face the same extrapolation problem as for the Clean Elections Index above. We (again) repeat the values observed in the last election and then replace all observations with 0 during electoral interruptions.

TABLE 5.3 *Measuring freedom of expression (BFA estimates)*

Indicator	Loadings (Λ)	Uniqueness (Ψ)
Print/broadcast censorship (*v2mecenefm*)	0.838	0.278
Harassment of journalists (*v2meharjrn*)	0.820	0.327
Media self-censorship (*v2meslfcen*)	0.828	0.314
Freedom of academic/cultural expr. (*v2clacfree*)	0.807	0.350
Freedom of discussion (*v2cldiscm + v2cldiscw*)	0.853	0.273
Media bias (*v2mebias*)	0.856	0.264
Print/broadcast media critical (*v2mecrit*)	0.867	0.250
Print/broadcast media perspectives (*v2merange*)	0.852	0.276

Note: Entries are factor loadings and uniqueness scores from a normal theory Bayesian factor analysis model; n = 24,028 country-years.

Table 5.3 demonstrates that these nine (reduced to eight) indicators are reflective of the latent trait "freedom of expression."[11] Hence, our index of freedom of expression and alternative sources of information (called *v2x_freexp_altinf*) is based on the point estimates from this BFA and converted to a probability (0–1) score by using the normal cdf.

5.1.2 Measuring the Whole: Aggregating the Components

Before delving into the aggregation of these five components of polyarchy, it is important to know how they co-vary. The lower diagonal in Table 5.4 displays the correlation coefficients using the entire set of country-year observations. The covariation is moderate to strong in most instances, but one cluster stands out: clean elections, freedom of association, and freedom of expression. The Elected Officials Index and suffrage both display systematically less strong correlation to these three components. One could suspect that this pattern is a result of the zeros imposed on the Clean Elections Index and on the multiparty elections indicator of the Freedom of Association Index, for periods of electoral interruptions. The upper diagonal in Table 5.4 therefore presents the correlations for election years only and, as expected, the correlations are overall weaker. Yet, the cluster with stronger bivariate correlations remains, separating the elected executive and suffrage components on the one hand from the clean elections, freedom of association and freedom of expression components on the other.

---

[11] One media indicator (*v2mecenefm*) was not included in the historical V-dem survey covering the time period prior to 1900. Scores for this variable are, however, imputed by our Bayesian factor analysis procedure prior to index construction.

TABLE 5.4 *Correlations among polyarchy components*

	Elected Officials	Suffrage	Clean Elections	Freedom of Association	Freedom of Expression
Elected Officials		0.392	0.219	0.335	0.332
Suffrage	0.633		0.238	0.164	0.163
Clean Elections	0.630	0.569		0.711	0.724
Freedom of Association	0.621	0.477	0.801		0.898
Freedom of Expression	0.582	0.437	0.769	0.916	

Note: Entries are correlation coefficients, in the lower diagonal for $n = 24{,}228$ country-years, in the upper diagonal for $n = 4501$ election years. Only sovereign counties are included in order to avoid the "break" in the data in 1900.

The results indicate that polyarchy is multidimensional, as argued by Coppedge and Reinicke (1990) and Coppedge et al. (2008), complicating the choice of aggregation rule. Had the correlations between all components been strong and consistent, the exact choice of aggregation rule would matter less. Since the different components demonstrably point in slightly different directions for different countries and time periods, however, the way we combine information from all of them matters more for the resulting index value.

The first and most important consideration for the choice of aggregation rule is whether the five components are treated as (partially) mutually substitutable aspects of polyarchy or as individually necessary conditions. The literature is divided on this issue. On one hand, there is a strong rationale in the literature for treating the components as necessary conditions (see Przeworski et al. 2000; Munck 2009; Boix et al. 2013). The argument holds that the degree of suffrage is not relevant if there is no freedom of association, if the election results are completely fabricated, *or* if the executive is not elected. Similarly, the freedom and fairness of elections should not count if only a tiny fraction of the population is enfranchised, and so on. According to this view, the two viable aggregation rules, which in the literature are typically considered most appropriate for capturing a set of necessary conditions, are either multiplication (see Munck and Verkuilen 2002: 24; Munck 2009: 32, 40–51) or taking the minimum (see Bowman et al. 2005: 956; Goertz 2006: 111–15). With dichotomous measures these two aggregation rules reduce to the exact same thing, but with graded information this is generally not the case. An important drawback of the minimum rule is that the value of a single

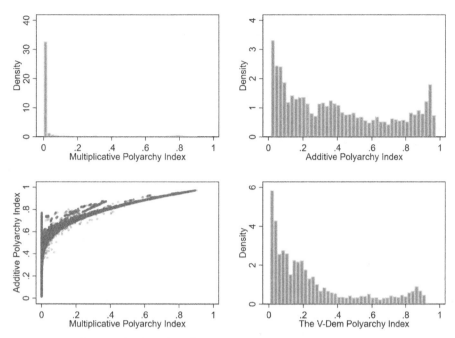

FIGURE 5.2 Aggregating to polyarchy.

indicator may determine the aggregated index value. The relative virtue of multiplication is that it combines information from all constitutive elements and hence relies on, and retains, more information. When all index components are scaled from 0 to 1, as in our case, it is also fairly easily interpretable, with each component indicator serving as a weight for the others. According to the "necessary conditions" logic, then, what we call the Multiplicative Polyarchy Index (MPI) is constructed as follows:

MPI = Elected Officials * Clean Elections * Freedom of Association * Suffrage * Freedom of Expression and Alternative Sources of Information. (5.1)

A low score on *any* of the component indices suppresses the value of this overall index. As a result, its distribution is heavily skewed toward zero (see the upper left quadrant of Figure 5.2). The measurement uncertainty of the lower-level component indices is propagated into this component index by multiplying the standard errors from the BFA posteriors of the Clean Elections, the Freedom of Association and the Freedom of Expression and Alternative Sources of Information Indices (since both Elected Officials and Suffrage are assumed to be measured without error).

However, there is also a second well-established strand in the literature on how to measure electoral democracy going back to Bollen (1980), Coppedge and Reinicke (1990), and Hadenius (1992). It argues that the polyarchy components are correlated and therefore somewhat interchangeable measures of the same underlying construct. The aggregation rule should thus be additive rather than multiplicative. This logic seems to have its strongest theoretical rationale when it comes to the components based on "freedoms" of different sorts, particularly with respect to O'Donnell and Schmitter's (1986) concept of "liberalization" – the phase in a transition to democracy when the first opening of the authoritarian regime occurs (such as a lifting of media censure and wider acceptance for expressions of popular discontent), before the first "founding election." If the extent to which such "liberalizations" count is made conditional on the electoral side of the equation – as implied by the multiplicative logic – we will not be able to observe them in the data. The additive or averaging logic, however, allows such openings to be counted in and of themselves.

Yet as already Dahl (1971) argued, and as recently demonstrated by Coppedge et al. (2008) and Miller (2013), there are other paths toward partial polyarchy. Another prominent route is the introduction of executive elections with universal suffrage, but with severe electoral manipulation, little or no competition at the polls, and severe repression of the freedom of expression. It is this mode of institutionalizing the trappings of electoral democracy without its safeguards that is driving the low correlations between elected officials and suffrage, on the one hand, and the other three polyarchy components on the other, in Table 5.4. If we generalize the additive logic to the full set of components, these two different paths would weigh approximately equally in the resulting index. While recognizing the value of an aggregation rule that also lets the polyarchy components influence the overall score independently of one another, we therefore favor a hybrid approach that lets the two components that can achieve high scores based on the fulfillment of formal-institutional criteria (elected officials and suffrage) together weigh half as much as the other components that enjoy a stronger independent standing in terms of respect for democratic rights (clean elections, freedom of association and expression). The Additive Polyarchy Index (API) is then constructed as follows:

API = [(Elected Officials + Suffrage) + 2 * (Clean Elections + Freedom of Association + Freedom of Expression and Alternative Information)]/8 = 0.125 * Elected Officials + 0.125 * Suffrage + 0.25 * Freedom of Association + 0.25 * Clean Elections + 0.25 * Freedom of Expression and Alternative Information.   (5.2)

The resulting index is somewhat bimodally distributed, as shown in the upper right quadrant of Figure 5.2. Measurement uncertainty is again taken into account by averaging the standard errors from the BFA estimates of Clean Elections, Freedom of Expression, and Freedom of Association.

The lower left quadrant of Figure 5.2 contrasts the two aggregation rules, demonstrating that they discriminate at two different ends of the underlying electoral democracy scale. Thus, what the additive index mostly does is to differentiate different degrees of democracy at the lower end of the multiplicative scale. Even when the latter is zero, the additive index can achieve as high a score as 0.77. Conversely, the multiplicative index mostly discriminates among countries already achieving high values on the additive scale. Thus, the variation on the multiplicative scale is from 0.16 to 0.90 when the additive scale is above 0.80. This has potentially highly significant implications for the results of many empirical analyses depending on which of the two indices are used.

Since both the multiplicative and the additive logic have support in the literature, and since they evidently have the virtue of discriminating at different ends of the spectrum of a foundational concept in political science that one would want to measure in full, we argue that a compromise – more specifically, the average – between the two is the preferred solution to the aggregation problem. The V-Dem Electoral Democracy (Polyarchy) Index is thus constructed by averaging (1) and (2), or more precisely:[12]

(1) Polyarchy (5.3)

= 0.5 * MPI + 0.5 * API = 0.5 * Elected Officials * Clean Elections * Freedom of Association * Suffrage * Freedom of Expression and Alternative Sources of Information + 0.0625 * Elected Officials + 0.125 * Clean Elections + 0.125 * Freedom of Association + 0.0625 * Suffrage + 0.125 * Freedom of Expression and Alternative Sources of Information.

As shown in the lower right quadrant of Figure 5.2, this index is still positively skewed, but far less so than the multiplicative version.

Since the choice of exact weights is a somewhat arbitrary decision, it is essential to assess how sensitive the outcome estimate of polyarchy is to this choice. In Figure 5.3 we provide simulation evidence showing that, on average, the overall index value only deviates by 0.047 from the proposed version depending on what weights are awarded to the individual subcomponents of the additive index (API). The average standard deviation depending on what weight is applied to the average (API) versus multiplication (MPI) component, however, is 0.082, and there is a particular sensitivity to this choice during the later parts of the "first wave of democratization" (Huntington 1991) in the late nineteenth and early twentieth centuries. Although the outcome is thus more sensitive to this latter choice (as already

---

[12] The measurement uncertainty is once again propagated into this overall index by averaging the standard errors from the API and MPI.

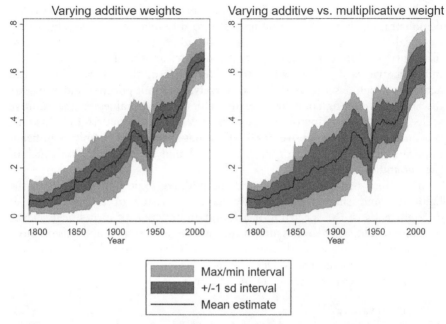

FIGURE 5.3 Sensitivity to aggregation rule of the Polyarchy Index. The left-hand graph simulates the effect of varying the weights of the five additive subcomponents of API in Eq. (5.3) from 0 to 0.5 in 0.05 increments (subject to the restriction that all five together should sum to 0.5; $n = 1001$ simulations for 11,738 country-year observations; $SD = 0.047$; average max/min range = 0.245). The right-hand graph instead simulates varying weights for the additive (API) versus the multiplicative component (MPI) of Eq. (5.3) from 0 to 1 in 0.001 increments (again subject to the constraint that they together should sum to 1; $n = 1001$ simulations for 11,738 country-year observations; $SD = 0.082$, average max/min range = 0.284). Only sovereign countries (where *v2svindep = 1*) are included to avoid a "break" in 1900.

Figure 5.2 would seem to indicate), the results are still not worlds apart. We encourage end users to test the robustness of their empirical results in a similar fashion.[13]

---

[13] Formally, the simulations are based on the following generic aggregation equation, which encompasses both MPI and the API above, as well as any possible combination of the two (and of weights for the components indices):

$$u_a * \frac{1}{k} \sum_{i-1}^{k} w_i * c_i + u_m * \prod_{i-1}^{k} c_i,$$

where u and w are weights and c are the k component variables. The first simulation (varying additive weights) then varies w_i from 0 to 1, subject to the restriction that $\Sigma w_i = 1$, while holding u_a and u_m constant at 0.5 ($N \approx 1000$). The second simulation (varying additive vs. multiplicative component weights) instead varies u_a and u_m from 0 to 1, subject to the restriction that $u_a + u_m = 1$, while holding w_i constant at $1/k$ ($N = 1001$).

5.1.3   Empirical Patterns

Table 5.5 lists the bottom and top five countries in the world covered by the V-Dem data in three years two centuries apart: 1812, 1912, and 2012. The exact rank orderings of countries should be taken with a grain of salt, since all index scores are also accompanied with confidence intervals (not displayed). But the countries that appear in the bottom and top positions still illustrate some general patterns. In 1812, the US was the most electorally democratic country in the world, followed by Sweden and the UK. In 1912, however, New Zealand, and Australia were, by wide margins, the most electorally democratic countries in the world, together with Finland being the only countries in the world at the time that provided universal or near-universal suffrage to both women and men. Other countries scoring high at the time were Switzerland, Belgium, and Denmark. In 2012, Switzerland and Denmark still hold a position as one of the world's most polyarchic countries, now accompanied by UK and the US, and one Latin American country: Uruguay.

What the table does not show, however, is a long string of highly electorally democratic countries scoring almost indistinguishably lower than Uruguay. The least electorally democratic – and sovereign – country in the world that we have data on in 1812 was the kingdom of Nepal, and in 1912 the Sultanate of Muscat and Oman. In 2012, that position goes to another monarchy: Saudi Arabia, one of the few countries in the world today not even holding any national elections.

Figure 5.4 depicts the aggregate trends in the Polyarchy Index and its five component indices since 1789 (our first year of measurement). Looking at the

TABLE 5.5 *Top- and bottom-five countries of polyarchy*

Top five					
1812:		*1912:*		*2012:*	
US	0.374	New Zealand	0.797	UK	0.940
Sweden	0.272	Australia	0.771	Switzerland	0.933
UK	0.268	Denmark	0.612	Uruguay	0.933
France	0.130	Belgium	0.585	US	0.928
Spain	0.107	Switzerland	0.574	Denmark	0.926
Bottom five					
1812:		*1912:*		*2012:*	
Portugal	0.022	Venezuela	0.045	Qatar	0.090
Morocco	0.022	Thailand	0.028	Laos	0.089
Korea	0.016	Ethiopia	0.018	Eritrea	0.085
Two Sicilies	0.015	Nepal	0.010	North Korea	0.083
Nepal	0.010	Oman	0.009	Saudi Arabia	0.022

Note: V-Dem also includes semisovereign entities such as colonies, but for the purpose of this table, only sovereign entities (*v2svindep=1*) have been included.

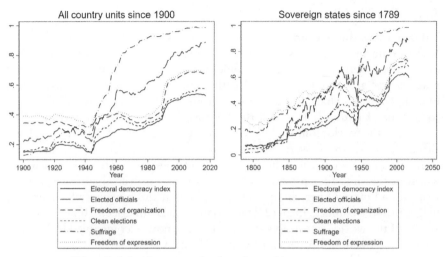

FIGURE 5.4 Historical development of polyarchy and its components.

composite index first (solid line), we can observe traces of all of Huntington's (1991) three waves of democracy, although with differences not seen before. First, when all country units are included in the analysis (left panel), the first wave in the early nineteenth century is much less pronounced. This is mainly a result of the fact that this panel treats semisovereign territories such as colonies on par with independent states. For the same reason, the V-Dem Polyarchy Index shows a much more gradual second wave stretching into the 1960s rather than erupting immediately after World War II, and displays very few signs of a reversed second wave. When only independent countries are included (right panel), the pattern is more similar to conventional wisdom, with the long and slow first wave peaking in the 1920s, and the second in the 1960s, in both cases followed by a more distinct setback. This is an important corrective to our understanding of the level and development of democracy in the world. When seen from the perspective of the population of the world, democratic development looks somewhat different than from when viewed from the perspective of independent states.

Second, the five subcomponents of polyarchy display slightly different trajectories, although they all trend upward in similar ways. Most importantly, again illustrating the distinctiveness of this democratic institution, suffrage reveals no reverse waves and peaks already after World War II, today being observed almost universally across the globe. Having nominally elected officials is second in the order of observance, again placing it among the "simpler" democratic accomplishments to achieve. The most difficult one, tracking the others at a lower rate almost throughout the nineteenth and twentieth centuries, and today falling distinctly below the others, is the organization of free and fair elections. This is thus the democratic institution of the world to which future developments will remain most sensitive.

5.2 THE LIBERAL PRINCIPLE

The liberal principle of democracy, although not lacking supporters, has never been theorized as distinctly as the more fundamental electoral democracy concept. With prominent intellectual roots in Montesquieu and the republican tradition, and perhaps most eloquently exposed in the *Federalist* papers, this principle embodies the intrinsic value of protecting individual and minority rights against potential a "tyranny of the majority" and state repression more generally. This is achieved through constitutionally protected civil liberties, strong rule of law, and effective checks and balances that limit the use of executive power. In terms of O'Donnell's (1998) famous distinction, the liberal tradition thus puts a premium on *horizontal* rather than *vertical* accountability, the latter being the primus motor of electoral democracy. As pointed out in Chapter 2, there are three critical components to consider: the protection of basic civil liberties, and legislative as well as judicial constraints on the executive. It is to the measurement of these features that we now turn. As in the former section, we then address the question of aggregation.

5.2.1 Measuring the Parts: Three Components of Liberal Democracy

The V-Dem data set includes indicators of 10 individual liberties that tap into the extent to which the state (or the executive of the state) encroaches on the private sphere of individuals. The first three are related to the individual's protection from the legal sphere, or what is commonly called "rule of law."[14] This includes (1) an impartial public administration (Rothstein and Teorell 2008), (2) transparent laws with predictable enforcement, and (3) access to justice (measured separately for women and men). Other heralded principles in the liberal tradition are of course (4) the right to private property (again measured separately for women and men); and respect for physical integrity rights (Davenport 2007: 487), more specifically measured as freedom from (5) torture and (6) political killings. Key to the protection of a private sphere is also (7) freedom from forced labor (measured separately for men and women) and freedom of movement, both (8) domestically (measured separately for men and women) and (9) across borders. Finally, one has to be granted the right to (10) exercise one's religion freely.

To test the proposition that these 10 indicators are reflections of an underlying concept, the protection of liberty in general, we ran a Bayesian

---

[14] The rule of law is often thought of as an "essentially contested concept," one in which "the proper use of [the concept] involves endless disputes about [its] proper uses on the part of [its] users" (Gallie 1955, as quoted in Waldron 2002). At the very least, the concept is multidimensional. In the abstract, there is general agreement the rule of law means that the people as well as officials of the state should obey the law and be guided by it (Raz 1977). Disagreements derive from how to give meaning to this broad idea. Our measure incorporates several dimensions of the concept that are used by scholars in the field. That law should be clear and predictable follows the desire that individuals should be guided by the law (Fuller 1969). That justice should be accessible is a key feature of how the United Nations understands the concept (www.un.org/ruleoflaw/). For a modern treatment of the conceptual and empirical challenges associated with the concept, see Rodriguez et al. (2009).

TABLE 5.6 *Measuring equality before the law and individual liberty (BFA estimates)*

Indicator	Loadings (Λ)	Uniqueness (Ψ)
Rigorous and impartial public administration (*v2clrspct*)	0.700	0.509
Transparent laws with predictable enforcement (*v2cltrnslw*)	0.791	0.373
Access to justice (*v2clacjstm, v2clacjstw*)	0.874	0.234
Property rights (*v2clprpty, v2clprptw*)	0.735	0.459
Freedom from torture (*v2cltort*)	0.778	0.396
Freedom from political killings (*v2clkill*)	0.770	0.409
Freedom from forced labor (*v2clslavem, v2clslavef*)	0.717	0.485
Freedom of religion (*v2clrelig*)	0.653	0.575
Freedom of foreign movement (*v2clfmove*)	0.758	0.425
Freedom of domestic movement (*v2cldmovem, v2cldmovew*)	0.783	0.386

Note: Entries are factor loadings and uniqueness scores from a normal theory Bayesian factor analysis model; $n = 24{,}880$ country-years. Where two indicator tags appear, separate questions have been asked for men and women, respectively, and then averaged.

factor analysis (BFA) the results of which are reported in Table 5.6. Although the fit is not quite as good as for the polyarchy component indices, there are no signs of multidimensionality. The resulting index (called *v2xcl_rol*) is, as before, rescaled to 0–1 through the normal cdf.

Next, we turn to measuring two types of constraints on the executive, one stemming from the judiciary, the other from the legislature. The critical feature of the judiciary is of course its independence, but as argued by Ríos-Figueroa and Staton (2014), judicial independence requires two things: autonomy (from other government institutions) and influence (over other government institutions). If the judiciary only does the bidding of the government, it is of course not independent. But, on the other hand, if the government never complies with the rulings of the courts, their autonomy is exercised in a vacuum and cannot fully constrain the executive. We therefore include indicators of both dimensions of judicial independence. In addition, we ask separately about the high (or highest) court and the lower courts in the country, since their status vis-à-vis the government could differ. Lastly, our index of judicial constraints includes a more behavioral measure, namely the extent to which the executive (the head of state and government together with cabinet ministers) respects the constitution in practice. As shown in Table 5.7, these five variables behave as reflective indicators capturing a unidimensional underlying construct (captured by the index *v2x_jucon*).

TABLE 5.7 *Measuring judicial and legislative constraints on the executive (BFA estimates)*

Indicator	Loadings (Λ)	Uniqueness (Ψ)
Judicial constraints:		
High court independence (*v2juhcind*)	0.752	0.431
Lower court independence (*v2juncind*)	0.766	0.413
Compliance with high court (*v2juhccomp*)	0.814	0.339
Compliance with lower courts (*v2jucomp*)	0.824	0.324
Executive respects constitution (*v2exrescon*)	0.625	0.577
Legislative constraints:		
Legislature questions officials in practice (*v2lgqstexp*)	0.711	0.495
Legislature investigates in practice (*v2lginvstp*)	0.873	0.242
Legislature opposition parties (*v2lgoppart*)	0.785	0.382
Executive oversight other body (*v2lgotovst*)	0.791	0.375

Note: Entries are factor loadings and uniqueness scores from a normal theory Bayesian factor analysis model; n = 21,313 (judicial constraints) and 16,472 (legislative constraints) country-years, respectively.

The other major institution that may be invested with powers to constrain the executive is of course the legislature (Fish and Kroenig 2009). First, the legislature must have the power to regularly question the government – to force it to explain its policies or testify, for example through the power of summons. Second, the legislature needs to be invested with the power to also investigate an executive accused of misconduct, and this investigation must also have the potential to result in a decision or report that is unfavorable to the executive. Third, not only the legislature as such but also the opposition parties in the legislature, not part of the ruling party or coalition, must be able to exercise oversight and investigatory functions against the wishes of that governing party or coalition. Fourth, and finally, there may be other bodies than the legislature exercising the questioning and investigative functions, such as a comptroller general, general prosecutor, or ombudsman. Although this final indicator is strictly speaking not part of the legislature, its existence is correlated with the other investigative powers of the legislature strongly enough to form one "system." That "system," as it were, is what the factor index (called *v2xlg_legcon*) is attempting to measure, and as is clear from Table 5.7, the expectation of unidimensionality is again borne out by the data.

5.2.2 Measuring the Whole: Aggregating the Components

Figure 5.5 illustrates the empirical relationships between the three components of the liberal principle. As one would expect, the protection of civil liberties

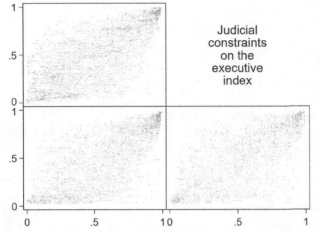

FIGURE 5.5 Relationships among the liberal subcomponent indices.

tends to go hand in hand with constraints on the executive. Although mostly driven by convergence at the end points, the correlations are overall moderate to strong (at 0.77 and 0.75 between civil liberties and legislative and judicial constraints on the executive, respectively; and at 0.74 between the two constraints). This implies that the choice of aggregation rule for how to combine them will be less critical than in the case of polyarchy.

We argue that the three liberal components can be viewed as partial substitutes. A high score on judicial constraints on the executive can thus compensate to some extent for a low score on legislative constraints. Similarly, if equality before the law and civil liberties are upheld in the absence of constraints on the executive, it should still count as a partial fulfillment of the liberal principle. Alternatively, we could argue that the three component indices should be seen as distinct measures of the same underlying theoretical construct. The implication is the same: that we form the Liberal Component Index by taking the average of the three. Thus

> Liberal = (Civil Liberties + Judicial Constraints + Legislative
> Constraints)/3 .   (5.4)[15]

---

[15] Eq. (5.4) ignores missing values by taking the average of all observations for at which least one component index has nonmissing data. Measurement uncertainty is, as before, taken into account by averaging the standard errors from the BFA estimates of Civil liberties, Judicial constraints, and Legislative constraints.

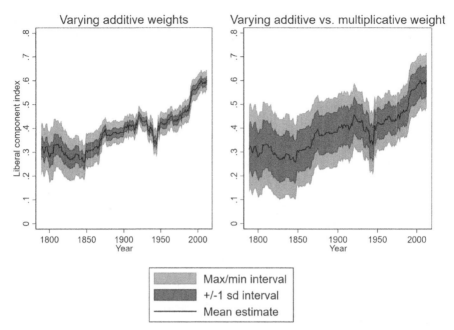

FIGURE 5.6 Sensitivity to aggregation rule of the Liberal Component Index. The left-hand graph simulates the effect of varying the weights w_k of the three additive subcomponents of a more generalized version of Eq. (5.4), Liberal = 0.5 * (w_1 * Civil liberties + w_2 * Judicial constraints + w_3 * Legislative constraints) + 0.5 * (Civil liberties * Judicial constraints * Legislative constraints), from 0 to 1 in 0.02 increments (subject to the restriction that all three w_k together should sum to 1; n = 1326 simulations for 13,359 country-year observations; SD = 0.027; average range = 0.119). The right-hand graph instead simulates varying weights for the additive versus the multiplicative part of the same equation from 0 to 1 in 0.001 increments (again subject to the constraint that they together should sum to 1; n = 1001 simulations for 13,359 country-year observations; SD = 0.077, average max/min range = 0.268).

In Figure 5.6, we provide simulation results for how sensitive this index is for the choice of aggregation weights and the aggregation rule. The left-hand graph shows the results from varying the weights applied to each subcomponent. Eq. (5.4) assumes equal weights, but one could also have contemplated other weights, such as proportional to the correlations between the subcomponents and an underlying latent factor, or a weighting system giving equal weight to the civil liberties component on the one hand and the two executive constraints components on the other. Since the three subcomponents are fairly strongly correlated, the outcome index is not very sensitive to the exact choice of weights, particularly not in later time periods, which is evidenced in the left-hand graph in Figure 5.6. The right-hand graph in the same figure, however, indicates that the choice between averaging or multiplication as the rule for how to aggregate the three subcomponents is more consequential, again particularly during the nineteenth century. Based on theoretical considerations, we have opted in favor of the average, but again end users may want to explore how robust their results are to this particular choice.

5.2.3 Empirical Patterns

In Table 5.8, we list the top- and bottom-five countries in the world in terms of the Liberal Component Index, as per 1812, 1912, and 2012. It should be stressed that this index is distinct from the Polyarchy Index, although we view electoral democracy as the most fundamental form of democracy at the national level, the one without which we cannot even talk about democracy in any other sense (more on this below). Despite being distinct in terms of its measurement, however, the liberal principle follows a pattern very similar to that for polyarchy. In 1812, the top three liberal countries in the world were also the most polyarchic, although Sweden is now higher ranked than both the UK and the US. In 1912, Switzerland comes out as the most liberal country in the world, closely followed by Denmark, Norway, the Netherlands, and Australia. In 2012, Germany and Sweden have taken the positions of Switzerland and the Netherlands on this list.

It may come as some surprise to some to see unitary, unicameral parliamentary countries with no constitutional court such as Denmark, Norway, and Sweden in this position. After all, these countries are seldom

TABLE 5.8 *Top- and bottom-five liberal countries*

Top five					
1812:		*1912:*		*2012:*	
Sweden	0.784	Switzerland	0.925	Denmark	0.983
UK	0.712	Denmark	0.923	Norway	0.981
US	0.679	Norway	0.922	Germany	0.978
Denmark	0.560	Netherlands	0.919	Sweden	0.977
Mecklenburg Schwerin	0.107	Australia	0.913	Australia	0.971
Bottom five					
1812:		*1912:*		*2012:*	
Burma	0.125	China	0.138	Uzbekistan	0.096
Paraguay	0.095	Ethiopia	0.062	Syria	0.086
Korea	0.075	Oman	0.061	Turkmenistan	0.061
Russia	0.070	Iran	0.051	Eritrea	0.038
China	0.040	Nepal	0.042	North Korea	0.027

Note: V-Dem also includes semisovereign entities such as colonies, but for the purpose of this table, only sovereign entities (*v2svindep=1*) have been included.

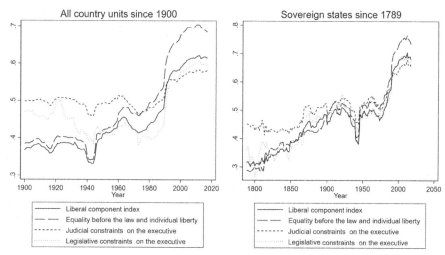

FIGURE 5.7 Historical development of the liberal principle and its components.

praised for bearing the hallmarks of Madisonian democracy. Although the empirical (if not intellectual) birthplace of the liberal principle of democracy, the US, scores almost as high (at 0.964, ranked eighth in the world), this is an important reminder of the type of institutions the Liberal Component Index does *not* pick up. The "liberal" principle cannot be equated with presidentialism and the type of institutional gridlock that such systems can sometimes end up with: divided government and executive vetoes. Also, "liberal" does not mean bicameral, which again with the US taken as a model can sometimes lead to two elected legislatures with opposing majorities. Finally, "liberal" does not mean federalism. As discussed in Chapter 2, these features should, if anything, be considered part of the consensual versus majoritarian principles of democracy (which V-Dem currently does not measure), not the liberal tradition. What makes a country such as Denmark "liberal" is thus the combination of highly secured civil liberties, a highly independent and consequential supreme court, and a legislature vested with strong executive review powers.

With the exception of Korea, the list of most illiberal countries is different from the list of electoral nondemocracies in 1812, but in 1912 the two overlap to a great extent, with Ethiopia, Oman, and Nepal appearing on both lists. North Korea is currently the most illiberal country in the world.

In Figure 5.7, we look at the historical trajectory of liberalism across the twentieth century. Although the overall pattern looks very similar to that of polyarchy, with a distinct three-wave pattern particularly visible for sovereign states, there are some deviations at the subcomponent level that deserve highlighting. First, particularly with respect to judicial and legislative constraints, the mid-twentieth century and in particular the 1970s marked a period of global deterioration as compared to the early twentieth century. Second, a reversal has occurred in terms of which liberal component is most easily safeguarded. In the nineteenth and early twentieth centuries, judicial independence was the most highly respected liberal principle. Today, it is the one that is least respected. Given the key importance in having a judicial system that can impartially uphold the right to civil liberty and keep an unfettered executive in check, this does not bode well for the future of liberalism in the world.

5.3 THE PARTICIPATORY PRINCIPLE

The participatory model of democracy arose in criticism of what were considered the unfulfilled promises of representative Western democracy in the 1960s and 1970s. Although not necessarily challenging the electoral and liberal principles of democracy as such, participatory democrats, inspired by practices of direct democracy in ancient Greece and by the writings of, e.g., Rousseau, sought to supplement Western democratic institutions with enriched popular participation, particularly at the local level. As mentioned in Chapter 2, four features in particular are critical to the participatory ideal: high levels of political engagement, both in electoral and nonelectoral modes of participation; the practice of direct decision-making; and decentralization. Due to lack of valid and reliable global data across time and space, one of these features is omitted from the V-Dem index of participatory practices: electoral turnout. Below, we describe how the other three have been captured.

5.3.1 Measuring the Parts: Three Components of Participatory Democracy

To measure the first component we have assembled an index of the extent of popular participation in civil society organizations (CSOs). This includes (1) the degree of decentralization of intraparty candidate nomination procedures; (2) the range of consultation of CSOs by central level policy makers; (3) the degree of popular involvement in CSOs; and, since there is typically a gender gap in political participation across the globe (Paxton and Hughes 2017), (4) the degree of women's participation in CSOs. To test the proposition that these four indicators are reflections of an underlying concept, we ran a Bayesian factor analysis the results of which are reported in Table 5.9. The overall fit of the model seems satisfactory. We call the resulting factor index the index of civil society participation ($v2x\_cspart$).

Since participatory democrats generally favor citizen participation in direct decision-making over the indirect influence exercised through voting for representatives, a second component of the participatory principle is a derived index tapping the extent to which citizens engage in means of direct popular voting (Altman 2017). This index results from the aggregation of the scores of four types of mechanisms of direct democracy: popular initiatives, popular

TABLE 5.9 *Measuring civil society participation (BFA estimates)*

Indicator	Loadings (Λ)	Uniqueness (Ψ)
Decentralization of intraparty candidate selection (*v2pscnslnl*)	0.502	0.753
CSO consultation (*v2cscnsult*)	0.780	0.392
CSO participatory environment (*v2csprtcpt*)	0.775	0.400
CSO women's participation (*v2csgender*)	0.600	0.642

Note: Entries are factor loadings and uniqueness scores from a normal theory Bayesian factor analysis model; n = 22,728 country-years.

referenda, obligatory referenda, and authorities' plebiscites. The index then measures: how easy it is to (1) initiate and (2) approve each type of popular vote, and (3) how consequential that vote is (if approved). Ease of initiation is measured by (1) the existence of a direct democracy process (Ǝ), (2) the number of signatures needed (1-S), and (3) time limits to collect signatures (CT). Ease of approval is measured by quorums pertaining to (1) participation, approval, and supermajority (1-SQS), and (2) district majority (AQ). Consequences are measured by (1) the legal status (decisiveness) of the decision made by citizens (D) and (2) the frequency with which direct popular votes have been used and approved in the past (T). Drawing on these seven features, based on 11 indicators, the formula for the subindex of each mechanism of direct democracy is

$$\text{Direct Popular Vote} = [\text{Ǝ} * (1 - S) * CT + (1 - SQS) * AQ] * D * T. \quad (5.5)$$

The final index value, scaled to range from 0 to 1, is then formed by taking a weighted average across the four mechanisms of direct democracy, with popular initiatives and popular referenda given the weight if 1.5, obligatory referenda and plebiscites the weight of 1. (See Altman 2017 for elaboration and details.)[16] Data for this index (called *v2xdd_dd*) has only been collected back to 1900, which is also the reason why V-Dem does not provide any estimates for the overall level of participatory democracy for the nineteenth century (although both the other component indices are observed going back to 1789).

A third and final critical feature of the participatory principle is a plea for decentralization, or local as opposed to national politics. We measure this aspect by looking into whether there are elected local and/or regional governments; and – if so – to what extent can they operate without interference from unelected bodies at that level. More specifically, we ask our Country Experts to assess, separately for the local and regional level (if both

[16] In the case of popular votes originating from above (obligatory referenda and plebiscites), the consequences measured by D and T drop out from the equation.

exist), (1) whether none of the government offices at that level is elected, only the executive is elected, only the assembly is elected, or both the executive and assembly are elected (*extent*). This construct is scaled to vary from 0–1 and then multiplied (weighted) by (2) the extent to which nonelected officials are subordinate to elected officials at that level (*relpower*, also scaled from 0–1). Since the existence of local and regional levels of government is in part determined by country size, and since they can be seen as functional equivalents for the purpose of achieving decentralization, we treat the two levels as perfect substitutes. The formula for creating the index is thus

$$\text{Elected Local/Regional Government} = \text{Max}(\text{extent}_{local} * \text{relpow}_{local}, \text{extent}_{regional} * \text{relpow}_{regional}). \tag{5.6}$$

5.3.2 Measuring the Whole: Aggregating the Components

As Figure 5.8 makes clear, there are ambiguous interrelationships between the three participatory subcomponent indices. Although civil society participation and elected local/regional government are decently related ($r = 0.69$), both these indices are only weakly associated with the direct popular vote ($r = 0.36$ and 0.32, respectively).[17] Nevertheless, we argue in favor of averaging the three to arrive at our index for the participatory principle. To the best of our knowledge, theorists of participatory democracy have not developed the concept enough to determine whether any of the three features are necessary conditions. Arguably, none of them in itself is a sufficient condition. As in the case of the liberal principle, we therefore view them as partial substitutes. Thus

$$\text{Participatory} = (\text{Civil Society Participation} + \text{Direct Popular Vote} + \text{Elected Local/Regional Government})/3. \tag{5.7}^{[18]}$$

The low correlations make the Participatory Component Index more sensitive to what weights to apply to each subcomponent, and increasingly so over time (see Figure 5.9). Whether the subcomponents are averaged or multiplied matters approximately as much on average, although considerably more so after the mid-twentieth century. As previously, end users should make their conclusions sensitive to these aggregation choices.

---

[17] One possible reason for this is that the direct popular vote index does *not* take into account the practice of direct democracy at the local level.

[18] Eq. (5.7) ignores missing values by taking the average of all observations for which at least one component index has nonmissing data. Measurement uncertainty is taken into account by averaging the standard errors from the BFA estimates of Civil society participation and the index of elected local/regional government (whereas direct popular vote is assumed to have been measured without error).

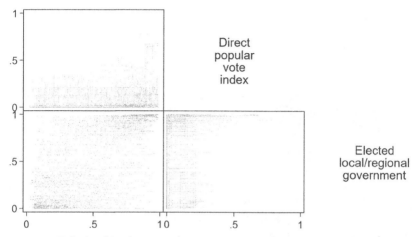

FIGURE 5.8 Relationships between the participatory subcomponent indices.

5.3.3 Empirical Patterns

There is one country that, very unsurprisingly, stands out as the most participatory country in the world, both in 1912 and in 2012, and that is Switzerland, as shown in Table 5.10. New Zealand is however a close runner-up, with a third position in 1912 and fourth in 2012. In modern times, Switzerland is also joined by two of the other most directly democratic countries in the world: Uruguay and Slovenia.

The bottom-five slot in 1912 is again crowded by countries very similar to the list for polyarchy and liberal, with Ethiopia and Nepal holding similar bottom positions. Saudi Arabia, Eritrea and, again, North Korea are the least participatory countries in the world today.

Figure 5.10 displays the historical development of participatory practices across the globe. We again see traces of the three waves, although less markedly so. Direct popular vote is by far the participatory principle that is least fulfilled, having significantly lower scores than the others at all times. Civil society participation and elected local government is the highest scoring component, with the former outperforming the latter in recent decades.

5.4   THE DELIBERATIVE PRINCIPLE

Following what is sometimes called the "deliberative turn" in the 1990s (Dryzek 2002), the deliberative vision of democracy enshrines the core values

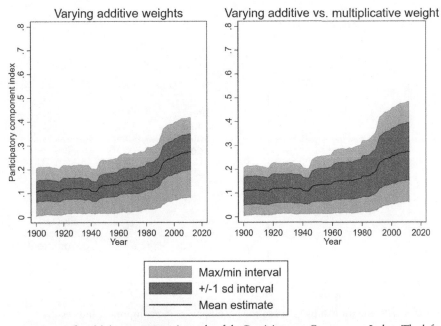

FIGURE 5.9 Sensitivity to aggregation rule of the Participatory Component Index. The left-hand graph simulates the effect of varying the weights w_k of the three additive subcomponents of a more generalized version of Eq. (5.7), Participatory = 0.5 * (w_1 * Civil society participation + w_2 * Direct popular vote + w_3 * Elected local/regional government) + 0.5 * (Civil society participation * Direct popular vote * Elected local/regional government), from 0 to 1 in 0.02 increments (subject to the restriction that all three together should sum to 1; $n = 1326$ simulations for 18,051 country-year observations; $SD = 0.057$; average max/min range = 0.253). The right-hand graph instead simulates varying weights for the additive versus the multiplicative part of the same equation from 0 to 1 in 0.001 increments (again subject to the constraint that they together should sum to 1; $n = 1001$ simulations for 18,051 country-year observations; $SD = 0.083$, average max/min range = 0.286).

that political decision-making in pursuit of the public good must be informed by respectful and reasonable dialogue rather than by emotional appeals or coercion. This is arguably one of the most, if not *the* most, difficult democratic principle to measure. The deliberative principle lacks clear institutional embodiments like elections, judiciaries, or mechanisms of direct democracy. Unlike civil liberties, for example, the extent to which the deliberative principle is fulfilled is also hard to observe, particularly for an entire country over long swaths of time.

Our approach to at least attempt a measure of deliberation is inspired by the so-called Discourse Quality Index (Steenbergen et al. 2003). We thus ask our Country Experts to assess (1) the extent to which political elites give public justifications for their positions on matters of public policy; (2) justify their positions in terms of the public good; (3) acknowledge and respect

TABLE 5.10 *Top- and bottom-five participatory countries*

Top five			
1912:		*2012:*	
Switzerland	0.849	Switzerland	0.885
Australia	0.697	Uruguay	0.836
New Zealand	0.625	Slovenia	0.823
Denmark	0.609	New Zealand	0.762
Canada	0.603	Italy	0.760
Bottom five			
1912:		*2012:*	
Nepal	0.076	Quatar	0.123
Iran	0.071	Uzbekistan	0.105
Ethiopia	0.058	Saudi Arabia	0.094
Thailand	0.046	North Korea	0.061
Venezuela	0.036	Eritrea	0.042

Note: V-Dem also includes semisovereign entities such as colonies, but for the purpose of this table, only sovereign entities (*v2svindep==1*) have been included.

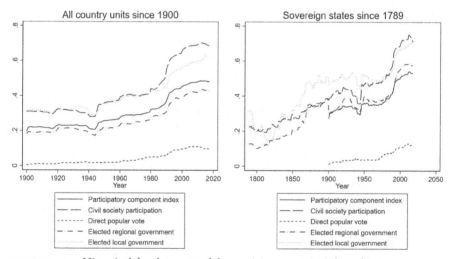

FIGURE 5.10 Historical development of the participatory principle and its components.

counterarguments; and how wide the range of consultation is at (4) the elite level; and (5) in society at large. Our hypothesis is that these five broad indicators tap into a general underlying phenomenon: the quality of deliberation. Table 5.11 strongly supports this contention. All five indicators,

TABLE 5.11 *Measuring deliberation (BFA estimates)*

Indicator	Loadings (Λ)	Uniqueness (Ψ)
Reasoned justification (*v2dlreason*)	0.818	0.332
Common good (*v2dlcommon*)	0.641	0.588
Respect counterarguments (*v2dlcountr*)	0.824	0.322
Range of consultation (*v2dlconslt*)	0.857	0.266
Engaged society (*v2dlengage*)	0.871	0.243

Note: Entries are factor loadings and uniqueness scores from a normal theory Bayesian factor analysis model; $n = 18,178$ country-years.

TABLE 5.12 *Top- and bottom-five deliberative countries*

Top five			
1912:		*2012:*	
Switzerland	0.949	Norway	0.991
Australia	0.903	Switzerland	0.987
Denmark	0.901	Denmark	0.983
Norway	0.807	Germany	0.980
Canada	0.798	Sweden	0.979
Bottom five			
1912:		*2012:*	
Dominican Republic	0.095	Laos	0.121
Ethiopia	0.061	Syria	0.099
Oman	0.035	Eritrea	0.096
Guatemala	0.018	Turkmenistan	0.063
Nepal	0.014	North Korea	0.027

Note: V-Dem also includes semisovereign entities such as colonies, but for the purpose of this table, only sovereign entities (*v2svindep==1*) have been included.

with the partial exception of references to the common good (which seems to be so common that it discriminates less well, at least for some time periods; see below), load on a single unidimensional construct. The factor index (called *v2xdl_delib*) capturing this construct, although only back to the year 1900, is our measure of the deliberative principle.

With a country like Switzerland scoring on top of both the participatory and deliberative principle in both 1912 and 2012, one might think that these two principles are not empirically distinct. Table 5.12 suggests that this is not the case, however. New Zealand, for example, the fourth most participatory country in the world in 2012, is only ranked 56th in terms of its quality of

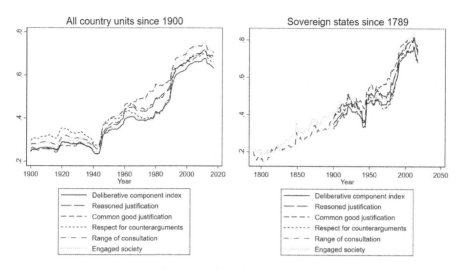

FIGURE 5.11 Historical development of the deliberative principle and its components.

deliberation. Mauritius, moreover, is ranked the eighth most deliberative country in 2012 but is far from the top-five position on all the other democratic principles (and scoring only 0.838 on polyarchy in 2012). The bottom part of the table produces results more consistent with the other democracy indices. Although none of the indicators are overlapping, Ethiopia and Nepal again come out among the least deliberative countries in the world in 1912, although here also joined by countries such as the Dominican Republic and Guatemala, which we have not seen on any other bottom rankings thus far. North Korea and Eritrea vie for a similarly consistent bottom-five position in 2012.

The historical trajectory of deliberative democracy (Figure 5.11) presents a trajectory that should look familiar by now. Particularly when zooming in on sovereign countries, there are clear signs of a first wave with reversal prior to World War II, a second wave with reversal prior to the 1970s, and a third wave with still no signs of a reversal since. A more peculiar feature of the Deliberative Component Index is that all its components move very much in tandem. Only in the 1960s to the 1990s is there a period when some components perform less well than others. Societal deliberation (engaged society) was then outperformed by elite-level deliberation (reasoned and common good justification). Almost without exceptions, respecting counterarguments has been the deliberative principle that is least well satisfied.

5.5 THE EGALITARIAN PRINCIPLE

The egalitarian principle cuts through just about every other conception of democracy in its emphasis on the principle of political equality. As old as democratic thinking itself, this conception, like the deliberative principle, looks beyond particular ways of institutionalizing democracy. Unlike the deliberative principle, it focuses on the distribution of power in society and resources needed to exercise of political rights. As pointed out in Chapter 2, there are three subcomponents of the egalitarian conception: the equal protection of rights and liberties across all groups; the equal distribution of access to power; and the equal distribution of resources (see Figure 2.7 of Sigman and Lindberg 2018).

5.5.1   Measuring the Parts: Three Components of Egalitarian Democracy

As argued by Sigman and Lindberg (2018), the fulfillment of the egalitarian principle of democracy requires equal influence over the governing process. This overall equality may be broken down into three constituent subcomponents. The first demands that the government protect the rights and freedoms of individuals equally across all groups. Since the standard of "all" groups is an ideal that would not be amenable to systematic measurement, V-Dem focuses on two distinct group categorizations: (1) socioeconomic status and (2) all "other" social group characteristics salient in the country, such as caste, ethnicity, language, race, region, religion, or some combination thereof. In addition, V-Dem attempts to measure (3) geographical inequalities in the protection of civil liberties by asking Country Experts what percentage of the population dwells in areas where respect for civil liberties is significantly weaker than the country average.

Second, egalitarian democracy not only demands equal protection of rights but also that these rights are actually being translated into actual access to power. We attempt to measure this by asking about the equality of power dispersion across the same two group distinctions as above: (1) socioeconomic status and (2) other social groups. In addition, we include an indicator on equal access to power by (3) gender.

The third requirement of egalitarian democracy is that the government must invest in or otherwise facilitate an equal distribution of power resources. Two critical resources in politics then come to the fore: (1) education and (2) health. Moreover, we explore two aspects of the welfare state most likely to affect the overall distribution of resources in society: (3) the public goods aspect of spending and (4) the use of universalistic rather than means-tested social benefit programs.

As indicated by Table 5.13, these indicators seem to tap into three unidimensional latent constructs: equal protection of rights (*v2xeg_eqprotec*); equal access to power (*v2xeg_eqaccess*); and equal distribution of resources (*v2xeg_eqdr*), the former two of which are measured all the way back to 1789.

5.5.2   Measuring the Whole: Aggregating the Components

The three subcomponents of the egalitarian principle correlate fairly strongly (at 0.76 between protection and access; at 0.80 between protection and resources; and at 0.79 between access and resources; see Figure 5.12). This again implies that the principle of egalitarian democracy should not be highly

TABLE 5.13 *Measuring equal protection, access, and distribution (BFA estimates)*

Indicator	Loadings (Λ)	Uniqueness (Ψ)
Equal protection of rights:		
Social class equality in respect for civil liberties (*v2clacjust*)	0.897	0.200
Social group equality in respect for civil liberties (*v2clsocgrp*)	0.644	0.584
Regional unevenness in respect for civil liberties (*v2clsnlpct*)	0.475	0.788
Equal access to power:		
Power distributed by gender (*v2pepwrgen*)	0.722	0.476
Power distributed by socioeconomic position (*v2pepwrses*)	0.731	0.466
Power distributed by social group (*v2pepwrsoc*)	0.746	0.445
Equal distribution of resources:		
Educational equality (*v2peedueq*)	0.874	0.236
Health equality (*v2pehealth*)	0.910	0.171
Particularistic vs. public goods spending (*v2dlencmps*)	0.567	0.680
Means-tested vs. universalistic policies (*v2dlunivl*)	0.614	0.624

Note: Entries are factor loadings and uniqueness scores from a normal theory Bayesian factor analysis model; n = 25,465 (equal protection), 25,374 (equal access), or 18,178 (resource distribution) country-years, respectively.

sensitive to the exact choice of aggregation rule. For simplifying purposes, we have again relied on the average of the three subcomponents, seeing the lack of one as partially substituting for the lack of the other. In other words (again following Sigman and Lindberg 2018),

$$\text{Egalitarian} = (\text{Equal Protection} + \text{Equal Access} + \text{Equal Distribution})/3. \qquad (5.8)^{[19]}$$

Figure 5.13 conveys a picture similar to that for the liberal aggregation rule above (cf. Figure 5.6). The choice of exact weights for the three subcomponents matters little, but whether the subcomponents are averaged or multiplied has larger significance, more so in later times. Again, end users may want to explore how robust their results are to this particular aggregation rule.

---

[19] Eq. (5.8) ignores missing values by taking the average of all observations for at which least one component index has nonmissing data. Measurement uncertainty is, as before, taken into account by averaging the standard errors from the BFA estimates of Equal protection, Equal access, and Equal distribution.

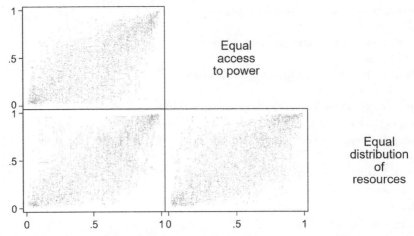

FIGURE 5.12 Relationships between the egalitarian subcomponent indices.

5.5.3 Empirical Patterns

That Scandinavian welfare states appear among the most egalitarian polities in the world, both in 1912 and 2012, should come as no surprise (see Table 5.14). Perhaps less expected is the appearance of Belgium – a society sometimes depicted as deeply divided between two ethnic groups, as short-listed at both time points. Switzerland holding the top position in 1912 is also slightly surprising given the status of women at the time. A couple of Latin American countries this time upholds the position as the least egalitarian countries in 1912. In 2012 that position is upheld by the newest member of the state system: South Sudan.

The development of egalitarianism over time is not a story of wave-like surges and backsliding but of constant progression, with the brief exception of the period around World War II (see Figure 5.14). The world is substantially more egalitarian today than it was a century ago. The most significant improvement has occurred in the field of equal access to power.

5.6   HIGHER-LEVEL AGGREGATIONS AND THE VARIATION
TRADE-OFF

It should be recalled that the liberal, participatory, deliberative, and egalitarian *component* indices presented above do not in themselves embody a *variety of democracy*. Following the canon in each of these four alternative traditions that argues that electoral democracy is insufficient, we agree that there is more to

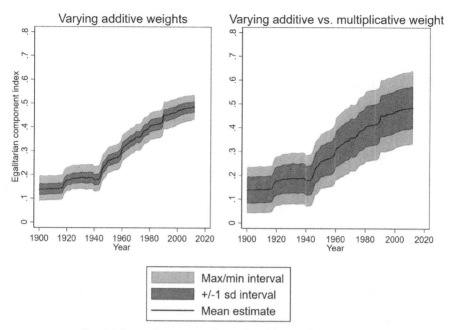

FIGURE 5.13 Sensitivity to the aggregation rule of the Egalitarian Component Index. The left-hand graph simulates the effect of varying the weights w_k of the three additive subcomponents of a more generalized version of Eq. (5.8), Egalitarian = 0.5 (w_1 * Equal protection + w_2 * Equal access + w_3 * Equal distribution) + 0.5 * (Equal protection * Equal access * Equal distribution), from 0 to 1 in 0.02 increments (subject to the restriction that all three w_k together should sum to 1; n = 1326 simulations for 17,954 country-year observations; SD = 0.024; average max/min range = 0.109). The right-hand graph instead simulates varying weights for the additive versus the multiplicative part of the same equation from 0 to 1 in 0.001 increments (again subject to the constraint that they together should sum to 1; n = 1001 simulations for 17,954 country-year observations; SD = 0.074, average max/min range = 0.258).

democracy than just elections. However, we also argue that there can be no democracy without elections. To construct the varieties of democracy indices, we thus view the Polyarchy Index as the foundation for the others. More specifically, we combine the scores for our Polyarchy Index with the scores for the components measuring deliberation, equality, participation, and liberal constitutionalism, respectively. This is not an easy task.[20] Imagine two components, P = Polyarchy and HPC = High Principle Component (liberal, egalitarian, participatory, or deliberative), that we want to aggregate into a more general high-level index, called an HLI (Deliberative Democracy Index, Egalitarian Democracy Index, and so on). As above, both P and HPC are scaled

---

[20] This section on how to aggregate to the higher-level indices of democracy is based on Coppedge et al. (2016b).

TABLE 5.14 *Top- and bottom-five egalitarian countries*

Top five			
1912:		*2012:*	
Switzerland	0.835	Denmark	0.975
Denmark	0.752	Norway	0.971
Norway	0.714	Sweden	0.968
New Zealand	0.696	Finland	0.957
Belgium	0.670	Belgium	0.951
Bottom five			
1912:		*2012:*	
Peru	0.062	Sudan	0.230
Bolivia	0.061	Somalia	0.215
Ecuador	0.060	Chad	0.214
Guatemala	0.057	Angola	0.179
Nicaragua	0.049	South Sudan	0.136

Note: V-Dem also includes semisovereign entities such as colonies, but for the purpose of this table, only sovereign entities (*v2svindep==1*) have been included.

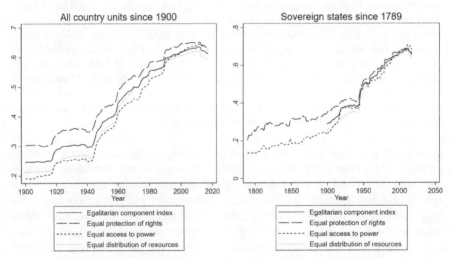

FIGURE 5.14 Historical development of the egalitarian principle and its components.

to a continuous 0–1 interval. Based on extensive deliberations among the authors and other members of the V-Dem research group, we have arrived at the following aggregation formula:

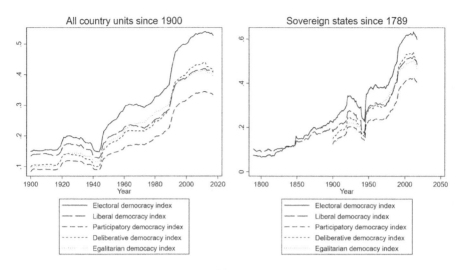

FIGURE 5.15 Historical development of five varieties of democracy.

$$HLI = 0.25 * P^{1.6} + 0.25 * HPC + 0.5 * P^{1.6} * HPC. \qquad (5.9)$$

The underlying rationale for this formula for all four HLIs is the same as that for the Electoral Democracy Index (polyarchy): equal weighting of the additive terms and the multiplicative term in order to respect both the necessary conditions logic and a family resemblance logic. For example, the degree of deliberation still matters for deliberative democracy even when there is no electoral democracy, and electoral democracy still matters even when there is no deliberation; but the highest level of deliberative democracy can be attained only when there is a high level of *both* electoral democracy and deliberation.

The more a country approximates polyarchy, the more the combined HLI score for that country should reflect the unique component. This perspective is a continuous version of theoretical arguments presented in the literature that polyarchy or electoral democracy conditions should be satisfied to a reasonable extent before the other democracy component contributes much to the high-level index values. At the same time, it reflects the view in the literature that when a certain level of polyarchy is reached, what matters in terms of, say, participatory democracy is how much of the participatory property of democracy the country has. This argument also resembles a widespread perspective in the quality of democracy literature emphasizing that fulfillment of some baseline democracy criteria is needed before it makes sense to assess the quality of democracy. (For an overview, see Munck 2016.) The question then becomes at what rate this influence should increase. We arrived at an exponent of 1.6 by defining an anchor point: When a country has a polyarchy score of 0.5 (that is, halfway between a closed dictatorship and a fully electoral democracy)

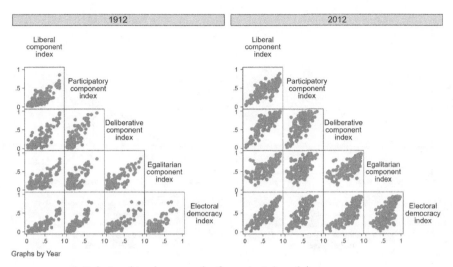

FIGURE 5.16 Relationships between the five principles of democracy.

and the HPC is at its maximum (1), the high-level index score should also be set at 0.5.[21]

Collectively, these thick versions of the five principles (also counting Polyarchy) capture five significant varieties of democracy. Figure 5.15 depicts their respective developments over time. The picture should be familiar by now. Particularly when restricting attention to sovereign countries, all three of Huntington's (1991) waves of democracy are clearly present. We can also see that electoral democracy is the most developed variety of democracy in the world, whereas participatory democracy is least developed. Liberal democracy, in the early nineteenth century the most developed variety, today lags behind the electoral core and is upheld to approximately the same extent as egalitarian and participatory democracy.

These and most other converging over-time trajectories, as well as the top/ bottom-five examples for the five democratic principles presented above, seem to point on an important conclusion. Democracy is not unidimensional. But is it also not as multidimensional empirically as it is theoretically. One variety of democracy seldom develops independently of the others. Another piece of evidence pointing in the same direction is presented in Figure 5.16, where we go back to the level of the component indices (so as not to inflate the correlations by already including polyarchy in the indices). The correlations between the five

---

[21] Define the power parameter as p. Setting Polyarchy = 0.5, HPC = 1, and HLI = 0.5 (the anchor point), and solving for HLI = 0.25 * Polyarchy^p + 0.25 * HPC + 0.5 * Polyarchy^p * HPC, p = log(base 0.5) of 0.25/0.75 ≈ 1.6.

TABLE 5.15 *Top- and bottom-five "Big-D" countries*

Top five			
1912:		*2012:*	
Switzerland	0.826	Switzerland	0.944
Australia	0.779	Denmark	0.917
Denmark	0.759	Sweden	0.903
New Zealand	0.741	Norway	0.902
Norway	0.708	Uruguay	0.902
Bottom five			
1912:		*2012:*	
Venezuela	0.104	Turkmenistan	0.178
Guatemala	0.089	Saudi Arabia	0.167
Ethiopia	0.062	Syria	0.159
Oman	0.059	Eritrea	0.152
Nepal	0.042	North Korea	0.109

Note: V-Dem also includes semisovereign entities such as colonies, but for the purpose of this table, only sovereign entities (*v2svindep=1*) have been included.

principles range from 0.67 (between participatory and egalitarian) to 0.88 (between participatory and electoral). They are also very stable over time.

The fact that all varieties of democracy are fairly closely related raises the question of whether we can move even one further level up in the tree of aggregation. Is it possible to speak of "democracy" *tout court*, or "Big-D," a combination of all five varieties of democracy for which V-Dem has collected empirical measures? One possible such measure of course readily suggests itself, namely to simply take the average across the five component indices:

"Big-D" = (Polyarchy + Liberal + Participatory + Deliberative + Egalitarian)/5. $(5.10)^{22}$

Table 5.15 lists the resulting top- and bottom-five countries as before. Taking a simple average across all five principles, Switzerland comes out on top as the most democratic country in the world, *tout court*, both in 1912 and 2012. Denmark is a close runner-up, ranking third in 1912 and a close second in 2012, together with Norway (fifth in 1912, fourth in 2012). At the bottom, as should be expected from the results above we find Nepal in 1912 and North Korea in 2012.

---

[22] Eq. (5.10) ignores missing values by taking the average of all observations for at which least one component index has nonmissing data.

TABLE 5.16 *Three levels of aggregation*

	Big-D	Principles	Components
Polyarchy:			
Elected Officials	1	1	1
Clean Elections	1	1	2
Freedom of Association	1	1	3
Suffrage	1	1	1
Freedom of Expression	1	1	4
Liberal:			
Civil Liberties	1	2	5
Judicial constraints	1	2	6
Legislative constraints	1	2	7
Participatory:			
Civil society participation	1	3	8
Direct popular vote	1	3	9
Elected local/regional government	1	3	9
Deliberative:			
Deliberative principle	1	4	10
Egalitarian:			
Equal protection	1	5	11
Equal access	1		12
Equal distribution	1	5	13
R-squared	0.574	0.640	0.706

Note: Results from three confirmatory factor analyses run with Stata 14's SEM-command. Numbers 1–13 signify the number of factors retained. Similar numbers signify that indicators within the given component load on the same factor (but on no other factor). To see which indicators are included for each component, see Tables 5.1–5.3, 5.6, 5.7, 5.9, 5.11, and 5.13. R-squared is the average squared loadings from each model. No. of observations = 12,368 country-years.

We would, however, like to end on a more cautionary note. There is no denying that there are benefits to aggregation. Without being able to move up the ladder of generality, very few general patterns would be discerned. Every single comparison would get lost in a jungle of indicators. Also, for the sake of scientific advancement, theoretical concepts need to be matched by measures capturing the same level of generality. If we theorize democracy at the level of polyarchy, the liberal and participatory principle and so on, we also need to develop measures, while based on lower-level indicators, that aggregate up to these concepts.

However, it must be kept in mind that significant amounts of information are being lost along the way. As a rule, the higher the level at which we aggregate, the more nuance and variation in the disaggregated indicators will be lost. To illustrate this, Table 5.16 presents results from three confirmatory factor analyses based on all 61 indicators (or merged indicators in case of similarly worded questions for men and women) presented in this chapter together with the three derived subcomponent indices (elected officials, direct popular vote, and elected local/regional government). At the most general level, we fitted a single-factor "democracy *tout court*" model to this data (across all nonmissing country-year observations). Although we do not present the exact results at the indicator-level (to preserve space), this model actually does not fit the data that poorly. As should be expected from all the moderate to strong correlations between indicators, components, and principles presented above, there is some justification to speak of a single factor of democracy. However, this factor only explains 57.4 percent of the variation in the underlying indicators.

If we instead fit the model at the level of principles, meaning one factor each for polyarchy, liberal, participatory, deliberative, and egalitarian, we improve the fit of the model and now explain 64.0 percent of the variation in the indicators. Finally, in the third column we fit a model at the level of the subcomponents of each principle, resulting in 13 different unique factors representing the 64 indicators or derived indicator indices.[23] This model again improves the fit and increases the level of explained variance in the underlying indicators to 70.6 percent.

There is thus a trade-off between the level of aggregation and the amount of variation in the data that can be retained. The higher the level of aggregation, the less unique information retained. Exactly where one prefers to strike a balance between these two entities can of course vary by the research question at hand. For certain types of analyses, a "Big-D" measure of democracy might serve a certain purpose. If we let theoretical guidance decide, however, we think one should refrain from going to the highest level of aggregation. To the best of our knowledge, no one has hitherto theorized democracy at the level of "Big-D." The literature has instead concentrated on the level of the varieties of democracy. This is thus the highest level of analyses at which we present indices in the V-Dem data set.

---

[23] To identify the factors representing derived indicator indices, we had to group elected officials and suffrage as well as direct popular vote and elected regional/local government together.

6

Data Validation*

6.1 INTRODUCTION

How do we know if our data are valid? Both scholars and policymakers, producing or consuming any data set, struggle with this question. As social scientists, our understanding of how institutions work and evolve relies fundamentally on the quality of our measures. Similarly, aid organizations disburse billions of dollars a year to promote democracy and governance in the developing world based on data-driven evaluations of each polity's current status, attributes, recent history, and future prospects. Both policymakers and scholars use sophisticated tools to evaluate causal relationships, seeking either to influence, or simply understand, the development process. Yet, even the most refined and sophisticated empirical analysis cannot overcome fundamental issues of data validity. It is therefore crucial to systematically assess, and incrementally improve, the validity of the measures produced by V-Dem.

V-Dem seeks to take a comprehensive approach to validation. In this chapter, we present our approach to comparative data validation – the set of steps we take to evaluate the precision, accuracy, and reliability of our measures, both in isolation and compared to extant measures of the same concepts (McMann et al. 2016).[1] As discussed throughout the chapter, our efforts build on the work of other scholars who have considered what constitutes valid data and how to evaluate the validity of a measure or data set (e.g., Bollen 1993; Adcock and Collier 2001; Munck and Verkuilen 2002;

---

* The lead author of this chapter is Brigitte Seim, with contributions by Michael Bernhard, Fernando Bizzarro Neto, Michael Coppedge, John Gerring, Staffan I. Lindberg, Matthew Maguire, Daniel Pemstein, Jan Teorell, and Eitan Tzelgov.
[1] All analysis in this chapter is based on v8 of the V-Dem data set, except where noted in individual tables and figures.

Schedler 2012a). Our approach assesses the degree to which measures align with shared concepts (content validation), shared rules of translation (data generation assessment), and shared realities (convergent validation). Within convergent validity, we execute two convergent validity tests. First, we examine convergent validity as it is typically conceived – assessing whether V-Dem measures align with existing measures of the same concepts by examining the aggregate correlation level. We extend this analysis to consider the predictors of differences across data sources. Second, we evaluate the level of convergence across coders, considering the individual coder and country traits that predict coder convergence rather than simply the aggregate level of convergence. We complete these coder-level convergent validity tests for the polyarchy and corruption indices, and then examine the robustness of our findings across 10 randomly selected indicators from the V-Dem data set.

Throughout this chapter, we focus on three indices included in the V-Dem data set: polyarchy, corruption, and core civil society. These three concepts collectively provide a "hard test" for the validity of our data, representing a range of existing measurement approaches, challenges, and solutions. Democracy has been measured many times, and much of the past debate surrounding validating democracy measures centers around issues of conceptualization and aggregation (which, we argue, are twin challenges). Corruption is similarly oft-measured, but its clandestine nature makes minimizing measurement error the primary validity issue. Finally, measuring civil society is a relatively recent undertaking, and here the primary challenge is to evaluate validity in a relative vacuum. The discussion in this chapter both illustrates the fundamental challenges inherent in measuring these concepts and provides empirical support for the quality of the measures that we have developed across the project. However, we hasten to add that considering only these three indices do not allow for a full validation of the V-Dem data. Instead, focusing on these three indices and delineating the validation tools we used for them simply illustrates the fundamental challenges inherent in producing and validating data on complex concepts.

6.2 V-DEM VALIDATION APPROACH

V-Dem's data validation approach provides a practical guide to measurement assessment. We evaluated the validity of the V-Dem data in three ways – content validity, data-generating process validity, and convergent validity – each of which illuminates the degree to which the measure is valid and reliable. Unlike several who differentiate validity and reliability (e.g., Adcock and Collier 2001), we include reliability in our assessment of validity because we see these as closely related in assessing data quality, broadly conceived. Validity can generally be thought of as accuracy or, more technically, as the absence of systematic measurement error. Reliability can be thought of as precision or the absence of unsystematic (or random) measurement error. Precision should not be overlooked when assessing the V-Dem data; while reliability is not useful in the absence of validity, neither is a valid, but unreliable, measure.

First, it is helpful to examine the extent to which the measure captures the higher-level theoretical concept. This can be done not only through a content validity assessment, where indicators are mapped to theoretical concepts, but also, as we suggest, by assessing the content validity of the measure relative to other available measures. In this chapter, we illustrate how we undertook content validity assessment in the V-Dem project by considering V-Dem's polyarchy, corruption, and civil society indices. Much of the content validity discussion regarding the Polyarchy Index was included in Chapter 5 of this book, so here we focus more on what additionally we can learn from assessing the content validity of the Corruption Index and Core Civil Society Index.

Second, we examine the data-generating process for evidence of bias, unreliability, and aggregation inconsistency. The assumption is that an unbiased and reliable data-generating process results in unbiased and reliable data. The strength of this approach is that it allows us to focus on something we can evaluate (i.e., the reliability of a process) rather than something we cannot (i.e., a measure's alignment with the truth). For example, though we cannot prove that a coder selected the "true" answer when coding Argentina's level of civil society freedoms in 1950, we can show that the process to recruit, engage, and synthesize data from that coder was unbiased and reliable. Though much was discussed regarding the data collection process in V-Dem in previous chapters, here we examine V-Dem's data management structure, data sources, coding procedures, aggregation methods, and geographic and temporal coverage more narrowly, specifically focusing on the implications for the reliability and validity of the data. As with the first exercise, described above, the data-generating process can be evaluated in isolation and its strengths and weaknesses can be assessed relative to other measures. We note that since the data-generating process was the same across all V-Dem measures, we do not distinguish between the polyarchy, corruption, and civil society indices in this section.

Third, we evaluate the convergent validity of the V-Dem measures. Here, we engage in three types of convergent validity assessments, two of which we discuss here and the third of which is described in McMann et al. (2016). We first complete the standard convergent validity assessment analyzing the level of convergence between V-Dem and other data sets. We extend this analysis to identify the determinants of this convergence and evaluate what this means for the validity of V-Dem data. Then, we examine the extent of coder convergence, considering the level and predictors of agreement across V-Dem coders for different indicators, countries, and years. Considering the individual coder traits that predict disagreement, rather than simply the aggregate level of convergence in coders, allows researchers to identify threats to validity that are a function of the composition of their coder pools. In McMann et al. (2016), we also considered the level of alignment (i.e., qualitative convergence) between

V-Dem data and actual cases. We completed this analysis for the Corruption Index through rigorous case studies completed by an independent coder who had not seen the V-Dem data and was therefore "blind." McMann et al. (2016) describe this approach in detail, but, given limited space, we merely summarize the findings here.

The three tools, guiding questions, and techniques are outlined in Table 6.1 and described in detail below, where we apply them to the V-Dem polyarchy, corruption, and civil society indices.

6.3 CONTENT VALIDITY ASSESSMENT

In our content validity assessment, our goal is to determine the extent to which the measure captures all relevant meanings while excluding ones irrelevant to the "systematized" concept (Adcock and Collier 2001) or accepted definition (Bollen 1993). We use face validity assessments, a qualitative exercise, and factor analysis, a quantitative approach, to make such determinations. A measure's content validity can also be assessed comparatively, so we examine the conceptual mapping between V-Dem measures and other measures.

6.3.1 Content Validity of the V-Dem Polyarchy Index

We first consider V-Dem's electoral democracy, or "polyarchy," index. Data for this index are available (in version 7.1) for a global sample of 181 countries from 1900 to the present. We have constructed the polyarchy scale on the basis of 36 individual variables, with on average five experts rating each indicator. By measuring the five components of "elected officials," "free and fair elections," "freedom of expression," "associational autonomy," and "inclusive citizenship" separately, we anchor this new index directly in Dahl's (1971) influential theoretical framework. We employ Bayesian factor analysis to aggregate indicators to component indices, preserving adequate information of measurement uncertainty. As previously stated, we do not extensively evaluate the content validity of the Polyarchy Index in this chapter, as this discussion is largely included in Chapter 5.

6.3.2 Content Validity of the V-Dem Corruption Index

V-Dem's corruption data also cover the same 181 countries and time period, from 1900 to the present. Except for microstates and recent years' updates, which are both in the pipeline, V-Dem has corruption indicators for all countries from 1900 to 2012. It contains six measures of corruption based on six survey questions: two each for the executive and public sector on (1) bribery and other corrupt exchanges and on (2) theft and embezzlement, making up four indicators. Then, there is a single indicator each for corruption in the

TABLE 6.1 *Tools to assess data quality*

Category	Guiding questions	Techniques
Content validity assessment	To what extent does the measure capture the higher-level theoretical construct it is intended to capture and exclude irrelevant elements? To what extent is the measure useful in research?	Evaluate the resonance, domain, differentiation, fecundity, and consistency of the measure. Evaluate the causal utility of the measure.
Data generation assessment	Does the data-generating process introduce any biases, reliability problems, or analytic issues? How does it compare to the data-generating process of alternative measures? Where multiple coders exist, to what extent do they generate consistent and converging information?	Evaluate data set management structure, data sources, coding procedures, aggregation methods, and geographic and temporal coverage for each question. Evaluate extent of disagreement among coders, whether disagreement varies systematically with level of difficulty, and extent to which coder characteristics predict their responses.
Convergent validity assessment	Does the measure accurately capture actual cases? To what extent do the data produced by the measure correlate with data produced by other measures of the construct, and are areas of low correlation thoroughly understood?	Evaluate data against original or existing case studies. Evaluate strength of correlations, any outliers, and the implications of differences across measures.

Note: A discussion of this validation approach is not available in this chapter, but it is described in detail for the Corruption Index in McMann et al. (2016).

legislature and judiciary. In a two-stage process, the V-Dem Corruption Index aggregates these six indicators to produce an overall measure of corruption.[2]

The systematized concept for the V-Dem Corruption Index aligns with the common academic definition of corruption, "use of public office for private gain." The index captures a wide variety of participants in corruption and

---

[2] The V-Dem Corruption Index uses all the corruption variables available from V-Dem except for one, which pertains to corruption in the media rather than corruption in the government.

TABLE 6.2 *Bayesian factor analysis for the Corruption Index components*

Indicator	Loadings (Λ)	Uniqueness (ψ)
Executive bribery (*v2exbribe*)	0.830	0.312
Executive embezzlement (*v2exembex*)	0.827	0.315
Public sector bribery (*v2excrptps*)	0.846	0.285
Public sector embezzlement (*v2exthftps*)	0.848	0.281
Legislative bribery/theft (*v2lgcrrpt*)	0.693	0.496
Judicial bribery (*b2jucorrdc*)	0.753	0.433

Note: Entries are factor loadings and uniqueness from a normal theory Bayesian factor analysis model, run through the MCMCfactanal( ) command in the MCMC package for R (Martin et al. 2011); n = 26,647 country-years.

a large number of illicit practices, including both top officials and public sector employees to capture both grand and petty corruption. The questions use specific language to indicate particular corrupt practices as well as more general language to capture other forms of illicit behavior. This language enables the survey questions to generate data that cover a wide range of meanings of the use of public office for private gain. However, the V-Dem measures do not capture "revolving door" corruption, where public sector positions are used to secure private sector jobs and vice versa. If researchers seek a measure of corruption that includes this specific form of corruption, other, broader indices (such as Transparency International's Corruption Perceptions Index) might be more suitable.

The V-Dem measures do, however, exclude meanings of corruption that are irrelevant to the systematized concept. The data do not capture uses of "corruption" outside the academic definition, such as egregious asset accumulation (perhaps a consequence of corruption but not necessarily corruption in and of itself). By specifying government officeholders, the indicators do not include the use of nongovernmental positions for private gain. By specifying types of personal gain, the instruments also exclude behaviors where there is no evidence of direct, immediate material gain, such as vote buying, which does not always result in direct, individual gain. Finally, the detailed nature of the survey questions excludes other unethical behaviors, such as personal scandal, that do not involve the use of public office for private gain.

Bayesian factor analysis also provides evidence that the six V-Dem corruption measures represent meanings relevant, and not irrelevant, to the systematized concept. As shown in Table 6.2, all six indicators strongly load on a single dimension, although the fit for both legislative and judicial corruption is somewhat weaker. This could, however, simply be an artifact of the over-representation this set of indicators gives to executive corruption.

In addition to the conceptualization required to develop the V-Dem corruption indicators, we also assess comparative content validity by comparing the Corruption Index to existing corruption indices. Here, it is important to bear in mind the conceptual specificity of the V-Dem Corruption Index. By their own descriptions, many of the other corruption data sets gather information about "public sector" or bureaucratic corruption, excluding executive, legislative, and judicial corruption, making them less general than V-Dem's. This includes Transparency International's Corruption Perception Index (CPI), the World Bank's Business Environment and Enterprise Performance Survey (BEEPS), and nearly all the barometers. It is also difficult to determine what some of the other data sets capture because of their ambiguous language: Transparency International's Global Corruption Barometer (GCB) combines data on the public sector with private "big interests," and International Country Risk Guides' Political Risk Services (ICRG) focuses on the "political system." The World Values Survey (WVS) offers a more transparent conceptualization, but also one that is more expansive than V-Dem's, as it includes petty and grand corruption and capture of government institutions by private interests. There is also a fundamental conceptual difference between WVS's measure of public perceptions of corruption based on mass survey data and V-Dem's effort to measure corruption more objectively using expert ratings. Problematically, some measures used in studies as general indices of corruption actually capture a very narrow slice of "the use of public office for private gain." For example, the International Crime Victims Survey asks only about exposure to bribery (Kennedy 2014). Narrower measures will provide different results because different countries are marred by corruption in different forms or sectors (Knack 2007; Gingerich 2013). This issue affects the V-Dem Corruption Index less because it is considerably more comprehensive. The exclusion of irrelevant meanings is also a strength of the V-Dem Corruption Index. Indicators from other data sets often include superfluous information. For example, the Worldwide Governance Indicators' Control of Corruption (WGI) mixes electoral corruption, which does not necessarily involve private gain, along with public sector corruption.

6.3.3   Content Validity of the V-Dem Core Civil Society Index

The third index considered in this chapter to illustrate the V-Dem validation approach is the V-Dem Core Civil Society Index (CCSI), a measure of the robustness of civil society across the same large number of states for the same period, from 1900 to 2016 (v7.1) (Bernhard et al. 2017). In assessing the content validity of the V-Dem CCSI, different conceptualization challenges come to light. Civil society is an entire set of actors in a state, whereas corruption is an action. Perhaps because of this difference, there is lower consensus on the definition of civil society. In V-Dem, we conceived of civil society as an essential intermediary sphere of the polity. It lies in the public space between the private sphere and the official sphere of the state. It is not the only set of actors that lie within the nonofficial public sphere – it shares this space with political society, a set of public actors who are consciously organized to contest the control of state power. While civil society has a degree of autonomy from the state (ranging from extensive to minimal), civil society is still regulated by the state. The state establishes a framework for the operation of civil society, and often intervenes in its life (though the degree of freedom of civil society is enhanced by less intervention).

Civil society is populated by groups of citizens organized to act in pursuit of their interests, broadly conceived. This would include both material interests (goal-oriented, *Zweckrational* in Weberian terms) and interests inspired by values (*Wertrational*) (Weber 1978: 25). We refer to these groups of self-organized interested citizens as civil society organizations (CSOs). CSOs include, but are by no means limited to, interest groups, labor unions, religiously inspired organizations (if they are engaged in civic or political activities), social movements, professional associations, charities, and other nongovernmental organizations. It is essential to distinguish between the public and private spheres in understanding what constitutes a civil society organization. Both routine spiritual and economic activity are not civic but private. The productive activity of firms is not part of civil society, nor is the spiritual activity housed in religious institutions. However, when producers, workers, or people who share a set of spiritually grounded political, moral or ethical beliefs organize on the basis of a shared set of interests and pursue their realization in the public space, such activity is assuredly part of civil society.

Given the inherently dependent relationship between civil society, citizens, and the state, our aim was to produce both a series of disaggregated civil society indicators that get at the different aspects of civil society as well as a general index of civil society robustness that covers a global sample of countries over an extensive period of time. To that end, there are 10 questions that gauge different disaggregated aspects of civil society in V-Dem's survey. The answers to three of the questions – (1) whether there is control of civil society organizations' (CSO) entry and exit, (2) what is the level of state repression of CSOs, (3) what is the participatory environment in civil society – have been aggregated into the general measure of robustness of civil society: the CCSI. With this conceptual mapping and the corresponding V-Dem indicators, our goal was twofold: (1) provide measures of conceptually distinct lower-level concepts (what Adcock and Collier 2001 term construct validity) and (2) ensure the indicators collectively depict the higher-level concept of civil society. Figure 6.1 maps the conceptual rationale behind the index.

As with the Corruption Index, the content validity exercise for the Core Civil Society Index can also be comparative. Unlike corruption, however, panel indices capturing civil society are comparatively rare, and potential substitutes measure concepts that are only peripherally related. For example, the most

FIGURE 6.1 Conceptual mapping of the Core Civil Society Index.

common measurement of civil society uses questions from the World Values Survey (WVS) on organizational and protest behavior. WVS and the various regional surveys and attitudinal barometers it has inspired are a major resource in the study of political culture. Similarly, event history coding of protest is also an important means to study the development of civil societies.

One of the most ambitious attempts is the CIVICUS Civil Society Index, which looks at civil society in 50 to 60 different countries since 1993. Its famous diamond consists of four different dimensions, "the organizational structure of civil society, civic engagement, perception of impact, practice of values and the enabling environment" (CIVICUS 2013). However, the geographic and historical coverage for this index is more limited.

The Enabling Environment Index (EEI) measures the "conditions that impact on the capacity of citizens ... to participate and engage in the civil society arena in a sustained and voluntary manner." The first report issued in 2013 includes 108 countries. The measure is composed of 53 indicators compiled over the period from 2005 to 2012, which capture three major dimensions (socioeconomic, socio-cultural, and governance) broken into 17 subdimensions. While ambitious in scope and useful for policy makers and activists, this measure, by its nature, is hard to use in statistical analysis except in basic cross-sectional terms (CIVICUS 2017).

The Center for the Study of Global Governance at the London School of Economics has compiled a Global Civil Society Index. In 2002, it published rankings for 33 countries in Europe and the Americas circa 2000 (Anheier and Stares 2002). To complicate things, there is also a second Global Civil Society Index compiled by the Center for Civil Society Studies at Johns Hopkins University. This index initially only covered 16 countries around 2000 (Center for Civil Society Studies 2004). Disaggregated components were compiled for 36 countries in an updated version (Salamon et al. 1999).

USAID has developed a Civil Society Organization Sustainability Index (CSOSI). It examines four to six dimensions in any given year including the legal environment, organizational capacity, financial viability, advocacy, service provision, infrastructure, and public image and ranks them on a scale of 1–5. The CSOSI is an average of the components. They have compiled the index for postcommunist Europe for the years 1997–2011 and for 20 countries in sub-Saharan Africa in 2009–11 (USAID 2012a, 2012b).

Freedom House's Nations in Transit Series (2012) also calculates a civil society score for the postcommunist countries. It ranks civil society on a scale from one to seven based on nine open-ended questions answered by experts. The ranking on the scale is originally determined by the author of the expert report and is then reviewed by outside readers and a board of academic advisors. Rankings are available for 1995 and 1997–2013 (Freedom House 2012).

The Bertelsman Transformation Index produces 49 scalar measures using expert opinion which are then compiled into a series of indices which gauge the extent to which the countries in question have transformed into liberal democratic market systems. After a pilot study in 2003 it has been compiled biennially since 2006 for 129 developing and transitional countries. It has four indicators relevant to the study of civil society – organizational freedom, the presence of interest group networks, social self-organization, and a civil society tradition (Bertelsmann Stifftung 2015: 122–27).

Last but not least, the International Institute of Social Studies in The Hague has created a set of "Indices of Social Development" (ISD) that measure aspects of civil society. They have compiled a "Civic Activism" indicator for 209 countries at five year intervals from 1990 to 2010. Seventeen percent of the observations are missing. It is compiled from a variety of answers to values and attitudes surveys, data on international nongovernmental organizations, the CIVICUS CSI, and data on communications technology (Indices of Social Development 2015a). The coverage of the subindicators is subject to a higher degree of missingness than the indicator itself. This problem is addressed through the use of percentile matching techniques rather than imputation (Foa and Tanner 2012). They have also compiled an indicator of "clubs and associations" from values and attitudes surveys. It is subject to a very high degree of missing observations – 55 percent (Indices of Social Development 2015a).

6.4 DATA GENERATION ASSESSMENT

In addition to considering the content validity of the underlying questions used in coding the data, we examine the degree to which the data-generating process aligns with shared rules of translation (Schedler 2012a). In this section, we assess whether different components of the process – data set management structure, data sources, coding procedures, aggregation methods, and geographic and temporal coverage – are both unbiased and reliable.

6.4.1 Data Set Management Structure

Leadership structures and funding sources can affect the validity of a data set. For example, Hawken and Munck (2009a) find that differences in corruption ratings are correlated with whether the organization providing the data is a commercial, public, or nonprofit enterprise. As discussed in Chapter 1 of this book, V-Dem is an academic venture, led by professors as PIs and more than a dozen scholars from universities in different countries as Project Managers, assisted by more than 30 (mostly) scholars from all parts of the world as Regional Managers, and the V-Dem Institute at University of Gothenburg, Sweden, as the organizational and management headquarters. A vast majority of the funding has been provided by research foundations and governments in Northern Europe, the European Commission and University of Gothenburg, with smaller contributions from organizations based in North America and South America, and global organizations with members from all regions of the world. Leadership that is academic, rather than political or for-profit, and funding that is from diverse regions of the world, rather than from a single region or country, help to ensure that the organizational structure generates unbiased and reliable data. Furthermore, V-Dem leadership represent diverse research interests within the political science discipline, precluding the tendency to generate data to test a particular theory. This openness to diverse perspectives, conceptualizations, and research aims is depicted in the introduction to this book and in Chapter 3, when discussing how the V-Dem research team was deliberately assembled with diverse strengths and areas of expertise in mind. It is also illustrated in Chapter 2, when discussing the conscious choice to embrace multiple meanings of democracy as a project. Not only do we see these choices as representing the gold standard in project management, we believe they improve the validity of our data as well.

6.4.2 Coding Procedures

Chapter 3 extensively discusses V-Dem's collaboration with expert coders, so the present chapter simply highlights a few points that have implications for data validation. In assessing the validity of a data source generated by coders, it is important to consider (1) the qualifications and potential biases of the coders themselves; (2) the transparency and thoroughness of the coding guidelines; and (3) the procedures for combining coder ratings into a single indicator or index (Treisman 2007; Martínez i Coma and van Ham 2015).

Regarding coder qualifications, several scholars have argued that expert-coded data are inferior to ordinary-citizen-coded "experience" data (Treisman 2007; Hawken and Munck 2009a, 2009b; Donchev and Ujhelyi 2014). Rather than privilege one type of coder over another, we recommend considering which type of coder is a good match for generating the data of interest and which techniques can reduce bias and increase reliability. For many of the concepts measured in V-Dem, including society-level characteristics such as the restrictions placed on civil society or politician behaviors such as corruption, ordinary-citizen coders offer certain disadvantages. Their perceptions are fundamentally limited because they interact with only certain kinds of officials and observe certain sectors of society. Moreover, ordinary citizens' conceptions (and maybe also thresholds) may exhibit greater variation than those of experts, and when not asked about their own factual behavior or experiences, ordinary-citizen knowledge of political phenomena is rather narrow (Marquardt et al. 2017). Furthermore, any potential disadvantage of far-removed experts coding conditions in a country can be addressed by relying on experts who are residents or nationals of the countries.[3] This is a priority of V-Dem, as discussed in Chapter 3 when presenting the V-Dem slogan, "Global standards, local knowledge."

To what extent, then, do V-Dem expert coding procedures produce valid data and measures? V-Dem relies on expert perceptions. The stringent selection criteria for experts could offset some of the biases common to other expert data sets. Our experts have been recruited based on their academic or other credentials as field experts in the area for which they code, and on their seriousness of purpose and impartiality. (See Chapter 4 in this volume.) Impartiality, in particular, is not a criterion to take for granted in political science research. Unsurprisingly, Martínez i Coma and van Ham (2015) noted that variance in estimates of election integrity in the Perceptions of Electoral Integrity data set was significantly higher when one of the coders was a candidate in the election. Understanding who the coders are and where they may provide biased data is critically important in evaluating data validity.

To summarize the traits and tasks of V-Dem's coders as it pertains to validity: V-Dem's data set is coded by more than 3000 Country Experts. Generally, at least three-fifths of the coders for a particular country either are nationals of or reside in the country – the "connection to the country" criterion discussed in Chapter 3. We aim to have at least five experts coding each question-year observation; 99 percent of the data meet this target. We thus tap into a local source of expertise and knowledge, avoiding the problem of far-removed experts and also the problem of citizens with limited experience and information. When data are based on ratings from multiple coders, we can evaluate quality by combining information across coders. We also deliberately ask them to self-evaluate the reliability of their data. They are provided a 0 to 100 percent confidence bar in the survey questions to report how certain they are that their answer is accurate. Researchers can use this information to adjust their analysis and inferences for measurement error, improving the quality of their analyses.

6.4.3 Aggregating Coder Ratings to Point Estimates

The key questions when evaluating the coder aggregation strategy for validity and reliability are whether the approach accounts for both systematic biases in how coders answer questions and whether it accounts for nonsystematic

---

[3] For civil society indicators, this issue might be moot, since there are few citizen-coded measures of civil society.

variation in coder reliability. For example, if coders provide ordinal ratings and they potentially vary in how they map those ratings onto real cases – perhaps one coder has a lower tolerance for corruption than another – then a strategy that models and adjusts for this issue will outperform a more naïve approach. This problem of differential item functioning (DIF) is discussed extensively in Chapter 4, and alluded to in Chapter 3 (in the discussion of cross-national comparability). It affects most survey-based approaches to data collection and reducing it is a frequent focus of the literature on data validation. (See, for example, the discussion regarding "establishing equivalence" in Adcock and Collier 2001.)

One should ideally weigh the contributions of more reliable raters more highly than those of especially error-prone coders when combining responses. However, most multicoder data sets simply average coder responses to provide observation-level estimates and – if they provide estimates of reliability – report simple standard deviations. These simple aggregation and reliability estimation procedures implicitly assume that there are no systematic differences in the way coders produce ratings, and treat coders as equally reliable. When these assumptions are wrong, such approaches will generate flawed point estimates and measures of reliability (Pemstein et al. 2010; Lindstaedt et al. 2016).

As delineated thoroughly in Chapter 4, in order to aggregate up from coders to the level of country-years, V-Dem uses statistical item response theory (IRT) techniques. They help model variation in coder reliability while allowing for the possibility that raters apply ordinal scales differently (Pemstein et al. 2015). In other words, coders may have varying error rates and be more or less strict than one another when making ordinal rating decisions. The model also uses bridge raters – who rate multiple countries for many years – and lateral coders – who, in addition to providing a time series for one country, provide single-year ratings for a number of other countries – to calibrate estimates across countries (Pemstein et al. 2014). V-Dem also incorporates anchoring vignettes into each annual update; the administration of vignettes is discussed extensively in Chapter 3.

By combining these tools, the V-Dem measurement model explicitly attempts to adjust for DIF across raters. Importantly, Marquardt and Pemstein (2018) show that using IRT models to aggregate expert ratings outperforms traditional averaging techniques when experts vary in reliability and exhibit DIF; these techniques also produce sound estimates when DIF is not a problem and experts are equally reliable. Finally, these methods allow V-Dem to produce estimates of uncertainty around measures that are available to users and that can assist researchers in weighing the relative quality of measures across cases.

6.4.4   Aggregating Indicators to Indices

Separate from the process of combining multiple coder ratings for each country-year-indicator observation, many data sets offer low-level indicators that they combine into higher-level indices. To assess the validity and reliability of resulting measures, it is important to consider (1) the choice of indicators to aggregate and (2) the aggregation rules. The aggregation models for the democracy indices are extensively discussed in Chapter 5. Therefore, in this section, we focus on the choice of indicators and how these are aggregated to an index for the CCSI and the Corruption Index.

6.4.4.1 *Aggregating Indicators in the Core Civil Society Index*

First, we examine the extent to which the measure captures the higher-level theoretical concept. The V-Dem Civil Society survey has 10 questions that gauge different disaggregated aspects of civil society, of which three have been aggregated into the CCSI. Two questions capture state constraints on civil society organization, i.e., whether there are (1) direct repression of organizations and activists (*v2csreprss*) and (2) what are the regulations on the entry and exit of CSOs into the public space (*v2cseeorgs*); the third and final question assesses (3) what is the participatory environment in civil society (*v2csprtcpt*). Country Experts provide multiple ordinal ratings for each of the variables that constitute the CCSI.

Do these questions provide robust estimates of the latent concept of civil society autonomy? The CCSI is defined as *the civil society's ability to establish autonomy from the control of the state and to create an environment where citizens pursue their collective interests actively*. The feature that makes CCSI a good index to capture the latent concept is its two-step aggregation process. In the first stage, multiple Country Experts answer the three questions above on ordinal-scale ratings and their ratings are aggregated by utilizing Bayesian measurement models. In the second stage, the output of these statistical models is aggregated into the CCSI using Bayesian factor analysis techniques. We briefly review each stage.

Since Country Experts provide multiple ordinal ratings for each of the variables that constitute the CCSI, the first measurement challenge is to aggregate the ordinal ratings into a unified, continuous, and reliable variable. Individual raters might vary with regard to the way they interpret the questions, and in terms of reliability and consistency. Thus, we utilize Bayesian item response theory models to aggregate their diverse ratings. These models are useful because they incorporate the information encoded in the variation in raters' perceptions, and in reliability levels across and within coders into the estimation process (Bollen and Paxton 2000; Jackman 2004). In the second stage, we generate the CCSI scores using Bayesian factor analysis. As before, utilizing the Bayesian framework is advantageous since it allows us to generate uncertainty estimates for the index. As can be seen by the results in Table 6.3, all three variables load strongly on the latent dimension (Core Civil Society Index).

6.4.4.2 *Aggregating Indicators in the Corruption Index*

The Corruption Index follows similar rules for choice of variables. We aggregate indicators into indices using the same two-stage approach. There

TABLE 6.3 *Bayesian factor analysis for the Core Civil Society Index components*

Indicator	Loadings (Λ)	Uniqueness (ψ)
CSO entry and exit (*v2cseeorgs*)	0.888	0.212
CSO repression (*v2csreprss*)	0.827	0.316
CSO participatory environment (*v2csprtcpt*)	0.733	0.463

Note: Entries are factor loadings and uniqueness from a normal theory Bayesian factor analysis model, run through the MCMCfactanal() command in the MCMC package for R (Martin et al. 2011); $n = 26,650$ country-years.

are six individual questions that capture each type of corruption: the first four are bribery in (1) the executive, (2) in the legislature, (3) in the judiciary, and (4) in the public sector – respectively, *v2exbribe, v2lgcrrpt, v2jucorrdc, v2excrptps*, while the last two are embezzlement in the (5) executive and (6) public sector – respectively, *v2exembez* and *v2exthftps*. They are first aggregated by fitting a Bayesian factor analysis model to the two indicators capturing executive branch corruption (*v2exbribe* and *v2exembez*) and, separately, to the two indicators capturing public sector corruption (*v2excrptps* and *v2exthftps*). The factor models estimate the posterior distribution of the latent factor score for each observation (country-year). One can use these posterior distributions to produce index point estimates (posterior averages) and estimates of uncertainty (standard deviations and highest posterior density regions). Thus, the six indicators are consolidated into four indicators, each capturing corruption within a sector or branch of government: legislature (*v2lgcrrpt*), judiciary (*v2jucorrdc*), executive (*v2x_execorr*), and public sector (*v2x_pubcorr*).

Finally, to construct the overarching Corruption Index (*v2x_corr*), V-Dem averages (1) the executive Corruption Index (*v2x_execorr*), (2) the public sector Corruption Index (*v2x_pubcorr*), (3) the indicator for legislative corruption (*v2lgcrrpt*), and (4) the indicator for judicial corruption (*v2jucorrdc*). In other words, V-Dem weights each of these four spheres of government equally in the resulting index (see Figure 6.2). This aggregation approach is a relative strength of V-Dem. Both the WGI and CPI choose indicators that reduce missingness (Hawken and Munck 2009a). V-Dem does not have such a constraint, as the level of missingness does not vary greatly from one indicator to another.

6.4.5   Coverage across Countries and Time

One potential threat to the validity of V-Dem data is the bias introduced by limitations in coverage across time and countries (Treisman 2007). Particularly with sensitive topics, such as corruption, the process of deciding which cases to include or exclude can introduce selection bias. Furthermore, we need to be able

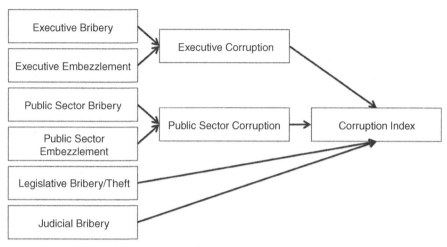

FIGURE 6.2 Conceptual mapping of the Corruption Index.

to evaluate how our measure anchors cases to a consistent scale (Treisman 2007). Thus, by eliminating selection, and allowing one to construct a scale based on the universe of cases, increasing country coverage also improves validity.

As previously discussed in several chapters, V-Dem performs well on the question of coverage. Version 7.1 covers 181 countries across the globe, avoiding biases in data sets of only a subset of countries (those easiest to code or those for which coders are readily available).[4] V-Dem also helps ensure reliability and unbiasedness by using the same coder recruitment procedures and data coding methods across countries and time. By asking the same questions of each coder for each country-year, V-Dem allows over-time and cross-country comparisons of corruption levels in the world back to 1900. As mentioned above, V-Dem enhances this cross-context comparability through the use of IRT methods, bridge and lateral coders, and anchoring vignettes.

6.4.5.1 Temporal Variation in the Corruption Index

The corruption literature, in particular, will benefit from improvements in comparability across time and space. Measures of corruption are typically taken at the country level, where comparisons across cases often come at the expense of comparisons over time (Christiane et al. 2006; Galtung 2006; Knack 2007). For example, WGI is calculated such that the global average is the same every year, meaning that changes in the level of corruption within a country are not revealed unless the change is so great as to move it up or down in the

---

[4] The only countries currently omitted from V-Dem are microstates, but they are already part of new research efforts to increase special coverage.

comparative rankings (Lambsdorff 2007). Kaufmann and Kraay (2002) estimate that half the variance in the WGI's index over time is the product of changes in the sources and coding rules used, rather than actual changes in corruption levels. Treisman (2007) notes that the CPI's aggregation strategies and sources have changed over time. Finally, the WGI's consistent global average over time, prevents, by construction, an understanding of trends.

Illustrating the V-Dem Corruption Index's relative validity in terms of coverage, we consider what we can learn about trends in corruption levels over time by analyzing the V-Dem Corruption Index. Figure 6.3 depicts a rather surprising global trend. According to the V-Dem measure, corruption levels have *risen* globally compared to the mid-twentieth century, with a peak just around the time when corruption appeared on the global reform agenda. In brief, the world thus looks much more corrupt today than it did 100 or 60 years ago. Yet, since 2000, worldwide corruption slightly declined.

So, does the trend in the V-Dem data depict the trend in reality? We think the global surge in corruption over the latter half of the twentieth century makes intuitive sense. First, the world economy is more monetized than it was half a century ago, leading one to expect higher corruption levels. Second, the collapse of the Soviet economies in the early 1990s, as well as a global rise of libertarian values, has led to a flurry of privatization reforms, also known to increase levels of corruption. Finally, the number of hybrid regimes rose (Teorell and Hadenius 2007), and we know from previous studies that corruption peaks in countries at the crossroads between authoritarianism and democracy (Montinola and Jackman 2002; Sung 2004; Bäck and Hadenius 2008; Rock 2007; Treisman 2007; Charron and Lapuente 2010).

Furthermore, reporting bias cannot completely account for this trend. Two pieces of evidence challenge the interpretation that the increase in corruption according to V-Dem data reflects greater media reporting about corruption in the mid-1990s, relative to earlier eras. The first is the downward trend we observe from around the year of 2000, since there is no reason to expect the media to have reported less on corruption during the last decade. Second, in the dashed line in Figure 6.3, we present the trend in corruption levels for a subsample of all countries where, according to the Whitten-Woodring and Van Belle (2014) measure, there was no freedom of the media. If reporting bias was driving the upward trend, we should expect a flat line (or perhaps even a decline) in countries where reporting was severely restricted. Yet, we observe the trend in these countries generally mirrors the overall trend.

6.4.5.2 Temporal and Regional Variation in the CCSI Index

The CCSI provides another test of V-Dem's validity over time. We used two approaches to examine whether CCSI behaved in conjunction with our expectations over large units of space and time. The first concern we had was how we expected the CCSI to develop over time. Our expectations were that

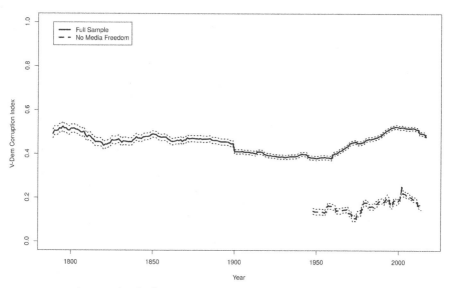

FIGURE 6.3 Average level of corruption over time. Trend lines depict global averages by year with 95 percent credible intervals.

civil society would be considerably weaker in the earliest part of the century, that it would drop off during waves of concentrated failure of democratic regimes and installation of harsh dictatorship (e.g., the heyday of totalitarianism and total war in the 1930s and 1940s and the wave of bureaucratic authoritarianism that hit Latin America in the late 1960s and early 1970s), and that it would grow extensively with the Third Wave of democratization.

We examine this in Figure 6.4, where we provide decade-by-decade boxplots for CCSI from the 1780s to the 2010s. As we had expected, the level of civil society development is significantly lower at the beginning of the time period than it is today. In the 1970s and 1980s, the global variation in civil society environment was greatest, before the onset of the Third Wave. With the global expansion of democracy that followed, we see civil society growing in strength globally from the 1990s until the present day.

We also have strong expectations about how civil society strength should vary geographically. Those regions which have had sustained histories of development, competitive politics, and political pluralism should have the strongest civil societies. Thus we expect from a historical point of view for strong civil societies to be prevalent in places like North America and Western Europe compared to other regions of the world. In regions in which there are long histories of harsh dictatorship, we would expect to see weaker civil societies over time. In Figure 6.5, we show the mean country-year CCSI scores for the major geographic regions of the world over time.

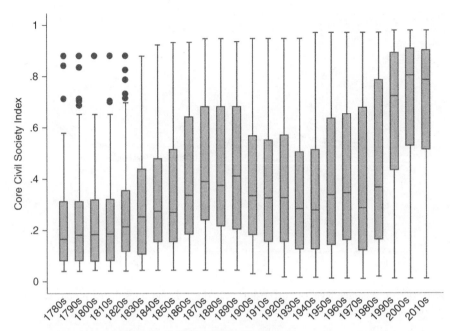

FIGURE 6.4 Average Core Civil Society Index by decade.

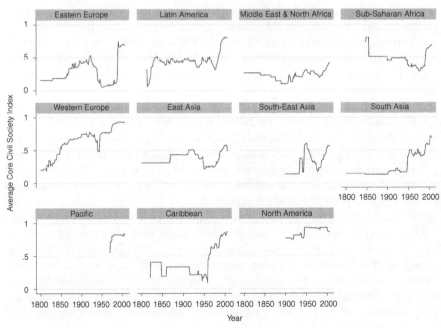

FIGURE 6.5 Average Core Civil Society Index by region over time.

Here again the picture presented by the data seems to indicate strong face validity. The most robust regions for civil society in the last century are Western Europe and North America. Eastern Europe, Latin America, sub-Saharan Africa, and the Caribbean have seen the most dramatic shifts in the last 50 years or so. East Asia and Southeast Asia, and South Asia remain somewhere in the middle of the distribution.

6.5 CONVERGENT VALIDITY ASSESSMENT

The third piece of the V-Dem validation approach is to assess convergent validity. Within convergent validity, we demonstrate two convergent validity tests. First, we examine convergent validity as it is typically conceived – assessing whether V-Dem measures align with existing measures of closely related concepts by examining the aggregate correlation level. We extend this analysis to consider the predictors of differences across data sources. Second, we evaluate the level of convergence across coders, considering the individual coder and country traits that predict coder convergence rather than simply the aggregate level of convergence. We walk through the convergent validity tests for the polyarchy, corruption, and civil society indices. Alternative measures of these concepts exist to varying degrees. Several alternatives comparable in coverage and conceptualization are available for the V-Dem Polyarchy Index, whereas the alternatives to the V-Dem Corruption Index are more restricted panel data sets, and the alternatives to the V-Dem CCSI are quite different, both conceptually and in terms of coverage. This variation in the availability of alternatives enables us to demonstrate how we assessed construct validity in different circumstances.

6.5.1 Cross-Measure Convergent Validity

Assessing this type of convergent validity is fundamentally about assessing whether various measures appear, on aggregate, to tap into the same concept. It is also about examining comparative advantage: When embarking on using a data set or measure for the first time, what are its strengths and weaknesses compared to existing data sets? What is gained by using this data set instead of others?

6.5.1.1 Cross-Measure Convergent Validity for the Polyarchy Index

We first consider the level of convergence between the V-Dem Polyarchy Index and extant alternatives. Figure 6.6 displays the bivariate descriptive pattern at country-year level, comparing the V-Dem Polyarchy Index to the Polity and Freedom House ratings, as well as the Unified Democracy Score (UDS), respectively. The latter is based on the majority of pertinent measures[5] of electoral democracy covering multiple countries and years (Pemstein et al.

---

[5] V-Dem's index is one of the few not included in UDS.

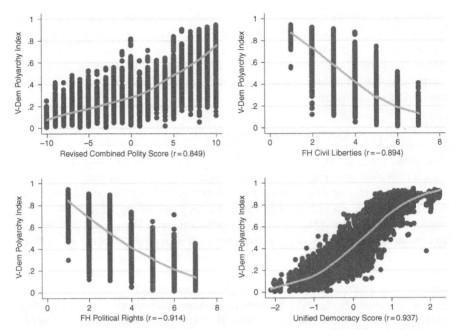

FIGURE 6.6 Comparing the Polyarchy Index with alternative electoral democracy indices.

2010). Overall, the measures converge. The pairwise correlations range from 0.85 for Polity to 0.94 for the UDS ratings. The gray smoothed lowess line of best fit also indicates a consistent pattern of monotonically increasing (albeit slightly nonlinear) levels of polyarchy, the higher the alternative measure of electoral democracy. The V-Dem Polyarchy Index thus seems to be measuring, broadly, the same underlying concept as these extant measures.

Nonetheless, the V-Dem Polyarchy Index regularly produces scores that differ from extant measures. The second step in assessing convergent validity, after demonstrating strong high-level correlations, is exploring the areas of divergence (Adcock and Collier 2001; Bowman et al. 2005). While one rarely has access to a "gold standard" against which to assess convergence, one can observe many aspects of the data-generating process. Researchers can use such indicators to model systematic determinants of divergence, elucidating where measures differ, and lending insight into potential threats to the validity of the measure under examination. A first such potential threat is the effect of coder characteristics, specifically the aggregate *composition* of coders for each country, estimated as the average coder characteristics at the country-year level (age, gender, education, nationality, ideology, understanding of democracy). Bollen (1993) refers to these as the "characteristics of judges" and finds them to be highly predictive of bias in measures of democracy. Second, we want to assess whether differences can be explained by three other prime predictors of the V-Dem data that vary by country and year: the average level of disagreement among coders, the number of coders, and the number of bridge/lateral coders.

Evidence presented in Table 6.4 refutes both explanations. The dependent variable in this analysis is the absolute value of the residuals resulting from regressing each V-Dem indicator on the extant scores (Polity, FH, or UDS). When controlling for individual-level characteristics (omitted from the table), there are only a few significant aggregate coder composition effects, and several

TABLE 6.4 *Predicting absolute deviations between the Polyarchy Index and Polity, Freedom House, and UDS*

	Deviation from Polity	Deviation from Freedom House	Deviation from UDS
Polity score	−0.135***		
	(0.028)		
Freedom House score		−0.225***	
		(0.028)	
Unified Democracy Score			−0.207***
			(0.036)
Share female coders	−0.084**	−0.047	−0.059
	(0.040)	(0.038)	(0.041)
Average age of coders	0.009	−0.004	0.012
	(0.015)	(0.012)	(0.015)
Average age^2	−0.000	−0.000	−0.000
	(0.000)	(0.000)	(0.000)
Share of PhD coders	−0.060	−0.022	−0.047
	(0.042)	(0.032)	(0.040)
Share of coders employed by government	−0.060	−0.066	−0.060
	(0.076)	(0.071)	(0.081)
Share of coders born in country	0.068	0.054	0.061
	(0.047)	(0.039)	(0.045)
Share of coders residing in country	−0.039	−0.110***	−0.053
	(0.036)	(0.041)	(0.038)
Share of Western coders	0.048	0.009	0.031
	(0.031)	(0.026)	(0.029)
Average free market support	0.004	−0.035**	−0.009
	(0.013)	(0.014)	(0.014)

(*continued*)

TABLE 6.4 *(continued)*

	Deviation from Polity	Deviation from Freedom House	Deviation from UDS
Average conventional understanding	−0.019	−0.007	−0.028
	(0.019)	(0.018)	(0.018)
Average alternative understanding	−0.026	−0.003	−0.024
	(0.016)	(0.014)	(0.017)
Coder disagreement	0.223***	0.214***	0.250***
	(0.015)	(0.015)	(0.016)
No. of coders	−0.002**	−0.003***	−0.006**
	(0.001)	(0.001)	(0.002)
No. of lateral coders	−0.003	0.003	−0.008
	(0.005)	(0.004)	(0.011)
R-squared	0.159	0.190	0.191
No. of countries	163	168	166
No. of observations	930,161	529,367	658,295

Note: Entries are regression coefficients, with standard errors, clustered on countries, in parentheses. The unit of analysis is country-year-coder-indicator. Coder-level controls for gender, age, education, born in/residing in country, Western origin, support for free market, conventional and alternative understanding of democracy, as well as year- and indicator-fixed effects included but omitted from the table. $*p < 0.10$. $**p < 0.05$. $***p < 0.01$. This analysis was produced with v5 of the V-Dem data set.

of them only affect a single component (this goes for share of female coders for Polity, as well as coders residing in country and free market support for FH). Coder disagreement at the country-year level is one of the few systematic predictors of absolute deviations, from Polity, Freedom House, and UDS. Not surprisingly, the differences between V-Dem's polyarchy score and the alternatives are greater for countries that are hard to code. This is noteworthy, but having more V-Dem coders in all instances shrinks the distance. Overall, the findings indicate that divergences are not due to the composition of our sample of coders, or how these coders assess electoral democracy. To the extent that the V-Dem polyarchy measure deviates from extant measures, we thus have good conceptual and operational reasons to believe that the deviation is not driven by any issue in particular.

6.5.1.2 *Cross-Measure Convergent Validity for the Corruption Index*

We perform an aggregate convergent validity test by systematically comparing V-Dem to the WGI and the CPI measures. Since non-V-Dem corruption indices

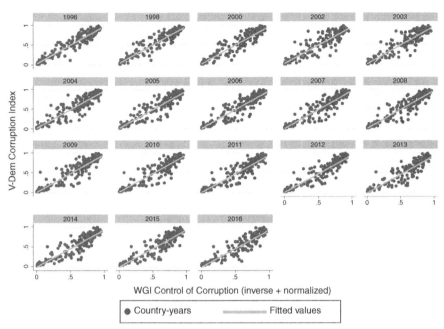

FIGURE 6.7 Comparing the V-Dem and Worldwide Governance Indicators (WGI) Control of Corruption.

explicitly discourage comparisons over time, we perform these comparisons on a year-by-year basis, starting in the first year of measurement for the corresponding measure (1996 and 1995, respectively). Generally, as Figures 6.7 and 6.8 show, V-Dem and alternative measures agree about which countries are more corrupt. Both pooled correlation coefficients are around 0.90. This seems to indicate strong convergent validity. Nonetheless, there are differences in how V-Dem compares to WGI versus CPI. The deviations from the WGI are more uniformly distributed over the Corruption Index, whereas the CPI tends to rate middle corruption countries as lower in corruption than does V-Dem but low- and high-corruption countries as higher in corruption than V-Dem.

Furthermore, V-Dem systematically rates some countries, such as Malaysia and Qatar, as more corrupt than do other extant measures. V-Dem considers others, such as Latvia and Lithuania, as consistently less corrupt. In general, two measures can be highly correlated at the aggregate level but systematically differ from one another in important ways. We therefore see standard quantitative convergent validity assessments – which generally consist of reporting simple scatter plots and correlation coefficients – as only the first step in a full-fledged convergent validity analysis.

As with the Polyarchy Index, in Table 6.5 we extend the analysis of the effect of coder-level determinants to explain deviations from the alternative corruption measure with the broadest coverage: WGI. We ask whether the composition of

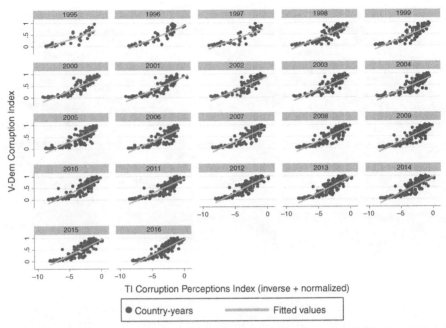

FIGURE 6.8 Comparing the V-Dem and Transparency International (TI) Corruption Perceptions Index.

V-Dem coders per country and year, measured with average coder traits, affects the tendency for the V-Dem Corruption Index to deviate from the WGI. Put in technical terms, what can explain the absolute residuals – the vertical distance to the regression line – in the year-by-year comparisons in Figure 6.7?

There are only a few systematic patterns pertaining to coder composition. Notably, V-Dem coder disagreement is a statistically significant predictor of the absolute residual between V-Dem and the WGI. When V-Dem experts disagree, so do the two measures. Thus, disagreement may be most common in hard-to-rate cases, a finding more indicative of stochastic error than systematic bias (an idea explored in detail in the next section).

On the other hand, WGI and V-Dem disagree less when V-Dem relies more heavily on PhD-holding coders and when V-Dem coders include more men. Thus, insofar as PhD holders or men are the "correct" set of experts to generate estimates of corruption, this result may indicate that the inclusion of practitioners and other coders may systematically bias V-Dem away from the concept in question. Yet overall, the pattern is clear: there are few systematic predictors of the deviations between the WGI and V-Dem measures.[6]

---

[6] Replicating the analysis presented in Table 6.5 for the CPI instead of the WGI yields similar findings (not included here).

TABLE 6.5 *Predicting absolute deviations between the V-Dem Corruption Index and WGI*

	Deviation from WGI
Share of female coders	0.052**
	(0.025)
Average age of coders	−0.002
	(0.009)
Average age of coders^2	0.000
	(0.000)
Share of PhD coders	−0.084**
	(0.023)
Share of coders employed by government	−0.068
	(0.042)
Share of coders born in country	−0.009
	(0.028)
Share of coders residing in country	0.010
	(0.027)
Average free market support	0.006
	(0.010)
Average electoral democracy support	0.001
	(0.015)
Average liberal democracy support	−0.005
	(0.013)
Mean coder discrimination (beta)	0.004
	(0.004)
Coder disagreement	0.345**
	(0.043)
No. of coders	−0.008**
	(0.002)
R-squared	0.099
No. of countries	164
No. of observations	54,235

Note: Entries are regression coefficients, with standard errors, clustered on countries, in parentheses. The dependent variable is the absolute residuals from regressing each V-Dem indicator on the WGI measure, including year-fixed effects. Individual-level coder traits are included; indicator-fixed effects are in the pooled model but omitted from the table. $*p < 0.10$. $**p < 0.05$. $***p < 0.01$. This analysis was produced with v4 of the V-Dem data set.

In sum, the results from these statistical analyses speak in favor of the validity of the V-Dem measures. First, the degree of coder disagreement is comparatively small; and, when disagreement does exist, it varies meaningfully by context. Second, with the infrequent exception of PhD degree or gender, coders are not systematically affected by background or ideological factors. V-Dem measures correlate strongly with other measures of corruption, and the deviations from those measures cannot, by and large, be explained by the composition of V-Dem coders.

6.5.1.3 *Cross-Measure Convergent Validity for the Core Civil Society Index*

In examining CCSI's convergent validity, or the degree to which the CCSI is related to extant measures, we examined several alternative measures, most available for only a very narrow subset of the country-years covered by V-Dem. The best coverage for an aggregate measure of civil society is provided by the USAID CSO Sustainability Index for postcommunist Europe and sub-Saharan Africa (USAID 2012a, 2012b). The correlation between CCSI with the USAID CSO Sustainability Index is 0.6781 ($p < 0.001$).

Next, we consider the association between the CCSI and V-Dem's Thick Freedom of Expression Index. Our expectation is that a stronger civil society and free expression should be strongly correlated. We abstain from making claims about whether one causes the other, that they are mutually constitutive, or that they are caused by an unnamed set of other factors. Figure 6.9 presents

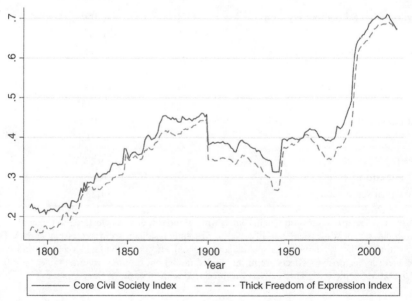

FIGURE 6.9 Association between the Core Civil Society Index and the Thick Freedom Of Expression Index over time.

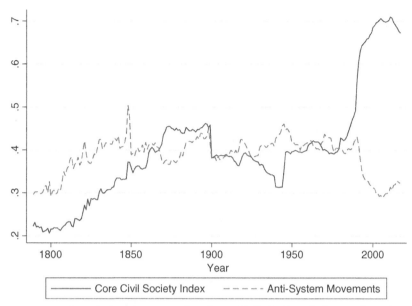

FIGURE 6.10 Association between the Core Civil Society Index and antisystem movements over time.

the global mean of each index by year. As can be seen, the two measures follow each other very closely ($r = 0.994$).

We also examined the covariation of CCSI with another indicator from the V-Dem Civil Society battery that captures the extent to which antisystem movements, which might present a threat to the regime, exist. We present the result in Figure 6.10. Our expectation is that more open polities, which have robust civil societies that can represent a broad range of interests, will be less likely to give rise to antisystem movements. As expected, we find a significant, yet not strong, negative correlation between the two ($r = -0.496$). The relationship seems to be strongest since 1980, where the flowering of civil society globally coincides with a downward trend in antisystem movements.

Finally, we consider convergence between the subcomponents of the CCSI and extant measures that might proxy for them. The closest match, conceptually, to the V-Dem Civil Society repression component is the CIRI Physical Integrity Right Index, which captures the extent to which the population of a state is subjected to extrajudicial killing, torture, disappearances, and political imprisonment (Cingranelli et al. 2014). The conceptual alignment between the two measures is not perfect, given that our repression index includes a number of lesser forms of harassment of CSOs and activists. The correlation between the two measures is 0.5664 ($p < 0.001$). For the V-Dem indicator on the freedom of CSO entry and exit, *v2cseeorgs*, we compare it to the Freedom of Assembly and Association Index, also from CIRI. Here the correlation is 0.6930 ($p < 0.001$). Comparing freedom of CSO entry and exit to the Bertelsmann question on freedom of assembly and association shows an even higher correlation of 0.8160 ($p < 0.001$) (Bertelsmann Stiftung 2014). For the CSO participation component, we compared it to the ISD Civic Activism measure (Indices of Social Development 2015a). This measure covers half-decades from 1990–2010, which we correlated with the corresponding country-year observations in the V-Dem data set. Given that their data are compiled over five year periods, we would expect the correlation to be weaker than if we were making country-year to country-year comparisons. Still the correlation is 0.5082 ($p < 0.001$).

The convergent validity tests for these three indices demonstrate the limits of such assessments. In the absence of existing measures of a concept, as is the case generally with the CCSI, analyzing cross-measure convergence is relatively uninformative.

6.5.2   Cross-Coder Convergent Validity

When data are produced by multiple coders, one can empirically examine the data-generating process by conducting an analysis of coder (dis) agreement. Assuming that our experts exercise independent judgment when translating their perceptions of the world into numerical ratings (Schedler 2012a), coder agreement could be interpreted as a sign of validity. Both Steenbergen and Marks (2007) and Martínez i Coma and van Ham (2015) compare ratings across coders as a test of validity. They argue that the less interexpert disagreement, or the less systematic sources of variation in interexpert judgments, the more valid the measure. We argue that intercoder agreement provides insight into both validity and reliability, and emphasize the advantages of multicoder data to examine both aspects of the data-generating process. Clearly, a measure is more reliable when intercoder disagreement is low. Intercoder agreement can also be seen as a measure of validity if one is willing to assume that multiple coders are unlikely to exhibit identical biases. Systematic cross-case patterns in intercoder disagreement also yield insights into the validity of the data-generating process. Finally, when coder traits predict disagreement systematically, this provides insight into potential sources of bias in the data. We explore several permutations of intercoder disagreement, in turn, below. At each step, we present the analysis for the polyarchy and corruption indices, and then for 10 randomly selected V-Dem indicators. This approach allows us to examine the robustness of the findings we obtained when validating the polyarchy and corruption indices and expand the validation exercise to the V-Dem data more generally.

Table 6.6 decomposes the variance for three indicators underlying the Polyarchy Index. The dependent variables on each column are the standard

TABLE 6.6 *Variance decomposition of coder disagreement for the Polyarchy Index components*

	Clean elections	Freedom of organization	Freedom of expression
Grand mean	1.400***	2.230***	1.650***
	(0.038)	(0.060)	(0.059)
Coder random effects	0.511***	0.409***	0.544***
	(0.015)	(0.019)	(0.013)
Indicator random effect	0.802***	0.904***	0.591***
	(0.007)	(0.009)	(0.005)
No. of indicators	8	6	9
No. of experts	1292	1863	1687
No. of observations	288,910	438,269	725,251

Note: Entries are variance components expressed as standard deviations, with standard errors in parentheses. Country- and year-fixed effects are included but omitted from the table. Estimates obtained from the "mixed" command in Stata. $*p < 0.10$. $**p < 0.05$. $***p < 0.01$. This analysis was produced with v5 of the V-Dem data set.

deviations of raw scores that coders have given to each country-year observation. Also expressed as standard deviations, the random effects coefficients are measured on the same ordinal zero-to-four scale as the original indicators to ease interpretation. Although statistically significant, they are all less than a point on a five-point scale, which does not suggest conspicuously high levels of disagreement among our Country Experts. One should recall that a decent share of this "raw" coder disagreement is known to be a reflection of varying thresholds for how to map perceptions on to the ordinal coding categories in the survey, and that the measurement model corrects a substantial share of this variance when aggregating these raw scores to the country-year level (Pemstein et al. 2015).

All V-Dem indicators rely on a measurement model that corrects for systematic threshold bias, or the tendency of coders to be more or less strict in their application of ordinal scales. Using this model, we can estimate coders' "perceptions" of corruption, after controlling for fixed threshold bias (Johnson and Albert 1999). Table 6.7 displays a variance decomposition of these adjusted perception ratings for the corruption data, scaled to vary from zero to one. Even correcting for different levels of coder rigor, we find little coder disagreement overall, evidenced again by the low magnitude of the expert coefficient across six indicators and the pooled index.

To examine the robustness of these findings, we ran the same variance decomposition exercises on 10 randomly selected variables from the V-Dem data set. We use the same perception measures as above. The results are

TABLE 6.7 *Variance decomposition of coder disagreement for the Corruption Index components*

	Exec. bribery	Exec. theft	Pub. bribery	Pub. theft	Legisl. corr.	Jud. bribery	Pooled
Expert	0.031***	0.044***	0.041***	0.053***	0.051***	0.029***	0.027***
	(0.002)	(0.003)	(0.002)	(0.003)	(0.003)	(0.002)	(0.002)
Indicator							0.030***
							(0.001)
No. of experts	924	600	903	847	877	872	1346
No. of observations	57,290	28,843	52,976	44,614	56,989	32,000	272,711

Note: Entries are variance components expressed as standard deviations, with standard errors in parentheses. Country- and year-fixed effects are included but omitted from the table. Estimates obtained from the "mixed" command in Stata. *$p < 0.10$. **$p < 0.05$. ***$p < 0.01$. This analysis was produced with v4 of the V-Dem data set.

reported in Table 6.8, and are consistent with the findings of the variance decomposition exercise for the polyarchy and corruption indices.

Next, again following Steenbergen and Marks (2007) and Martínez i Coma and van Ham (2015), we examine whether interexpert disagreement varies systematically with the level of difficulty of the coder task. Two potential sources of "level of difficulty" stand out. The first is the availability of information (e.g., Bollen 1986, 1993; Bollen and Paxton 2000). There are (at least) two ways to proxy for the availability of information on corruption. The first proxy is time: we would, ceteris paribus, expect the experts to have more information about present-day than historical corruption, both because of their own lived experience and through the availability of other studies. The second proxy is media freedom or, more generally, freedom of expression. In closed authoritarian systems, all else being equal, there should be less information available about the political sphere, since one of the goals of censorship is to conceal the extent and nature of government action. A second potentially systematic source of variation in coder-level disagreement is the level of the trait in question. Extreme conditions should be more easily identifiable than the "muddled middle"; hence coders should be likely to disagree more at intermediate levels of whatever aspect of the country they are assessing.

We test these assertions in Tables 6.9–6.11. Except for the effect of time, we find support for our expectations across different V-Dem variables. Our findings are consistent for the raw and measurement model adjusted ratings; we therefore omit the results for raw scores. The standard deviation of coder disagreement is statistically significantly lower in countries with widespread freedom of expression. Coder disagreement is also lower in countries representing extremes. Adding coders increases the level of disagreement.

TABLE 6.8 *Variance decomposition for 10 randomly selected indicators*

Panel A

	Health equality	Judicial accountability	Transparent laws with predictable enforcement	Compliance with high court	Respect counterarguments
Expert	0.047***	0.103***	0.031***	0.075***	0.021***
	(0.0025)	(0.006)	(0.002)	(0.004)	(0.001)
No. of experts	997	915	1059	913	1029
No. of observations	94,922	61,433	94,547	65,260	101,575

Panel B

	Disclosure of campaign donations	Access to justice for men	Freedom of religion	Religious organization repression	Election losers accept results
Expert	0.050***	0.030***	0.038***	0.038***	0.026***
	(0.002)	(0.002)	(0.002)	(0.002)	(0.002)
No. of experts	1125	1050	1073	1063	985
No. of observations	115,299	97,982	110,934	88,897	68,002

Note: Entries are variance components expressed as standard deviations, with standard errors in parentheses. Country- and year-fixed effects are included but omitted from the table. Estimates obtained from the "mixed" command in Stata. $*p < 0.10$. $**p < 0.05$. $***p < 0.01$. This analysis was produced with v4 of the V-Dem data set.

TABLE 6.9 *Predicting coder disagreement for the Polyarchy Index*

	Clean elections	Associational autonomy	Freedom of expression
Year	−0.000	−0.001***	−0.001**
	(0.000)	(0.000)	(0.000)
Media access	−0.003***	−0.003***	−0.003***
	(0.001)	(0.001)	(0.000)
Level	0.053***	−0.052***	0.030***
	(0.011)	(0.010)	(0.008)
Level^2	−0.112***	−0.097***	−0.083***
	(0.006)	(0.005)	(0.003)
No. of coders	0.006**	0.010**	0.019***
	(0.003)	(0.005)	(0.005)
No. of indicators	8	6	9
Adjusted R-squared	0.289	0.331	0.334
No. of countries	171	173	173
No. of observations	49,390	80,450	139,046

Note: Entries are regression coefficients, with standard errors, clustered on countries, in parentheses. The unit of analysis is country-year-indicator. Indicator-fixed effects are included but omitted from the table. $*p < 0.10$. $**p < 0.05$. $***p < 0.01$. This analysis was produced with v5 of the V-Dem data set.

There are a few notable exceptions to these patterns. Freedom of expression does not significantly predict coder agreement for several of the randomly selected variables, including several that seemingly would rely on freedom of expression to obtain accurate coding: Freedom of Religion and Religious Organization Repression. Furthermore, the number of coders does not always significantly predict an increase in coder disagreement. Rather than developing post hoc justifications for these isolated findings, we instead focus on general patterns that speak to validity. Mid-level cases seem to result in greater coder disagreement, as do countries with low freedom of expression. There is some evidence that coder disagreement may increase going back in time and with the number of coders, but this finding is not robust.

We extend the analysis by modeling the determinants of individual coder deviations from typical responses, illuminating sources of coder bias, and identifying potential threats to validity. If certain types of coders systematically disagree with one another, and coder types vary systematically across cases, then the data-generating process will exhibit bias, undermining the validity of the resulting measures. On the other hand, if patterns of disagreement are stochastic, we need not worry that certain types of coders

TABLE 6.10 *Predicting coder disagreement for the Corruption Index*

	Corruption Index
Year	–0.000
	(0.000)
Freedom of Expression Index	–0.039***
	(0.009)
Level	–0.003
	(0.003)
Level^2	–0.042***
	(0.003)
No. of coders	0.001
	(0.002)
Adjusted R-squared	0.234
No. of countries	173
No. of observations	69939

Note: Entries are regression coefficients, with standard errors, clustered on countries, in parentheses. Indicator-fixed effects are omitted from the table. $*p < 0.10.$ $**p < 0.05.$ $***p < 0.01.$ This analysis was produced with v4 of the V-Dem data set.

are over- or under-represented across cases. In practice, we can model the extent to which coder characteristics bias the coders away from the "true," or typical, score. By including country- and year-fixed effects we fix the comparisons to the same countries and time periods. Moreover, we can model the coder point estimates as a function of coder characteristics. Dahlström et al. (2012) take this approach, and model expert survey responses to questions on bureaucratic recruitment patterns as a function of gender, age, education, state employment, and whether the expert was born or resides in the country coded.

Table 6.12 predicts adjusted coder ratings for the Corruption Index, focusing on the same coder characteristics as Dahlström et al. (2012), plus three attitudinal measures that might tap into ideological biases when coding a country's level of corruption: support for a free market; support for the principle of electoral democracy; and support for the principle of liberal democracy. Table 6.13 replicates this analysis for the 10 randomly selected variables from V-Dem's data set.[7]

---

[7] We omit the results for the democracy indicators because the models are less comparable across concepts. Although they hold constant coder traits, the other control variables are democracy related, such as the difference between alternative and traditional concepts of democracy.

TABLE 6.11 *Predicting coder disagreement for 10 randomly selected indicators*

| | Panel A | | | | |
	Health equality	Judicial accountability	Transparent laws with predictable enforcement	Compliance with high court	Respect counterarguments
Year	-0.000	-0.000	-0.000**	0.000	-0.000
	(0.000)	(0.000)	(0.000)	(0.000)	(0.000)
Freedom of Expression Index	-0.009	0.019	-0.074***	-0.106***	-0.078**
	(0.015)	(0.027)	(0.025)	(0.025)	(0.031)
Level	0.014***	0.033***	0.023***	-0.005	-0.001
	(0.004)	(0.009)	(0.008)	(0.008)	(0.011)
Level^2	-0.053***	-0.084***	-0.044***	-0.059***	-0.070***
	(0.003)	(0.007)	(0.004)	(0.005)	(0.005)
No. of coders	0.002**	0.001	0.002**	0.001	0.002*
	(0.001)	(0.003)	(0.001)	(0.001)	(0.001)
Adjusted R-squared	0.363	0.206	0.315	0.325	0.264
No. of countries	173	173	173	173	172
No. of observations	15,813	15,595	15,612	15,547	15,665

	Disclosure of campaign donations	Access to justice for men	Freedom of religion	Religious organization repression	Election losers accept results
Year	0.000	-0.000	-0.000**	-0.000	0.000
	(0.000)	(0.000)	(0.000)	(0.000)	(0.000)
Freedom of Expression Index	-0.014	-0.040*	-0.033	-0.027	-0.064***
	(0.022)	(0.022)	(0.023)	(0.018)	(0.017)
Level	-0.001	0.011*	0.006	-0.015**	-0.019***
	(0.009)	(0.006)	(0.007)	(0.006)	(0.005)
Level^2	-0.082***	-0.049***	-0.051***	-0.070***	-0.043***
	(0.005)	(0.003)	(0.004)	(0.004)	(0.005)
No. of coders	0.002**	0.001	0.001	0.001	0.003***
	(0.001)	(0.001)	(0.002)	(0.001)	(0.001)
Adjusted R-squared	0.381	0.432	0.361	0.489	0.387
No. of countries	172	173	173	173	167
No. of observations	15,502	15,576	15,710	15,916	3128

Panel B

Note: Entries are regression coefficients, with standard errors, clustered on countries, in parentheses. Indicator-fixed effects are included in the pooled model but omitted from the table. $^* p < 0.10.$ $^{**} p < 0.05.$ $^{***} p < 0.01.$ This analysis was produced with v4 of the V-Dem data set.

TABLE 6.12 *Predicting coder ratings with coder traits for the Corruption Index*

	Corruption Index
Gender	–.029***
	(0.011)
Age	–0.004
	(0.003)
Age^2	0.000
	(0.000)
PhD education	–0.004
	(0.012)
Government employee	0.001
	(0.021)
Born in country	0.024*
	(0.012)
Resides in country	0.018
	(0.013)
Supports free market	0.005
	(0.004)
Supports electoral democracy	–0.003
	(0.005)
Supports liberal democracy	–0.007
	(0.005)
Mean coder discrimination (beta)	–0.010
	(0.007)
R-squared	0.529
No. of countries	173
No. of observations	319,266

Note: Entries are regression coefficients, with standard errors, clustered on countries, in parentheses. Year- and country-fixed effects and indicator-fixed effects are omitted from the table. *$p < 0.10$. **$p < 0.05$. ***$p < 0.01$. This analysis was produced with v4 of the V-Dem data set.

With few exceptions, coder characteristics do not predict our coders' adjusted score for the Corruption Index nor for our 10 indicators, holding country and year constant. While female coders rate countries lower than men for the Corruption Index, this trend is not systematically present in the other indicators. Interestingly, there is no "democratic bias" in our coders' adjusted ratings of corruption and other variables – captured by the statistically insignificant coefficients on "supports electoral democracy."

Finally, we consider coder and country traits in combination in predicting coder ratings. This allows us to test for a potential form of

TABLE 6.13 *Predicting coder ratings with coder traits for 10 randomly selected indicators*

			Panel A		
	Health equality	Judicial accountability	Transparent laws with predictable enforcement	Compliance with high court	Respect counterarguments
Gender	-0.024*	0.000	-0.017	-0.013	-0.014
	(0.013)	(0.022)	(0.013)	(0.011)	(0.014)
Age	-0.003	0.012**	-0.002	-0.007	-0.007*
	(0.004)	(0.006)	(0.003)	(0.005)	(0.004)
Age^2	0.000	-0.000**	0.000	0.000	0.000
	(0.000)	(0.000)	(0.000)	(0.000)	(0.000)
PhD education	-0.024	0.016	0.008	0.025	0.009
	(0.015)	(0.017)	(0.013)	(0.017)	(0.015)
Government employee	-0.023	-0.011	-0.022	-0.030	0.000
	(0.022)	(0.029)	(0.033)	(0.031)	(0.030)
Born in country	0.007	0.025	0.016	0.042	0.017
	(0.016)	(0.024)	(0.016)	(0.027)	(0.016)
Resides in country	-0.008	-0.037*	0.002	0.025	-0.020
	(0.018)	(0.020)	(0.016)	(0.023)	(0.014)
Supports free market	0.006	0.002	0.003	0.001	0.008
	(0.006)	(0.008)	(0.005)	(0.007)	(0.006)
Supports electoral democracy	-0.005	-0.001	-0.006	0.004	0.007
	(0.007)	(0.008)	(0.006)	(0.014)	(0.006)

(continued)

TABLE 6.14 (continued)

	Health equality	Judicial accountability	Transparent laws with predictable enforcement	Compliance with high court	Respect counterarguments
Supports liberal democracy	0.007	0.013	0.003	0.009	-0.002
	(0.006)	(0.008)	(0.006)	(0.006)	(0.006)
Mean coder discrimination (beta)	0.018*	0.072***	-0.007	-0.018	0.001
	(0.010)	(0.014)	(0.009)	(0.011)	(0.012)
Adj. R-squared	0.695	0.644	0.529	0.685	0.488
No. of countries	173	172	172	172	172
No. of observations	86751	79486	87043	78859	86328

Panel B

	Disclosure of campaign donations	Access to justice for men	Freedom of religion	Religious organization repression	Election losers accept results
Gender	-0.018	-0.030*	0.024*	0.016	0.015
	(0.013)	(0.013)	(0.014)	(0.014)	(0.012)
Age	-0.002	-0.001	-0.002	-0.004	0.004
	(0.005)	(0.003)	(0.005)	(0.004)	(0.004)
Age^2	0.000	0.000	0.000	0.000	-0.000
	(0.000)	(0.000)	(0.000)	(0.000)	(0.000)
PhD education	-0.005	-0.009	0.003	-0.002	-0.036**
	(0.016)	(0.016)	(0.016)	(0.019)	(0.015)
Government employee	-0.011	-0.021	0.044	-0.019	-0.018
	(0.023)	(0.025)	(0.029)	(0.028)	(0.029)

(continued)

Born in country	0.006	0.041**	0.021	−0.000	0.038**
	(0.019)	(0.017)	(0.016)	(0.016)	(0.017)
Resides in country	−0.010	−0.020	0.005	0.019	−0.002
	(0.015)	(0.015)	(0.016)	(0.015)	(0.018)
Supports free democracy	0.004	0.001	−0.010	0.007	0.009*
	(0.007)	(0.005)	(0.006)	(0.006)	(0.005)
Supports electoral democracy	−0.003	−0.009	0.002	−0.005	−0.002
	(0.006)	(0.007)	(0.007)	(0.006)	(0.006)
Supports liberal democracy	0.005	0.009	0.014*	0.000	−0.012**
	(0.007)	(0.006)	(0.007)	(0.006)	(0.006)
Mean coder discrimination (beta)	−0.036***	0.022***	0.035***	0.005	0.004
	(0.013)	(0.008)	(0.013)	(0.014)	(0.013)
Adj. R-squared	0.589	0.570	0.536	0.522	0.559
No. of countries	172	172	172	173	167
No. of observations	97,552	87,320	88,206	88,223	69,760

Note: Entries are regression coefficients, with standard errors, clustered on countries, in parentheses. Year- and country-fixed effects are omitted from the table. $*p < 0.10$. $**p < 0.05$. $***p < 0.01$. This analysis was produced with v4 of the V-Dem data set.

bias that Bollen and Paxton (2000: 72) call "situational closeness," or the idea that "judges will be influenced by how situationally and personally similar a country is to them." In other words, we test whether ideological bias is geared toward certain types of countries. One could, for example, imagine that a strong believer in free markets would have no general tendency to rate countries as more or less democratic or corrupt, but a more specific tendency to rate countries with free markets as more democratic or less corrupt. The V-Dem postsurvey questionnaire allows us to assess three such interactions: one between support for free markets and a proxy for openness to trade (data from the Correlates of War project); the other two between support for electoral/liberal democracy and the level of electoral/liberal democracy (data from V-Dem).

The results of this analysis for the Polyarchy Index, the Corruption Index, and the 10 randomly selected indicators appear in Tables 6.14–6.16. Coders consider more liberal countries to be less corrupt and perform better on all of the randomly selected indicators. However, this effect is not stronger among those who report stronger support for liberal democracy. Similarly, coders consider more open economies to have cleaner elections, lower associational autonomy, and less corruption. However, once again, this effect is not stronger among those with a free market ideological bias, and this effect also does not hold across all of the randomly selected variables. In summary, ideological bias does not appear to drive coder ratings. Of course the strength of this analysis rests on the availability of the observable coder-level covariates that V-Dem collects. One should always consider the possibility that unobserved coder traits might predict coder ratings or disagreement, even when some coder-level covariates are available for analysis.

6.6 CONCLUSION

The V-Dem approach to validation has been designed to reveal strengths and weaknesses in V-Dem measures. This approach assesses the degree to which measures align with shared concepts (content validation), shared rules of translation (data generation assessment), and shared realities (convergent validation). Content validation and data generation assessment are undertaken in other chapters and only briefly reviewed in this chapter. Our focus in here is the latter part, making sure that V-Dem's indices are not only internally valid, by comparing and contrasting differences across coders, but also externally valid, by measuring and explaining the deviations between V-Dem's and other extant indices.

In assessing convergent validity, the first important task is a check of cross-measure correlation. We compared V-Dem's Polyarchy Index to Polity's, Freedom House's, and UDS's. The pairwise correlations ranged from 0.87 to 0.93. For corruption, the correlation coefficients are close to 0.90 with the Worldwide Governance Indicators and Transparency International measures.

TABLE 6.14 *Predicting coder ratings with coder and country traits for the Polyarchy Index*

	Clean elections		Associational autonomy		Freedom of expression	
Gender	-0.079	-0.018	-0.012	-0.029	-0.060	-0.090***
	(0.050)	(0.046)	(0.041)	(0.041)	(0.041)	(0.033)
Age	-0.017	-0.029*	-0.004	0.002	0.004	0.004
	(0.013)	(0.015)	(0.011)	(0.012)	(0.011)	(0.009)
Age^2	0.000	0.000**	0.000	-0.000	0.000	-0.000
	(0.000)	(0.000)	(0.000)	(0.000)	(0.000)	(0.000)
PhD education	-0.037	-0.028	-0.020	-0.041	-0.039	-0.028
	(0.056)	(0.056)	(0.039)	(0.047)	(0.038)	(0.036)
Government employee	-0.105	-0.104	0.087	0.089	-0.085	0.082
	(0.088)	(0.089)	(0.080)	(0.080)	(0.077)	(0.059)
Born in country	0.180***	0.145**	0.085*	0.082	0.060	0.068
	(0.065)	(0.070)	(0.044)	(0.053)	(0.051)	(0.050)
Resides in country	0.020	0.005	-0.064*	-0.058	0.027	-0.023
	(0.062)	(0.063)	(0.036)	(0.045)	(0.048)	(0.043)
Born in Western country	-0.021	0.007	-0.083	-0.004	-0.041	-0.041
	(0.070)	(0.084)	(0.051)	(0.060)	(0.063)	(0.055)
Free market support	0.019	0.030	0.022*	-0.007	0.031*	0.006
	(0.021)	(0.023)	(0.013)	(0.015)	(0.016)	(0.019)
Conventional understanding of democracy	-0.006	-0.014	-0.001	-0.042	-0.002	-0.022
	(0.023)	(0.053)	(0.015)	(0.034)	(0.016)	(0.032)
Alternative understanding of democracy	-0.008	0.013	-0.029*	0.035	-0.033**	-0.016
	(0.022)	(0.050)	(0.015)	(0.038)	(0.016)	(0.031)

(continued)

TABLE 6.14 (*continued*)

	Clean elections	Associational autonomy	Freedom of expression
Western country	0.135*	−0.319***	−0.174
	(0.072)	(0.085)	(0.129)
Born in Western country × Western country	−0.084	0.115	0.125
	(0.121)	(0.091)	(0.114)
Openness to trade	0.024*	−0.020*	−0.002
	(0.014)	(0.010)	(0.010)
Free market support × Openness to trade	−0.006*	0.002	−0.002
	(0.003)	(0.003)	(0.003)
Conventional democracy score	1.921***	2.890***	2.819***
	(0.322)	(0.315)	(0.261)
Conventional understanding × Score	0.027	0.056	0.060
	(0.085)	(0.060)	(0.049)
Alternative democracy score	1.835***	−0.243	0.903***
	(0.356)	(0.349)	(0.258)
Alternative understanding × Score	−0.075	−0.105*	−0.025
	(0.075)	(0.062)	(0.045)
Country-fixed effects?	Y N	Y N	Y N
R-squared	0.211 0.458	0.104 0.299	0.161 0.545
No. of countries	173 147	174 149	174 149
No. of observations	245,039 160,998	383,763 228,557	635,567 370,224

Note: Entries are regression coefficients, with standard errors, clustered on countries, in parentheses. The unit of analysis is country-year-coder-indicator. Year and indicator-fixed effects are included but omitted from the table. Models 1, 3, and 5 include country-fixed effects. $^*p < 0.10$. $^{**}p < 0.05$. $^{***}p < 0.01$. This analysis was produced with v5 of the V-Dem data set.

TABLE 6.15 *Predicting coder ratings with coder and country traits for the Corruption Index*

	Corruption Index
Supports free market	0.019**
	(0.009)
Openness to trade	0.000**
	(0.000)
Supports free market × Openness to trade	−0.000
	(0.000)
Supports electoral democracy	−0.032**
	(0.014)
Electoral Democracy Index	−0.038
	(0.155)
Supports electoral democracy × Electoral Democracy Index	0.041
	(0.028)
Supports liberal democracy	0.015
	(0.018)
Liberal Component Index	0.605**
	(0.144)
Supports liberal democracy × Liberal Component Index	−0.023
	(0.025)
R-squared	0.408
No. of countries	149
No. of observations	204,684

Note: Entries are regression coefficients, with standard errors, clustered on countries, in parentheses. Year-fixed effects are included, and indicator-fixed effects are in the pooled model, but they are omitted from the table. $*p < 0.10$. $**p < 0.05$. $***p < 0.01$. This analysis was produced with v4 of the V-Dem data set.

This is the first piece of evidence that V-Dem's indices have high convergent validity.

Next, we go beyond just looking at aggregate correlations across measures to assess the drivers of the residual deviations. Following Adcock and Collier (2001) and Bowman et al. (2005), we test whether coder characteristics, such as gender, age, or education, are significant predictors of deviations. Special focus is devoted to the average level of coder disagreement, the number of coders, and the number of bridge/lateral coders.

Deviations for the Polyarchy Index from other democracy indices are consistently explained by the level of coder disagreement, but this is

TABLE 6.16 *Predicting coder ratings with coder and country traits for 10 randomly selected indicators*

			Panel A		
	Health equality	Judicial accountability	Transparent laws with predictable enforcement	Compliance with high court	Respect counterarguments
Supports free market	0.029**	0.009	0.006	-0.007	-0.006
	(0.014)	(0.014)	(0.007)	(0.012)	(0.009)
Openness to trade	0.000***	-0.000	0.000	0.000**	-0.000
	(0.000)	(0.000)	(0.000)	(0.000)	(0.000)
Supports free market × Openness to trade	-0.000	-0.000	-0.000	-0.000	0.000
	(0.000)	(0.000)	(0.000)	(0.000)	(0.000)
Supports electoral democracy (ED)	-0.041*	-0.028	0.008	0.039*	0.021
	(0.024)	(0.024)	(0.016)	(0.021)	(0.014)
Electoral dem. component (EC)	0.005	-0.619***	0.049	-0.021	0.347**
	(0.194)	(0.224)	(0.148)	(0.174)	(0.137)
Supports ED × EC	0.056	0.114**	0.020	-0.047	-0.033
	(0.036)	(0.048)	(0.027)	(0.032)	(0.028)
Supports liberal democracy (LD)	0.010	0.050*	0.007	-0.024	0.000
	(0.024)	(0.029)	(0.017)	(0.019)	(0.013)
Liberal component (LC)	0.368**	1.016***	0.934***	0.947***	0.657***
	(0.160)	(0.175)	(0.110)	(0.152)	(0.101)
Supports LD × LC	0.008	-0.061	-0.023	0.040*	0.021
	(0.034)	(0.046)	(0.021)	(0.022)	(0.022)

(continued)

	Adj. R-squared	No. of countries	No. of observations
	0.301	149	49528
	0.342	149	46417
	0.578	149	49976
	0.546	149	46274
	0.549	149	50250

Panel B

	Disclosure of campaign donations	Access to justice for men	Freedom of religion	Religious organization repression	Election losers accept results
Supports free market	0.006	0.000	-0.038***	-0.026***	0.012
	(0.010)	(0.007)	(0.010)	(0.009)	(0.010)
Openness to trade	0.000	0.000	-0.000***	-0.000*	0.000
	(0.000)	(0.000)	(0.000)	(0.000)	(0.000)
Supports free market × Openness to trade	-0.000	0.000	0.000***	0.000*	-0.000*
	(0.000)	(0.000)	(0.000)	(0.000)	(0.000)
Supports electoral democracy (ED)	-0.013	0.000	-0.036*	-0.001	-0.011
	(0.021)	(0.019)	(0.020)	(0.021)	(0.021)
Electoral dem. component (EC)	0.001	-0.007	0.120	0.225	0.415**
	(0.202)	(0.141)	(0.166)	(0.167)	(0.178)
Supports ED × EC	0.053	0.000	0.043	-0.001	0.034
	(0.047)	(0.027)	(0.032)	(0.030)	(0.033)
Supports liberal democracy (LD)	0.002	0.002	0.030	0.019	0.011
	(0.021)	(0.021)	(0.028)	(0.023)	(0.025)
Liberal component (LC)	0.325*	0.906***	0.660***	0.648***	0.496***
	(0.170)	(0.118)	(0.185)	(0.148)	(0.159)

(continued)

TABLE 6.14 (continued)

	Disclosure of campaign donations	Access to justice for men	Freedom of religion	Religious organization repression	Election losers accept results
Supports LD × LC	0.031	0.003	−0.037	−0.007	−0.016
	(0.044)	(0.025)	(0.038)	(0.029)	(0.031)
Adj. R-squared	0.392	0.605	0.439	0.498	0.469
No. of countries	147	149	149	149	145
No. of observations	58,828	50,113	50,390	50,407	51,609

Note: Entries are regression coefficients, with standard errors, clustered on countries, in parentheses. Year-fixed effects are included, and indicator-fixed effects are in the pooled model, but they are omitted from the table. * p < 0.10. ** p < 0.05. *** p < 0.01. This analysis was produced with v4 of the V-Dem data set.

attenuated by increasing the number of coders. The share of female coders and the share of local coders drive deviations from one other democracy index, but not for all. Deviations between the V-Dem Corruption Index and other corruption indices follow the same patterns, but the share of PhD coders is also a significant predictor of cross-measure deviations.

Finally, we check for cross-coder convergence following Steenbergen and Marks (2007) and Martínez i Coma and van Ham (2015). Our main measure is intercoder disagreement: the standard deviations in country-indicator-year coder ratings. There are three levels in the analysis of intercoder disagreement: expert judgment, measured by coder-specific random effects coefficients; level of information, whose proxies are distance in time of coding to time of observation and freedom of the media; and, lastly, country and coder characteristics, measured by a vector of socioeconomic characteristics with different aggregation levels. Except for coder random effects, there is no systematic effect of any of these predictors on intercoder disagreement. Even in the case of random effects, all coefficients have an effect size of at most 0.5 on a zero-to-four scale for each indicator in V-Dem's data set. Most importantly, a large portion of this deviation is due to heterogeneous thresholds for mapping coders' perceptions on to ordinal categories in the survey, which are addressed by V-Dem's measurement model described by Pemstein et al. (2015).

All in all, V-Dem's indicators fare well even when submitted to rigorous validation tests such as those carried out in this chapter. In Chapter 7, we present some points to consider when incorporating V-Dem data in explanatory analysis.

7

Explanatory Analysis with Varieties of Democracy Data[*]

7.1 INTRODUCTION

General advice for analysis with longitudinal data such as Varieties of Democracy (V-Dem) can be found in standard textbooks and review papers (e.g., see Wooldridge 2002; Diggle et al. 2002; Beck and Katz 2011). However, there are four characteristics of V-Dem data that present distinct opportunities and challenges for analysis: (1) the large number of democracy indicators (i.e., variables), (2) the measurement of concepts by multiple coders filtered through the V-Dem measurement model, (3) the large number of years in the data set, and (4) the ex-ante potential for dependence across countries (generically referred to as spatial dependence). These characteristics have a number of implications for analysis that we describe below.

We discuss these four characteristics, and the opportunities and challenges (as well as strategies for overcoming these challenges) that each of these characteristics bring, in turn. We hold that the opportunities outnumber the challenges. The main challenges are that (1) the large number of variables makes it easier to capitalize on chance, (2) it is possible that scores contain some bias associated with the characteristics of the experts who assigned them, and (3) the long time series increases the need to model or rule out causal heterogeneity across historical periods. Nevertheless, it is advantageous (4) to have many disaggregated variables that make it possible to precisely test hypotheses and specific causal mechanisms and (5) to perform robustness checks; (6) to be able to account for measurement uncertainty in any kind of analysis; (7) to leverage large samples to obtain greater statistical power, (8) to reduce omitted variable

---

[*] The lead authors of this chapter were (alphabetically) Michael Coppedge, Adam Glynn, Carl Henrik Knutsen, and Daniel Pemstein.

bias, and (9) to have less risk of Nickell bias in models with fixed effects and a lagged dependent variable. The many variables and large-N environment of V-Dem also offers more possibilities for designing (10) differences-in-differences tests, (11) synthetic control type analyses, (12) using the Generalized Method of Moments, and to (13) test complex models that can differentiate between true spatial dependence and other processes that generate similar patterns in the data.

At the end of this chapter, we also discuss three assumptions that are implicit in most analyses of this type (i.e., analyses of observational indicators of macro-features, and more specifically political institutions measured at the national level), which aim to draw conclusions about causal relationships. We also offer a potential interpretation of results when these assumptions do not hold.

7.2 LARGE NUMBER OF DEMOCRACY INDICATORS

The V-Dem data set contains many indicators, measuring different dimensions of democracy. A wealth of choices confronts researchers who want to analyze these data. In particular, the disaggregated nature of V-Dem data and the large number of indicators mean that one can choose or construct outcome variables to fit more closely to research hypotheses focusing on any particular dimension of democracy. Let us provide a hypothetical example: If researchers want to study the effects of X on Y_1, V-Dem more likely provides an indicator for Y_1 as opposed to Polity, which might conflate the Y_1 and Y_2 dimensions in a more aggregated measure; or instead of Freedom House, which might focus more on Y_2. Put another way, V-Dem enables users to drill down from general indices to several levels of more specific variables, making it possible to test more specific hypotheses and specific causal mechanisms.

One example of such an application is Knutsen et al. (2019), which analyzes the relationship between income and different dimensions of democracy. These authors present an argument – centering on how economic development alters the relative power resources of citizens vis-à-vis leaders, *and* how elections enable citizens to solve collective action problems in challenging leaders – implying that the electoral aspect of democracy is strongly related to income. However, the argument has no clear implications for other dimensions of democracy or for composite measures incorporating various democracy dimensions. Knutsen et al. find a robust relationship between measures closely centered on electoral aspects of democracy, such as V-Dem's Clean Elections Index, whereas composite measures and measures focusing on other dimensions are less clearly related to income. The authors also employ the more fine-grained indicators composing the Clean Elections Index to gauge the potential mechanisms at work. They find, for example, that richer countries experience less election violence and less vote buying. In contrast, higher income does not seem to improve the quality of elections through the quality of the vote registry or the capacity or autonomy of the election monitoring board. In sum, this paper shows how V-Dem data allows for more nuanced tests by distinguishing among different dimensions of democracy, and among specific institutional indicators, to get closer to the mechanisms at work.

Another advantage is that the large number of available outcome variables can increase opportunities for placebo tests. Returning to the aforementioned hypothetical study, if we believe that X should primarily have an effect on Y_1, then we might expect X not to have an effect on Y_3. If we find that in fact X does not appear to have an effect on Y_3 (and we assume that any bias is similar for the Y_1 and Y_3 analyses), then this nonfinding for our placebo test will give us more confidence in our finding for Y_1. We refer to Hartman and Hidalgo (2018) for recent advice on how to conduct placebo tests and Sofer et al. (2016) for advice on how to convert placebo tests into a difference-in-differences style analysis.

The V-Dem data set provides the possibility for variants on this kind of logic, such as additional robustness checks in either new or old studies (i.e., replication analysis). One example is provided by Bizzarro et al. (2018), who analyze how the strength of political parties influences economic growth rates. The authors find a substantial, positive coefficient on their party strength measure in their benchmark regression. Yet, there is a voluminous literature on the institutional determinants of growth, with different scholars highlighting the relevance of everything from private property rights protection to an impartial state administration to a low level of corruption. Bizzarro et al. thus conduct a range of robustness tests that corroborate the baseline results even when controlling for these alternative institutions (which are also explicitly measured in the V-Dem data set).

However, there are two complications with the use of V-Dem data in this manner. First, there is measurement error inherent in many of the V-Dem indicators. (Of course, there is measurement error in all democracy indicators. V-Dem data differ by providing abundant estimates of the size of measurement error by indicator, country, and year.) The next section of this chapter will discuss techniques that account for this measurement error, but the assessment of robustness may be complicated when control variables are measured with error. For example, if a result is robust to the inclusion of the V-Dem variable (assuming no measurement error), but is not robust once the extra uncertainty due to measurement error is considered, then we may be fundamentally uncertain as to the robustness of the finding. Second, while the large number of variables provides the opportunity for many robustness checks, it also provides the opportunity for fishing expeditions and p-hacking. Hence, as with all data sets that contain a large number of variables, uncritical analysis using V-Dem data will be particularly susceptible to abuse through capitalizing on chance, selectively reporting large effects after extensive specification searches. The use of well-formed theories and techniques that penalize over-fitting would help prevent abuse. Publicly registering a research agenda before undertaking an analysis can be an additional safeguard.

7.3 ACCOUNTING FOR MEASUREMENT UNCERTAINTY

One of the unique features of V-Dem data is that they include measures of uncertainty that are useful to researchers who wish to account for measurement error into their analyses. The political institutions that V-Dem measures by using expert ratings are difficult to observe directly; they represent latent, or directly unobservable, constructs that experts perceive, and report, often differently from one another.

As we discuss in Chapter 4, and briefly review here, these differences in perceptions and reporting are likely to stem from two causes. First, even when experts perceive cases similarly, they may translate their perceptions onto ordinal scales differently, because of variation in how experts place ordinal thresholds onto the same continuous latent scale. This is what we call differential item functioning (DIF). Recall that a simple example of such differences is when one expert maintains systematically higher or lower standards than another when translating observations to reported ordinal scores. In other words, expert A's "2" might correspond to expert B's "3," and so on. DIF also occurs when experts systematically and consistently perceive cases differently; for example, a "glass half-empty" rater would see cases in a uniformly more pessimistic light than her "half-full" counterpart. Second, rater disagreement may stem from random rater error. Such random error might reflect idiosyncratic differences in the information available to raters, or simple mistakes or oversights. Some raters might also be more prone to such random mistakes than others.

The V-Dem measurement model provides a systematic framework for modeling expert disagreement in light of DIF and random rater error.[1] One way to think about this model is as an explicit set of assumptions about what causes experts to disagree that provides systematic guidance about how to generate latent trait point estimates while summarizing uncertainty around those estimates. V-Dem provides this information in the form of random samples from the posterior distributions of each latent trait that it measures.

---

[1] V-Dem's modeling framework cannot, of course, account for all possible causes of expert disagreement. In particular, we assume that experts share conceptual frames and that they do not exhibit biases that vary systematically across cases. One exception is the likely difference between expert coders, who code different time intervals – notably "historical" and "contemporary" V-Dem expert coders – where one would expect to observe differences in "institutional quality"; experts might adjust their scales to the variation in institutional quality across the observations that they consider. Chapter 4 discusses how the V-Dem measurement model is adjusted to account for such differences between experts coding different time periods (see also Knutsen et al. 2018). Regarding other potential differences in frames between experts, if an expert had personal disagreements with a given regime in her country of expertise, and systematically penalized that country's scores only when that regime was in power, V-Dem would not accurately model disagreement between raters. This is a fundamentally different problem than either DIF or random error. We are unaware of *any* expert-survey project in political science that compensates for such biases.

This strategy is highly advantageous, in that it allows analysts to apply a reasonably simple computational approach to uncertainty propagation, known as the method of composition, when computing any statistic that is a function of the V-Dem scores. This approach allows a researcher to accurately represent uncertainty – conditional on the assumptions inherent in V-Dem's measurement model – in everything ranging from simple aggregations of V-Dem measures, to coefficients estimated for complex generalized regression models with V-Dem measures on either (or both) side(s) of the regression equation.

Moreover, because V-Dem provides raw expert ratings, sophisticated users who are not happy with the assumptions inherent in the V-Dem measurement model can alter that model to fit other assumptions about what drives expert disagreement. The tools that we describe here could eventually allow researchers to quantify uncertainty using alternative models of V-Dem Country Expert disagreement, or even ensembles of models of the expert coding process.

The V-Dem approach to quantifying measurement uncertainty improves on disciplinary norms. In particular, while it is not unusual for expert-based measures of political institutions to rely on – and average across – the perceptions of multiple experts (e.g., Bakker et al. 2015), they rarely provide measures of uncertainty that are particularly useful for use in downstream analysis (Lindstädt et al. 2016). Most such data sets provide some measure of rater agreement, or case-level uncertainty, typically reporting the standard deviation of expert responses for each observation. While one can use expert averages and standard deviations to propagate measurement uncertainty into subsequent analyses, doing so requires heroic assumptions. Specifically, one must assume that experts exhibit neither differential item functioning (DIF), nor variation in reliability (again, see Chapter 4), in such an approach. Such assumptions are unlikely to prove robust (Lindstädt et al. 2016; Marquardt and Pemstein 2017).

Furthermore, while expert surveys generally provide some measure of uncertainty, the standard approach to analyzing data that include latent, or uncertain, measures is simply to ignore that uncertainty. Studies that engage measurement uncertainty seriously are vanishingly rare within the discipline. But researchers who ignore such uncertainty have the potential to mislead themselves and others, and careful users of the V-Dem data set should always account for measurement uncertainty when drawing conclusions from these data.

While the V-Dem approach to quantifying measurement uncertainty – using Bayesian computational techniques to draw random samples from posterior distributions of our various expert-based measures – is general, flexible, and extensible, it relies on statistical methods that are unfamiliar to many social scientists. This is a potential disadvantage because many V-Dem users are unable to effectively leverage the information that we provide, at least out of the box. On the other hand, the simpler approach of providing standard deviations around expert averages has also been largely unsuccessful at convincing users to incorporate measurement uncertainty in analyses. Researchers, in general, simply ignore this information (Trier and Jackman 2008; Desbordes and Koop 2016). The goal of this section of this book is to convince V-Dem users to pay attention to measurement uncertainty and to provide the data set's users with the skills necessary to leverage this information effectively. To that end, we introduce the method of composition and apply it in a series of example analyses, demonstrating its flexibility and utility for researchers who use V-Dem data.

Researchers should propagate measurement uncertainty into their analyses simply because it is the right thing to do: relying only on point estimates has the potential to produce misleading results, or to exaggerate confidence in findings. Indeed, Desbordes and Koop (2016) show that using multiple imputation to account for the uncertainty around the World Governance Indicators (WGI) can substantially alter the conclusions that researchers draw from these data.[2] Making use of V-Dem's uncertainty estimates can encourage other data-providers to better model, and report, uncertainty, thereby raising measurement standards in the discipline. Users who do not incorporate measurement uncertainty into their analyses using V-Dem data take the risk that their findings will be overturned in a future meta-analysis. As recent work on listwise deletion of missing data in studies of comparative and international political economy demonstrates (Lall 2016), this can be an embarrassing exercise for scholars who fail to adopt known best practices when conducting research.

7.3.1 Method of Composition

To explain how to use the method of composition in research, we will work within the context of a regression analysis. After introducing some notation, we'll show how such an analysis fits into the framework described above. Then we will walk through a simple regression analysis to illustrate the technique in practice. We provide an overview of the process here. Interested readers can find an expanded step-by-step tutorial, with Stata code, and more complicated examples at https://kellogg.nd.edu/content/workshop-varieties-democracy-data-incorporating-measurement-error.

We focus on an arbitrary V-Dem "C" indicator (i.e., an indicator coded by Country Experts), z. Specifically z is a vector of country-year observations of some such C indicator – say freedom of discussion for women (*v2cldiscw*). Thus, each z_i is a function of a vector of expert ratings, r_i. The V-Dem measurement model produces samples from the posterior density $f(z|R)$, where R is the $m \times e$ matrix of ratings, where m is the number of country-years in the data set, and e is

---

[2] The WGI provide standard error estimates that researchers routinely ignore.

the number of raters. Given the assumptions discussed above, and in Chapter 4, the software that implements the V-Dem measurement model draws S samples[3] from the marginal density $f(z|R)$. This produces an $m \times S$ matrix:

$$\mathbf{Z} = \begin{matrix} z_1^{(1)} & z_1^{(2)} & z_1^{(3)} & \cdots \\ z_2^{(1)} & z_2^{(2)} & z_2^{(3)} & \cdots \\ \vdots & \vdots & \vdots & \ddots \end{matrix}$$

It is important to stress here that V-Dem "C" indicators are random variables, and the V-Dem measurement model defines a density function for generating draws (each column in the above matrix) from these random variables. The point estimates for these indicators within the basic V-Dem data set are summaries of $\mathbf{Z}$, specifically the median of each z_i. They therefore oversimplify, sometimes dramatically, the information provided by the matrix of expert ratings, $\mathbf{R}$. Clearly, these point estimates ignore measurement uncertainty, but they also ignore the shape of the density $f(z|R)$. In many cases this density is symmetric and roughly normally distributed, but in some cases distributions are skewed. In particular, country-years with ratings at the extremes of the ordinal scales – observations that all raters consider top or bottom-level cases – tend to have skewed distributions. Medians outperform means at summarizing posterior densities under these circumstances, but simple summaries of posterior error, such as standard deviations of each row in $\mathbf{Z}$, will be misleading.

It is difficult to predict how ignoring the fact that "C" indicators are random variables will affect inferences in applied research. Certain intercase correlations may be robust across draws from $f(z|R)$ while others may not. Thus simple summaries of relationships across cases, and between z and other measures – say the correlation between freedom of discussion for women and infant mortality – that hold for point estimates may not hold for individual draws from $f(z|R)$, or, they may hold for many draws of the random variable, but not for point estimates.[4] Ignoring all the information provided by the V-Dem measurement model and working with point estimates can bias coefficients and cause both over- and under-confidence in inferences and descriptive statistics.

Note that this explanation is at odds with the story about ignoring measurement error (in regression models) that many readers will have encountered in their introductory econometrics classes. The standard errors-in-

---

[3] Readers can find sets of posterior samples for each "C" variable in the V-Dem data set at https://curate.nd.edu/show/1z40ks6792x. The tutorial at https://kellogg.nd.edu/content/workshop-varieties-democracy-data-incorporating-measurement-error explains how to download and import these data into Stata.

[4] This latter possibility is unlikely but can occur when posterior densities are skewed or cross-correlations across draws have complex structures.

variables (EIV) problem is that assuming away measurement error in independent variables causes attenuation bias in coefficients (a bias toward zero, at least in the context of a bivariate regression, whereas predicting the direction of the bias is more involved when there is more than one regressor). Therefore, researchers often underestimate the size of their regression coefficients. Furthermore, ignoring errors in dependent variables causes no bias, although it does reduce the precision of coefficient estimates. This treatment of measurement error is based on the idea that each independent variable is contaminated by some random error, drawn from a density with a mean of zero.

The V-Dem measurement model makes a similar assumption about expert errors and thus addresses the classical EIV problem by incorporating information from multiple raters, and explicitly modeling this source of measurement error. Nonetheless, the model relaxes the core assumption in classical EIV that measured variables are unbiased, by accounting for DIF. The relationship between measurement uncertainty in "C" indicators and regression coefficients is therefore more complicated than the "textbook" analysis leads us to expect. In other words, incorporating measurement uncertainty into your work with V-Dem data will not always increase the size of your coefficients, nor will it always decrease your standard errors.

The method of composition is a general technique for simulating random draws from the distribution function of a random variable that can be expressed as a mixture of other random variables that are easier to sample than the variable that you are interested in. More formally, say that you have a vector of random variables $\theta = \theta_1, \theta_2, \ldots, \theta_n$, and a data vector y, where the joint density of the random variables is $f(\theta|y)$. If you want to sample from the density $f(\theta_1|y)$, you can use the method of composition to sample from that density as long as you know how to sample from the densities $f(\theta_1|\theta_{-1}, y)$ and $f(\theta_{-1}|y)$, where $\theta_{-1} = \theta_2, \theta_3, \ldots, \theta_n$, or every item in θ except θ_1 (see, e.g., Tanner 1993). In particular, one can apply the following algorithm to draw S samples from $f(\theta_1|y)$:

For each $s \in 1, 2, \ldots, S$,

1 sample $\theta_{-1}^{(s)}$ from $f(\theta_{-1}^{(s)}|y)$

2 sample $\theta_1^{(s)}$ from $f(\theta_1^{(s)}|\theta_{-1}^{(s)}, y)$

Now, to understand where the method of composition fits in, note simply that fitting any regression model using V-Dem data is identical to sampling from the density $f(\beta, z|X, R)$, where β is a coefficient vector and X is a matrix of variables – appearing on either side of the regression model – that are measured without uncertainty. We take advantage of the decomposition

$$f(\beta, z|X, R) = f(\beta|X, R, z)f(z|X, R),$$

while assuming

A1 $f(\beta|X, R, z) = f(\beta|X, z)$

and

A2 $f(z|X, R) = f(z|R)$.

These assumptions maintain that the latent variables capture all the information in the expert ratings that is relevant for our regression, and that none of the other variables in the regression equation affect the relationship between expert ratings and the latent variable. The assumptions allow us to apply the method of composition directly. Our vector of random variables $\theta = \beta, z$ and our quantity of interest is $f(\beta|X)$. The V-Dem measurement modeling software conducts the first composition step, sampling S draws from $f(z|R)$. Now, remembering that regression coefficients are normally distributed, for each of these $s \in 1, 2, \ldots S$ draws, sample from $f(\beta|X, z)$ by

1 fitting your regression model to the data $X, z^{(s)}$, yielding partial likelihood estimates $\hat{\mu}^{(s)}$ and $\hat{\Sigma}^{(s)}$, and
2 drawing a random sample from the density $\beta^{(s)} \sim N\left(\hat{\mu}^{(s)}, \hat{\Sigma}^{(s)}\right)$.

In other words, you run your regression model once for every draw from the density of the V-Dem variable and then plug the coefficient vector and variance-covariance matrix that you estimate for that draw into a multivariate normal random number generator, producing one draw from the density $f(\beta|X)$ at each iteration. After completing this process, you are left with S random draws of β, which you can summarize like any other sample of a random variable. Specifically, you can produce point estimates by taking the average or median of these draws, and standard errors are simply the standard deviations across draws. While we describe this process for a single "C" indicator here, it is quite general. You can include multiple "C" indicators on either side of the regression equation – even on both sides – using the same basic procedure.

A simple example illustrates this technique. Specifically, say we think that women's voice in society predicts state performance in providing reproductive health care. As an initial descriptive test of this argument, one might fit the fixed effects regression model

Infant Mortality$_{cy} = \alpha_c + \beta_1$Free Discussion Women$_{cy} +$
$\beta_2 \ln(\text{GDP Per Capita})_{cy} + \epsilon_{cy}$,

where cy indexes country-years, with the expectation that β_1 will be negative. That is, controlling for development and fixed state characteristics, we would expect a negative relationship between women's free expression and infant mortality, if states where women are freer to express themselves provide better reproductive health services.

Figure 7.1 displays partial regression plots of infant mortality on free discussion for women, drawing on V-Dem data from the year 1900 onward, from version 8. The left-most panel shows the partial regression line based on simple point estimates. The middle panel adds, in gray, regression lines representing a few passes of the above-described algorithm. The right-most

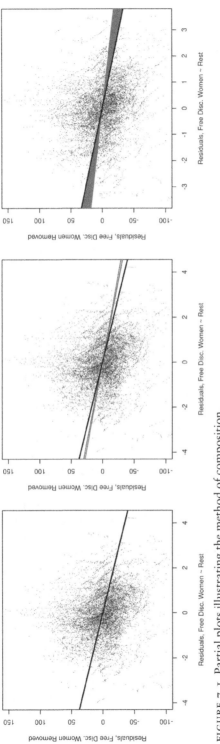

FIGURE 7.1 Partial plots illustrating the method of composition.

TABLE 7.1 *A sample application of the method of composition*

Coefficient	Point estimate	MoC min.	MoC avg.	MoC max,	MoC *SD*
Free disc. W.	−6.1	−6.6	−4.9	−3.1	0.5
Log GDP PC	−50.0	−53.3	−51.1	−48.6	0.8

panel shows the regression lines produced by running this algorithm for all 900 draws from the posterior distribution of the freedom of discussion for women indicator.

Table 7.1 presents the full results of the application of the method of composition to this model. The second column in the table provides coefficients for the basic model using V-Dem point estimates, while the remaining columns summarize the distribution of coefficients that we calculated using the method of composition. Note that while the point-estimate-based coefficient for log GDP per capita is close to the center of the sampling distribution, when we take measurement uncertainty into account, the point estimate for women's free discussion is not. Indeed, as Figure 7.1 illustrates, the regression line based on point estimates is out in the tail of the distribution of lines produced by composition. The full analysis indicates that the estimate of β_1 using V-Dem point estimates is likely too large in magnitude. After accounting for measurement uncertainty, and the shape of the distribution of z, we would estimate $\beta_1 = -4.9$ (the β_1 distribution average), with a standard error of 0.5 (the β_1 distribution standard deviation) around that estimate.

In this case, the substantive distinction between using point estimates and the composition technique is small: both approaches indicate a negative relationship between women's free discussion and infant mortality. Our results nonetheless illustrate the potential for analyses based on point estimates to misrepresent the full information provided by the V-Dem measurement model. Indeed, the estimate of β_1 computed using point estimates falls well over two standard deviations outside of the distributions of β_1 that we constructed through composition. In other contexts, similarly large statistical discrepancies could be substantively important.

7.3.2 Coder on Both Sides

The method of composition described above is easily generalized to multiple V-Dem indicators, occurring on either side of the regression equation. Nonetheless, researchers should exercise caution when modeling one V-Dem indicator with another. To the extent that coders exhibit biases that are not consistent with DIF, relationships between V-Dem variables may represent those biases rather than actual relationships between measured concepts. In particular, questions within a single V-Dem survey are generally coded by the same set of coders within each country. In addition, each Country Expert usually codes several surveys, so one cannot be absolutely sure of avoiding this issue when modeling concepts that inhabit different surveys. To assist readers in assessing risk, Table 7.2 summarizes patterns in cross-survey coding by experts. Each cell in the table describes the proportion of experts who coded the column survey who also coded the row survey. With only one close exception, more than half of the experts coded at least two surveys. Fewer experts would be found to have completed three, four, or especially five or more surveys; but an overlap of even two surveys is sufficient to advise caution.

In principle, analysts can eliminate this sort of potential bias by removing experts who code questions on both sides of a proposed model from the analysis. This would require working with the coder-level data set that V-Dem provides and, potentially, refitting the V-Dem measurement model to these coder-level data, with the overlapping experts removed or restricted to one or the other variable. A simpler, but less convincing, approach would be to check the sensitivity of country-year expert coding averages and standard deviations to the removal of variable-bridging experts. In other words, if country-year averages and standard deviations are largely immune to such removals, then one might argue that they are unlikely to bias results.

7.4 LONG PANEL STRUCTURE

In general, leveraging time series information allows for drawing stronger inferences than when relying on cross-sectional comparisons (see, e.g., Gerring and McDermott 2007). Using (within-unit) variation across time allows, for example, for drawing on the notion that causes typically precede effects temporally as well as avoiding inferences drawn from comparing units that are not truly comparable (in ways that we often cannot observe and control for). In principle, using panel data may thus open up opportunities for designs and analyses that help researchers reduce the influence of various sources of bias when estimating causal relationships.

Yet, this scenario may be infeasible in many practical settings. Drawing on time series information presents challenges, especially when dealing with variables that are slow-moving or variables that change infrequently. When time series are short, this leaves little relevant variation for estimating relationships of interest, which, in turn, means that the inferences drawn may be associated with high degrees of uncertainty. When time series are long, however, there may be enough variation for precise estimation, even for slow-moving or infrequently changing variables.

Since various institutions and other features of democracy fit the description of either slow-moving or infrequently changing variables, the considerations above suggest that studies on the causes and effects of democracy benefit immensely from democracy being measured across long periods of time. This points to one clear advantage with the V-Dem data set relative to extant

TABLE 7.2 *Percentages of experts for column survey who were also experts for the row surveys*

Survey	Civil liberties	Civil society	Deliberation	Elections	Executive	Judiciary	Legislative	Media	Political equality	Parties	Sovereignty
Civil Liberties	100	63	61	54	61	89	61	63	66	56	90
Civil Society	65	100	57	56	57	64	57	91	92	58	66
Deliberation	60	55	100	65	89	63	89	56	58	66	63
Elections	58	58	70	100	73	61	74	60	60	93	60
Executive	59	53	86	65	100	65	93	54	56	68	62
Judiciary	77	54	55	49	58	100	60	55	56	52	81
Legislative	57	52	84	64	90	65	100	53	55	68	61
Media	61	87	56	55	55	63	56	100	91	57	65
Political Equality	64	88	57	55	57	64	57	90	100	58	66
Parties	57	58	68	88	72	61	74	59	61	100	61
Sovereignty	85	61	60	53	61	89	61	63	64	56	100

Source: V-Dem Disaggregated Data Set, v.7.

Note: These figures are based on longitudinal, lateral, and bridge coders and do not include coders for Historical V-Dem (who code separate surveys). The percentages are only slightly smaller when based on longitudinal coders only.

democracy data sets – though we note that some such data sets extend back to the early nineteenth century (see Marshall et al. 2016; Boix et al. 2013; Skaaning et al. 2015) – as the longest time series in V-Dem, from v8 and onward, extend all the way from the year 1789 to the present. Only a modest number of polities have time series that do not extend back at least to the year 1900. Let us illustrate this point with one much-debated and important example, namely how long time series allows democracy researchers to account for country-fixed effects in their analyses.

In the presence of short time series, insisting that estimates of the causes and effects of democracy draw strictly on within-country comparisons can render analyses infeasible. This relates to the very nature of how democratic institutions change over time. Some features associated with democracy, such as the protection of various civil liberties, typically change very slowly, whereas others, such as the introduction or termination of multiparty elections, typically happen very infrequently.

As a result, measures of democracy with time series that extend for a handful of decades (such as Freedom House's indices, which extend back to the early 1970s) may carry relatively little relevant within-country information for some countries.[5] The lack of variation, in practice, leads to relatively large standard errors if one tries to account for country-fixed effects and draw strictly on within-country variation across time. This problem of accounting for country-fixed effects in the presence of sluggish or infrequently changing variables – and the influence it may have on conclusions on key questions within the discipline – is widely appreciated by political scientists (e.g., Beck and Katz 2001; for discussions on the effects of popular values on democratization, see Dahlum and Knutsen 2017a, 2017b; Welzel et al. 2017).

The traditional "solution" to this issue has been to estimate the causes and effects of democracy without accounting for country-fixed effects; that is, by drawing on cross-country variation. Indeed, many of the early statistical studies on the causes and effects of democracy, such as Lipset's (1959) seminal study on income and democracy, either compared means across different categories of countries or ran cross-country regressions.

While including cross-country information alleviates the above-described problem of slow-moving variables and highly uncertain estimates, it presents an arguably even more ominous problem, that of omitted variable bias affecting results. When comparing, say, the income and democracy levels of Afghanistan and the US to inform the relationship between income and democracy, we may

---

[5] Even measures of democracy extending back to 1946, such as the binary measures of Cheibub et al. (2010) and Geddes et al. (2014), display relatively little intra-country variation for most countries – only a handful of countries have experienced more than a couple democratization and de-democratization episodes after World War II according to these measures. For some aspects of democracy, such as suffrage, even extending the time series back to the early twentieth century might be insufficient for generating the requisite variation to draw clear inferences.

fail to account for the various other relevant ways in which these countries differ, and which may jointly determine their democracy and income levels (e.g., differences in culture, geography, or political history). Thus, key debates in the literature on the causes and effects of democracy, including on the effects of income (Acemoglu et al. 2008; Gassebner et al. 2009; Heid et al. 2012) or education (e.g., Acemoglu et al. 2005) on democracy, have centered on the appropriateness of incorporating cross-country variation in the analysis.

Measuring democracy for long time intervals helps alleviate the dilemma of whether or not to account for country-fixed effects when studying the causes and consequences of democracy. Even if various democratic features are slow-moving or change infrequently, the amount of change may be sufficient for producing fairly efficient estimates if we include a century or more of data. With V-Dem extending all the way back to 1789, this enables the possibility for studies of democracy that account for omitted variable bias due to country-fixed effects while at the same time keeping standard errors fairly low. As a result, we recommend that panel regression analysis on the causes and effects of democracy, or different features of democracy, using V-Dem data should consider the use of country-fixed effects. However, as with all fixed effects analyses, one must consider the possibility of bias amplification discussed in Middleton et al. (2016).

7.4.1 Simplifications with Long Panels

The above discussion highlighted one key benefit of the long time series of the V-Dem data. Yet, the long time series also present democracy researchers with other opportunities. Long panels allow for a number of techniques and strategies that would be inefficient, or even produce biases, when relying on short panels. Let us very briefly discuss three specific instances, namely fixed effects regressions with lagged dependent variables included as controls (autoregressive models), differences-in-differences (diff-in-diff) designs accompanied by sufficient parallel trends checking, and synthetic control with sufficient length to justify key assumptions.

First, researchers may sometimes want to include a lag (or multiple lags) of the dependent variable in their regressions. Adding a lagged dependent variable as a regressor may be a simple and feasible way of correcting for various biases.[6] Yet, including a lagged dependent variable leads to a particular issue in panel regressions that include unit-fixed effects, even though doing so is often appropriate when studying the causes and effects of democracy. Specifically, researchers working with dynamic panel data with a short time series must

---

[6] For instance, we are interested in studying the effect of an independent variable X on a sticky institution I, but we are concerned about reverse causality. If so, we may (to some extent) guard against the possibility that it is really the (historical) presence of the institution that is driving any observed relationship between X and I by including I_{t-1} as a control.

contend with Nickell bias (Nickell 1981), in which regressors (particularly a lagged dependent variable) are not independent of the error term because all the variables contain information about the mean value of the dependent variable for each unit. While this bias may be substantial for short time series, it diminishes as the length of the time series increases (although the size of the bias depends also on how strongly autocorrelated the dependent variable is). When the time series is longer than 200 years, as is the case for V-Dem – or even when it is about 120 years, as is the case for indicators and polities not covered by Historical V-Dem – the Nickell bias will likely be negligible. Hence, including lagged dependent variables in an OLS fixed specification is less problematic when using V-Dem data than when using measures of democracy with short time series.

Second, the long time series of V-Dem data may open up opportunities for the appropriate use of difference-in-difference designs, for example when studying the effects of some treatment variable on democratization. By considering both a control group and observations that receive the treatment, such designs aim to achieve consistent estimates even in the presence of unit- and time-specific effects through "[replicating] the classic setting of an experiment with pre- and post-tests" (Gerring 2012: 280). The change in the outcome variable from before the treatment to after the treatment is calculated both for the observations that received the treatment and for the control group. The resulting difference in outcomes for the control group is subtracted from the difference for the treatment group (see, e.g., Wooldridge 2002: 130).

Whether or not such a design yields consistent estimates of the treatment effect relies on the assumption that the introduction of the treatment (in other words, the selection into the treatment group) is uncorrelated with other factors that are not controlled for and that affect the outcome. More generally, this design assumes that the mean change in the outcome in the control group is a measure of the mean change in the outcome that the treatment group *would counterfactually have experienced* if it had not received the treatment. This assumption is often referred to as the parallel trends assumptions. One way of checking the plausibility of this assumption is to investigate the similarity of the pretreatment trends in the outcome variable for the treatment and control groups; if they are fairly similar over extended periods of time, it gives credence to the notion that we are making a relevant comparison. This claim requires that we have extensive time series for which we can make such comparisons. If not, it will be hard to assess the degree of similarity in pretreatment trends, given that the outcome variable is stochastic. Thus, the long V-Dem time series makes it possible to use and better assess the plausibility of difference-in-difference designs.

In addition to allowing the assessment of the parallel trends assumption, a time series in the treatment and control groups allows for violations of the parallel trends assumption to be corrected. This can be done in a number of ways (including synthetic control). See Xu (2017) for a discussion of these techniques.

While we have so far highlighted various benefits of the long time series contained in the V-Dem data set, estimating the causes and effects of democracy over a time span of more than two centuries also raises some critical issues. We continue by describing perhaps the key issue – related to the possibility of heterogeneous causal effects over time – and discuss how researchers may turn this challenge into a source of new insights.

7.4.2   Heterogeneity over Time

Scholars studying the causes and consequences of democracy often (explicitly or implicitly) assume that the relationships that they study are constant over time. However, this is often not a realistic assumption. To take one example, the relationship between income and democratization may very well have changed over the last two centuries, due to various developments in the international system (Boix 2011).

Researchers sometimes do account and test for potential changes in relationships over time. Sometimes this is done with sensitivity tests on whether a relationship that is proposed to be general holds in different (prespecified) parts of the time period. At other times, this is done by testing for systematic changes in relationships that are expected to occur at some point during the time period. One common, and easy to comprehend, way of checking the sensitivity of a relationship to particular time intervals is to split the sample and rerun the original model on these limited time intervals. One issue with directly interpreting tests from such split-sample analysis, is that a clear test statistic for whether the estimated relationship differs is not directly available. (One is typically then considering whether the relationship has the same sign and is clearly different from zero or not in the different time periods.) A second issue is that this approach limits the information/variation that is employed in each model.

Hence, a more informative way of testing for structural changes at prespecified points in time is by running so-called Chow tests in a standard regression framework. This is equivalent to taking the original model and adding a set of dummy variables for each relevant time period (except one). For example, if one expects a particular relationship to have changed after World War II and then again with the end of the Cold War, one could include a dummy for 1946–89 capturing the Cold War era, and a dummy for 1990 onward capturing the post–Cold War era. Furthermore, multiplicative interaction terms between these time period dummies and the independent variable of interests are also added, and one typically evaluates evidence for any structural break by investigating the size and statistical significance of these interaction dummies.

Chow tests are straightforward and easy to integrate in common regression setups. However, they are associated with a significant drawback. Researchers need to be well informed in advance concerning the factors that may generate such "structural breaks" in the relationship of interest in order to specify the correct model. Basically, the example model above would work very well if 1946 and 1990 mark the only relevant points in time in which the relationship under study may have changed. But if the relationship changed substantially in, say, 1970, the setup above may fail to pick this up, and even if the model suggests that the relationship changed in 1990, it could still be that the true structural break came in, e.g., 1988 or 1993.

One type of model that alleviates the latter issue is a change-point model. We will not go into the more technical aspects of such models here (see, e.g., Western and Kleykamp 2004; Park 2013) but basically these models more inductively search for structural breaks in the relationship between dependent and independent variables. Tests can assess whether (and when) there are structural breaks in the explanatory model, in some combination of parameters, or in a single parameter. Consider the example of whether the relationship between a proposed determinant of democracy, say income level measured as GDP per capita, and level of democracy has been systematically different in different periods of modern history. The regression coefficient β_{GDP} captures the estimated effect of income on democracy, but this relationship might be stronger or weaker (or even change signs) in different periods of modern history, for example due to differences in the number of great powers and the identity of these great powers (Boix 2011). The relevant test in a change-point model, for a time series $y_1, \ldots, y_T, \ldots y_n$, considers a point in time, $t = T$, after which a structural break may occur. More specifically, it does so by assessing whether the parameter $\beta_{GDP, \, t \leq T}$ is different from $\beta_{GDP, \, t > T}$. Such tests are conducted for all possible structural breaks, for example, replacing $t = T$ with $t = T + 1$, $t = T + 2$, etc. Hence, these types of models may be used not only to estimate whether structural breaks in a relationship occur over the time series, but also how many such breaks there seem to be and when they occur. This means that unexpected structural breaks may also be detected, which could spur new theorizing and insight about how a relationship is contingent on contextual variables.

7.4.3 Generalized Method of Moments (GMM)

As indicated by the discussion above, the so-called Nickell bias is mitigated if researchers use the whole time series of V-Dem. However, researchers may sometimes be interested in studying developments only across a limited time interval. This may be for pragmatic (e.g., lack of data on other variables entering the analysis), theoretical (e.g., the phenomenon is only of interest in the post–Cold War era) or other reasons (e.g., replicating an extant analysis that only used limited time series). One type of dynamic panel data estimator developed especially to handle short time series are the so-called Generalized Method of Moments (GMM) estimators. However, we describe below how one can adjust the length of the panels, constructing, e.g., 10-year panels, to effectively employ GMM models to the full V-Dem time series as well.

There are different kinds of GMM estimators, and a large literature assessing the relative performance of such models under different contexts (e.g., Blundell and Bond 1998). GMM models have long been popular in economics, but are also becoming more commonly used by political scientists. We will not go into the technical aspects of such estimators here (see, e.g., Arellano and Bond 1991; Blundell and Bond 1998; Roodman 2009a), but rather illustrate their use and highlight a few assumptions that need to be considered and investigated by those who want to employ such models using V-Dem data.

To take one relevant example, GMM models have played a central role in the recent debate on "modernization theory" and whether there is stringent evidence of any causal effect of income level on democracy, following the prominent contribution by Acemoglu et al. (2008). Acemoglu and coauthors used the most standard GMM model – alternatively called the Arellano-Bond or the Difference GMM model (Arellano and Bond 1991) – as a robustness test of their benchmark OLS fixed effects results, corroborating the main finding that income is not related to democracy. However, later work has suggested that another GMM estimator – the so-called Blundell-Bond or System GMM estimator (Blundell and Bond 1998) – is more appropriate than the Difference GMM model for studying the particular relationship between income and democracy. (We will explain why below.) Indeed, subsequent analysis finds a positive relationship between income and democracy when employing System GMM specifications (e.g., Heid et al. 2012).

As Roodman (2009a: 86) describes, both the Difference and System GMM models are designed to handle situations "with 1) 'small T, large N' panels, meaning few time periods and many individuals; 2) a linear functional relationship; 3) one left-hand-side variable that is dynamic, depending on its own past realizations; 4) independent variables that are not strictly exogenous, meaning they are correlated with past and possibly current realizations of the error; 5) fixed individual effects; and 6) heteroscedasticity and autocorrelation within individuals but not across them." The fact that such models aim to handle unit-fixed effects (although there is debate over the extent to which the System GMM models actually do so) and the fact that they can be used to model nonexogenous regressors make them relevant for many questions pertaining to causes or effects of political regimes (or more specific institutions). This is especially so in situations where researchers are unable to identify a separate, valid instrument for their endogenous independent variable, which means that instrumental variable techniques such as two-stage least squares (2SLS) regression are not viable, and estimators assuming exogenous regressors (such as OLS regression), when these regressors are, in fact, endogenous, will yield inconsistent estimates.

Basically, the "solution" provided by the GMM models is to employ instruments based on lagged values of the instrumented variable. Past realizations of levels (several periods in time back) are used to instrument for current first differences, and – in the System GMM model – lagged differences in variables can be used to instrument for current levels. This means that GMM models can be specified to include a large number of instruments based on lags of variables that are already included in the model (but one may also add additional instruments if they can be identified). Standard specification tests for assessing the validity of these instruments, are described below.

One difference between Difference and System GMM models is that the latter is more efficient, although this comes at the cost of making the additional assumption that the first differences of instrument variables are uncorrelated with the unit-fixed effects (Roodman 2009a: 86). In practice, this may have particular consequences for variables that are very "sluggish," and simulations suggest that the System GMM models often outperform Difference GMM models in such settings (e.g. Blundell and Bond 1998). Democracy is often considered to be such a variable that (depending on the measure used) either moves very slowly or seldom. This is the reason why, for instance, Heid et al. (2012) advocate for using System GMM rather than Difference GMM when studying the effect of income and democracy, and this is one possible reason that these authors pick up a positive effect that the models of Acemoglu et al. (2008) do not. This feature could make System GMM a particularly interesting model also for many research questions that involve using V-Dem data.

However, all GMM models rely on strong assumptions, so different tests are recommended for getting a better handle on whether the model is well-specified or not. For instance, Sargan or Hansen J tests of the overidentifying restrictions should be conducted to see whether the model may yield inconsistent estimates.[7] Furthermore, Arellano-Bond autocorrelation tests are often conducted to assess the assumptions of the model (again, low p-values suggest problems with the specification), and the relevant tests pertain to AR(2) if one lag of the dependent variable is included as a regressor; AR(3) if two lags are included as regressors; and so forth. Finally, researchers should pay attention to the number of instruments included (Roodman 2009b): a too-high instrument count yields various problems (e.g., it artificially blows up p-values on overidentification tests). The rule of thumb is not to have more instruments than cross-section units, and different adjustments can be made to reduce the instrument count, such as reducing the number of lags used for instrumentation (Roodman 2009b).

In the latter regard, the long time series of V-Dem data may actually become a problem. Since longer time series yield more instruments, running GMM models on a standard country-year setup can lead to an explosion in the instrument count, and thus noncredible results. There is, however, a fairly simple "trick" that alleviates this issue. Instead of employing annual panels,

---

[7] Low p-values suggest that the overidentifying restrictions are violated, and typical practice is to require far higher p-values than the standard 0.05 threshold to conclude that the model is well specified. For cross-country data such as V-Dem, Hansen J-tests are typically recommended, as the Sargan test will yield low p-values also in the presence of heteroscedasticity.

one may calculate 5- or 10-year panels (e.g., by measuring the average over the relevant time period or taking only the scores for the first year), or perhaps even longer panels for analysis including the entire V-Dem time series from 1789 onward. Taking 10-year panels will reduce a time series of 200 years to a time series with 20 time observations, often enabling more credible GMM models. While this reduces the amount of information that panel models can draw upon, potentially glossing over interesting developments within shorter time frames, this is sometimes proposed to have other benefits, such as reducing measurement error and noise. Hence, some scholars, including many economists working in the economic growth literature (who are, e.g., eager to smooth out "business cycles" when studying long-term growth), prefer using 5- or 10-year panels rather than annual also when employing estimators such as OLS. Nonetheless, the relative benefits of employing longer panels are clearer for GMM models.

7.5   SPATIAL DEPENDENCE

Most analyses of democratization implicitly assume that countries are independent: that democracy in one country is unaffected by democracy in other countries.[8] While this independence may hold for some V-Dem indicators, unfortunately, almost all studies that have examined this assumption for higher-level measures of democracy suggest that it is probably false (Bernhard et al. 2004; Bollen and Jackman 1985; Brinks and Coppedge 2006; Finkel et al. 2007; Gassebner et al. 2009; Gleditsch and Ward 2006; Leeson and Dean 2009; Levitsky and Way 2010; Mainwaring and Pérez-Liñan 2013: 93–123; Miller 2012; O'Loughlin et al. 1998; Pevehouse 2002; Starr and Lindborg 2003; Teorell 2010). There are several good theoretical reasons to expect such empirical relationships to exist (Huntington 1991; Starr 1991; Whitehead 1986). Simmons and Elkins (2004) provide a conceptual framework for theorizing about diffusion that can be applied to the diffusion of democracy, specifically. First, some states seek to force other states to become democratic using either *hard coercion*, such as occupation, or *soft coercion*, such as sanctions and diplomacy. Second, one state may pursue democracy to seek a *competitive advantage* over another, such as qualifying for foreign aid or joining an alliance. Third, states can *learn* (from experiences abroad) that democracy actually brings its own rewards, such as legitimacy, stability, or contented citizens. Fourth, some states may *emulate* democracies, either believing that democracy is inherently desirable or believing that it may bring rewards such as economic growth and greater social equality.[9] In all of these

---

[8] For simplicity, this section deals with analyses in which democracy is the dependent variable, but similar issues are likely to arise when democracy is a predictor.

[9] Franzese and Hays (2008) add a fifth model of diffusion, migration, but we see this as just one possible channel for transporting ideas and benefits, similar to trade and communication, all of which could serve as pathways for learning or emulation.

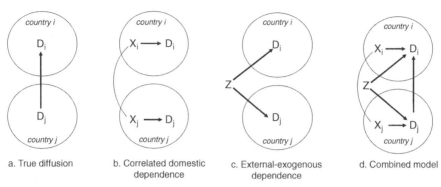

a. True diffusion   b. Correlated domestic dependence   c. External-exogenous dependence   d. Combined model

FIGURE 7.2 Diffusion contrasted with similar relationships.

pathways, democracy is believed to be spatially dependent, i.e., affected by democracy in other countries. Figure 7.2a depicts a pathway that qualifies as true diffusion. Here, democracy in country I (D_i) depends on democracy in country j (D_j).

Empirically, however, it is difficult to distinguish these kinds of true diffusion, in which democracy in one country depends on democracy in other countries, from two similar patterns. In one pattern, depicted in Figure 7.2b, domestic determinants of democracy $(X_i$ and $X_j)$ are spatially correlated, as indicated by the curved line: even though all the causes of democracy come from within national borders, democracy in countries i and j is still correlated.[10] For example, Western European countries could be democratic because they are all high-income, educated societies, not because each country promotes and protects democracy in its neighbors. If these domestic determinants are omitted variables, then the error term will contain spatial correlation. In another pattern (Figure 7.2c), which Franzese and Hays (2008) call "external-exogenous causation," many states alter their political regimes in similar ways in response to some international shock (Z) that is not itself directly pertaining to democracy and is not located in one country, such as the Great Depression, a world war, or globalization.

A first step toward distinguishing true diffusion from other processes masquerading as diffusion is to combine all three processes in a single model, as in Figure 7.2d. The relationships in this figure, adding in the time dimension of V-Dem's dynamic panel data and an error term, can be expressed as

$$D_{it} = \rho \sum_{j \neq i} w_{ij} D_{jt} + \boldsymbol{\beta}_x' x_{it} + \boldsymbol{\beta}_z' Z_t + \boldsymbol{\beta}_{zx}' (x_{it} \otimes z_t) + \varepsilon_{it}. \qquad (7.1)^{11}$$

---

[10] We leave aside the question of whether some other diffusion process accounts for the cross-national correlations among domestic determinants.

[11] Adapted from Eq. (7) of Franzese and Hays (2008).

The second term $(\boldsymbol{\beta}'_x \boldsymbol{x}_{it})$ represents all the domestic determinants of democracy. The third and fourth terms $[\boldsymbol{\beta}'_z \boldsymbol{z}_t + \boldsymbol{\beta}'_{zx}(\boldsymbol{x}_{it} \otimes \boldsymbol{z}_t)]$ represent external-exogenous dependence on international forces ($\boldsymbol{Z}$), which are allowed to have different consequences for different countries. These two processes are already easily addressed using techniques that are common in the literature: specifying domestic predictors and global year-fixed effects, which can be interacted with national characteristics if desired.

The first term $(\rho \sum_{j \neq i} w_{ij} D_{jt})$, however, represents diffusion: democracy in source countries D_{jt} has an impact ρ on other countries to which they are connected via a network. This kind of process requires models that are less well known. Any diffusion network can be defined by a matrix of diffusion weights, $\boldsymbol{W}$, which contains a column for each country and a row for each country; each weight w_{ij} represents the degree of connectedness between source country j and target country i (Neumeyer and Plümper 2016). Countries that are not connected in the network have a weight of zero. If all the countries are weighted equally, the matrix consists of ones and zeros. Continuous weights can be used to represent trade dependence, ratios of GDP or population or military power, and so on.

The most commonly examined networks in democracy diffusion are geographic: countries in the same region or immediate geographic neighbors, or sometimes longer spatial lags such as neighbors of neighbors. But countries can be networked in nongeographic ways, too, through trade, migration, investment, colonial heritage, language, religion, media, and other linkages.

It would be wonderful if diffusion hypotheses could be tested simply by estimating Eq. (7.1). Unfortunately, as Franzese and Hays (2008) warn, Eq. (7.1) yields estimates that are likely to contain two kinds of bias (as well as inefficiency and inconsistency). First, because diffusion, domestic dependence, and external-exogenous dependence could all produce very similar correlations among levels of democracy across countries, estimates are sensitive to how well each term in the model is specified. If domestic determinants are well modeled and the diffusion process is not, then the domestic determinants get too much credit for the outcomes and the diffusion process gets too little (and vice versa if the diffusion process is well modeled and domestic determinants not). The extreme, yet common, instance of this problem is to not specify diffusion relationships at all, which yields estimates of domestic influences that are likely to be exaggerated. The same issue, with respect to diffusion versus external-exogenous dependence, is known as Galton's Problem (although it is our problem, too!). This issue cautions researchers to pay close attention to the specification of all aspects of their models; otherwise, estimates can be unstable and unreliable.

Second, there is a near-certainty of simultaneity bias whenever country j affects country i in the same period that country i affects country j, or indeed whenever country j's influence passes through several countries on the way to country i, and vice versa, in the same period. If this is likely to be happening, instrumental variables regression is strongly advised. In the case of democracy diffusion, this would mean finding a variable that is a good predictor of democracy in country j and related to democracy in country i only because of its influence on democracy in country j. Domestic determinants for country j in an earlier time period may be good candidates for instruments in this application. Such models can be estimated with two-stage least squares or more complex structural-equations models (SEMs). However, when democracy (or the probability of democracy, or change in democracy, etc.) is the dependent variable, then a simpler model may suffice. This is because political regimes are sticky: once established, they tend to persist; most changes in V-Dem scores (on most of our indicators) tend to be small, and large changes are rare. This pattern suggests that the impact of external forces, such as regime changes in neighboring countries, are not likely to be realized in the same year. Transitions and breakdowns tend not to happen suddenly. It takes time to negotiate the surrender of power, to organize a coup coalition, to convoke and administer an election and inaugurate the winner, and so on. If this theoretical reasoning is sound, lagging the diffusion variable or variables reduces simultaneity bias and makes instrumental variables less important.[12] However, this reasoning cannot always be assumed to be sound, and if it is not, then democracy in every country is, in effect, indirectly endogenous to democracy in every other country. This is why instrumental variables are strongly recommended.

One example of diffusion research with V-Dem data is the paper by Coppedge et al. (2017), who specify multiple networks through which electoral democracy may diffuse: immediate geographic neighbors, military alliances, trading partners, and colonial networks. Each network requires its own W matrix, which is used to compute the expected change in each country's electoral democracy score in year t. Only one vector of predictions is required for each of the neighbors, alliances, and trading networks, but the authors construct more than 50 colonial network diffusion variables in order to allow colonial diffusion to vary by empire, pre- and postindependence, the direction of influence (colonizer to colony and colony to colonizer), and the type of colony (occupation, settlement, or forced settlement). All the diffusion variables are calculated as the gap between the source and target countries' electoral democracy scores, and the authors specify change in electoral democracy as the dependent variable. Thus, in these models, gaps between countries explain change within countries. The authors lag all diffusion variables two years, and include several domestic controls and two corrections for selection bias. Their estimates suggest that the neighbor network has the strongest influence, followed

---

[12] The R package "spdep" implements many techniques for analyzing spatial and temporal dependence for one W matrix at a time. Stata 15, released in June 2017, comes with a suite of commands specially designed for spatial and temporal analysis, including tools to construct network matrices for calculating diffusion variables. It makes it possible to test multiple Ws in the same model but cannot handle all of the country-year observations available in V-Dem data.

by alliances and trade. Colonial ties matter for the long-lasting and most recent colonial empires, but not for the most short-lived experiences with colonial rule. However, this paper does not incorporate the most advanced techniques for distinguishing between true country-to-country influence and spatially correlated errors due to omitted variables.

7.6 IMPLIED CAUSAL ASSUMPTIONS

Most of the aforementioned discussions on using V-Dem data for drawing inferences about causal relationships make three simplifying causal assumptions that can have important implications for the interpretation of results. First, they assume either causal homogeneity (that the same cause produces the same effect in all cases, regions, time periods, etc.) or that the estimated casual effect is true on average. More precisely, the implicit assumption is that unmodeled heterogeneity will result in estimates that can be interpreted as average effects. As we discuss below, there are cases where estimates cannot be interpreted as averages of effects, cases where estimates may be interpreted as weighted averages but where the weights are difficult to estimate and/or interpret, and many cases where it is unknown whether estimates can be interpreted as averages of any sort. Second, the above discussions assume implicitly that even in the absence of causal heterogeneity, statements such as "the effect of democracy" have some kind of meaningful interpretation. As we discuss below, from a strict causal inference perspective, it is unclear what such statements mean unless they can be expressed in terms of real or hypothetical interventions that could change democracy without having a separate effect on the outcome that democracy allegedly causes. Otherwise, we lack a good reason to expect that it is really democracy that is causing the outcome. Essentially there must be real or potential instruments. In the following subsections, we discuss the implications that this requirement has for the discussion of substantive significance. Third, the discussions above implicitly assume that all estimated effects refer to single-shot causes and not the effects of treatment histories. For example, an analysis that examines the effect of the number of years of being a democracy is implicitly analyzing the effect of the entire democratic history. When treatments are defined over time in this manner, then time-varying covariates can function simultaneously as posttreatment variables and pretreatment confounders. Blackwell and Glynn (2018) discusses this situation in detail.

7.6.1 Implications of Unmodeled Heterogeneity

The causal inference literature has devoted a great deal of attention to the implications of unmodeled heterogeneity for interpretation of findings. In some cases (e.g., marginally randomized experiments), estimated "effects" can be interpreted as estimates of average treatment effects, so that the interpretation of findings is more nuanced, but largely unchanged.[13]

In other cases, the estimated "effects" can be interpreted as weighted averages where the weights can be described. For example, in a cross-sectional additive regression, where the selection-on-observables assumption holds, the regression coefficient of interest can be interpreted as a weighted average of effects, where the weights are determined by the variance of the explanatory variable of interest within levels of the control variables. As shown in Aronow and Samii (2016), these weights can be estimated for each country in the analysis, so the weighted average can at least be characterized. In still other cases, results can be thought of as weighted averages, but the weights cannot be estimated for each country. For example, even in a cross-sectional instrumental variables analysis, with a randomized instrument, monotonicity of first stage effects, and an exclusion restriction holding (i.e., no direct effect of the instrument on the outcome), the results from a 2SLS analysis will produce a "local average treatment effect" (see Angrist and Pischke 2008 for a textbook treatment), where the meaning of "local" for each country cannot be estimated directly (although some information about what "local" means can be learned through kappa weighting, as in Abadie 2003).

Finally, for some analyses, estimates cannot even be thought of as weighted averages. For example, when first stage monotonicity does not hold for the aforementioned 2SLS analysis, the coefficient estimate can no longer be thought of as a weighted average because some of the "weights" will be negative.

The extension of these types of results to the more complicated analyses considered in Sections 7.4 (long panels) and 7.5 (spatial dependence) of this chapter, is to our knowledge, still incomplete. Therefore, when using these techniques one must either assume that unmodeled heterogeneity is minimal, or admit that the analysis is essentially exploratory in nature. For example, one might interpret the results as *robust dependencies* that may indicate the potential findings from a more explicit causal analysis.

7.6.2 Indirectly Manipulable and Latent Treatment Variables

The second assumption, that "effects" are well defined, will be important when V-Dem variables are used as the explanatory variable of interest rather than as the dependent variable. Many V-Dem variables are conceptualized as latent variables and are therefore not directly manipulable (even hypothetically). If

---

[13] The interpretation of standard errors, estimated standard errors, p-values, and confidence intervals in the presence of unmodeled heterogeneity is quite a bit more complicated and depends critically on a precise statement of the population of interest (e.g., see Gerber and Green 2012 for a textbook discussion in the experimental context). Although traditional approaches to the assessment of uncertainty can sometimes be seen as, at worst, conservative in simple contexts (again, see Gerber and Green 2012), the implications for some of the more complicated analyses considered in this chapter, is to our knowledge, an open area of research.

one wants to posit an effect for such a variable, we have to assume the existence of an instrument that could have indirectly manipulated the latent variable without directly affecting the outcome. As an example, consider an analysis where we estimate an "effect" of free and fair elections on the rate of economic growth. In order for the estimate from this regression to correspond to a causal effect, we must assume that there exists some form of intervention (maybe election monitors or the threat of sanctions) that could increase the fairness of elections without *directly* affecting economic growth.

Furthermore, we note that this requirement has implications for considerations of substantive significance. When assessing substantive significance, it is typical to consider changes in the explanatory/treatment variable of a standard deviation or sometimes changes from the minimum value to the maximum value. Given the requirement above, such changes only make sense if a hypothetical instrument could have changed the variable by a standard deviation while also not directly changing the outcome. If V-Dem variables are used as causal variables, then this assumption should be discussed explicitly. Alternatively, as with the issue of unmodeled causal heterogeneity, one could simply report findings as robust dependencies that are suggestive of potential causal relationships.

7.7 CONCLUSION

In general, the large size of the V-Dem data set, which reflects the large number of variables and countries, the long time series, and the thousands of Country Experts, creates new opportunities for quantitative analysis of the nature, causes, and consequences of democracy. Research with these data face the same kinds of challenges to rigorous inference and interpretation that all observational data projects face, but there are enhanced opportunities for using the abundant data and greater statistical power to get at causal mechanisms, check robustness, incorporate measurement uncertainty, rule out some confounders, and understand spatial dependence. The real pitfall in using V-Dem data would be continuing to run simplistic, familiar analysis rather than taking advantage of the new opportunities that it makes possible.

References

Abadie, Alberto. 2003. "Semiparametric Instrumental Variable Estimation of Treatment Response Models." *Journal of Econometrics* 113(2): 231–263.

Acemoglu, Daron, Simon Johnson, James A. Robinson, and Pierre Yared. 2005. "From Education to Democracy?" *American Economic Review* 95(2): 44–49.

Acemoglu, Daron, Simon Johnson, James E. Robinson, and Pierre Yared. 2008. "Income and Democracy." *American Economic Review* 98(3): 808–842.

Adcock, Robert, and David Collier. 2001. "Measurement Validity: A Shared Standard for Qualitative and Quantitative Research." *American Political Science Review* 95(3): 529–546.

Ake, Claude. 2000. *The Feasibility of Democracy in Africa*. Dakar: CODESRIA Books.

Almond, Gabriel, and Sidney Verba. (1963) 1989. *The Civic Culture: Political Attitudes in Five Western Democracies*. Newbury Park, CA: Sage.

Altman, David. 2011. *Direct Democracy Worldwide*. Cambridge, UK: Cambridge University Press.

Altman, David. 2017. "The Potential of Direct Democracy: A Global Measure (1900–2014)." *Social Indicators Research* 133(3): 1207–1227.

Altman, David, and Aníbal Pérez-Liñán. 2002. "Assessing the Quality of Democracy: Freedom, Competitiveness, and Participation in Eighteen Latin American Countries." *Democratization* 9(2): 85–100.

Alvarez, Michael, José Antônio Cheibub, Fernando Limongi, and Adam Przeworski. 1996. "Classifying Political Regimes." *Studies in Comparative International Development* 31(2): 3–36.

Alvarez, Michael, José Antônio Cheibub, Fernando Limongi, and Adam Przeworski. 1999. ACLP Political and Economic Database and ACLP Political and Economic Database Codebook.

Angrist, Joshua D., and Jörn-Steffen Pischke. *Mostly Harmless Econometrics: an Empiricist's Companion*. Princeton, NJ: Princeton University Press, 2008.

Anheier, Helmut, and Sally Stares. 2002. "Introducing the Global Civil Society Index." In *Global Civil Society 2002*, eds. Marlies Glasius, Mary Kaldor, and Helmut Anheier. Oxford: Oxford University Press.

Arellano, Manuel, and Stephen Bond. 1991. "Some Tests of Specification for Panel Data: Monte Carlo Evidence and an Application to Employment Equations." *Review of Economic Studies* 58(2): 277–297.

Aronow, Peter M., and Cyrus Samii. 2016. "Does Regression Produce Representative Estimates of Causal Effects?" *American Journal of Political Science* 60(1): 250–267.

Bäck, Hanna, and Axel Hadenius. 2008. "Democracy and State Capacity: Exploring a J-Shaped Relationship." *Governance* 21(1): 1–24.

Bagehot, Walter. (1867) 1963. *The English Constitution*. Ithaca, NY: Cornell University Press.

Bakker, Ryan, Catherine de Vries, Erica Edwards, Liesbet Hooghe, Seth Jolly, Gary Marks, Jonathan Polk, Jan Rovny, Marco Steenbergen, and Milada Vachudova. 2015. "Measuring Party Positions in Europe: The Chapel Hill Expert Survey Trend File, 1999–2010." *Party Politics* 21(1): 143–152.

Bakker, Ryan, Seth Jolly, Jonathan Polk, and Keith Poole. 2014. "The European Common Space: Extending the Use of Anchoring Vignettes." *The Journal of Politics* 76(4): 1089–1101.

Barber, Benjamin R. 1988. *The Conquest of Politics: Liberal Philosophy in Democratic Times*. Princeton, NJ: Princeton University Press.

Beck, Nathaniel, and Jonathan N. Katz. 2001. "Throwing Out the Baby with the Bath Water: A Comment on Green, Kim, and Yoon." *International Organization* 55(2): 187–195.

Beck, Nathaniel, and Jonathan N. Katz. 2011. "Modeling Dynamics in Time-Series–Cross-Section Political Economy Data." *Annual Review of Political Science* 14: 331–352.

Beetham, David. 1994. *Defining and Measuring Democracy*. Thousand Oaks, CA: Sage.

Beetham, David. 1999. *Democracy and Human Rights*. Cambridge: Polity Press.

Beetham, David, Sarah Bracking, Iain Kearton, and Stuart Weir, eds. 2001. *International IDEA Handbook on Democracy Assessment*. The Hague: Kluge Academic.

Beitz, Charles R. 1990. *Political Equality: An Essay on Democratic Theory*. Princeton, NJ: Princeton University Press.

Behmer, Markus. 2009. "Measuring Media Freedom: Approaches of International Comparison." In *Press Freedom in Europe: Concepts and Conditions*, eds. A. Czepek, M. Hellwig, and Eva Novak. Bristol: Intellect.

Berg-Schlosser, Dirk. 2004. "Indicators of Democracy and Good Governance in Africa: A Critical Appraisal." *Acta Politica* 39(3): 248–278.

Bernhard, Michael, Fernando Bizzarro, Michael Coppedge, John Gerring, Allen Hicken, Carl Henrik Knutsen, Staffan I. Lindberg, and Svend-Erik Skaaning. 2018. "Party Strength and Economic Growth." *World Politics* 70(2): 275–320.

Bernhard, Michael, Christopher Reenock, and Timothy Nordstrom. 2004. "The Legacy of Western Overseas Colonialism on Democratic Survival." *International Studies Quarterly* 48(1): 225–250.

Bernhard, Michael, Timothy Nordstrom, and Christopher Reenock. 2001. "Economic Performance, Institutional Intermediation, and Democratic Breakdown." *Journal of Politics* 63: 775–803.

Bernhard, Michael, Eitan Tzelgov, Dong-Joon Jung, Michael Coppedge, and Staffan I. Lindberg. 2017. "Making Embedded Knowledge Transparent: How the V-Dem Dataset Opens New Vistas in Civil Society Research." *Perspectives on Politics* 15(2): 342–360.

Bernstein, Eduard. [1899] 1961. *Evolutionary Socialism: A Criticism and Affirmation*. New York: Schocken Books.

Bertelsmann Stiftung. 2014. Bertelsmann Transformation Index 2003–2014 Scores.

Bertelsmann Stiftung. 2015. Bertelsmann Stiftung Transformation Index (BTI), 2003–2016. [online] Available at: www.bti-project.org/en/index [Accessed February 15, 2017].

Bessette, James M. 1980. "Deliberative Democracy: The Majority Principle in Republican Government." In *How Democratic Is the Constitution?*, eds. Robert A. Goldwin and William A. Schambra. Washington, DC: American Enterprise Institute.

Birch, Sarah. 2011. *Electoral Malpractice*. New York: Oxford University Press.

Bizzarro, Fernando, John Gerring, Carl Henrik Knutsen, Allen Hicken, Michael Bernhard, Svend-Erik Skaaning, Michael Coppedge, and Staffan I. Lindberg. 2018. "Party Strength and Economic Growth." *World Politics* 70(2): 275–320.

Bizzarro, Fernando, Daniel Pemstein, and Michael Coppedge. 2016. "Incorporating V-Dems Uncertainty Estimates in Regression Analysis." Unpublished manuscript.

Blackwell, Matthew, and Adam N. Glynn. 2018. "How to Make Causal Inferences with Time-Series Cross-Sectional Data under Selection on Observables." *American Political Science Review* 112(4): 1067–1082.

Blundell, Richard, and Stephen Bond. 1998. "Initial Conditions and Moment Restrictions in Dynamic Panel Data Models." *Journal of Econometrics* 87(1): 115–143.

Bohman, James. 1998. "The Coming of Age of Deliberative Democracy." *The Journal of Political Philosophy* 6(4): 400–425.

Boix, Carles. 2003. *Democracy and Redistribution*. Cambridge: Cambridge University Press.

Boix, Carles. 2011. "Democracy, Development, and the International System." *American Political Science Review* 105(4): 809–828.

Boix, Carles, and Susan C. Stokes. 2003. "Endogenous Democratization." *World Politics* 55(4): 517–549.

Boix, Carles, Michael K. Miller, and Sebastian Rosato. 2013. "A Complete Data Set of Political Regimes, 1800–2007." *Comparative Political Studies* 46(12): 1523–1554.

Bollen, Kenneth A. 1980. "Issues in the Comparative Measurement of Political Democracy." *American Sociological Review* 45(3): 370–390.

Bollen, Kenneth A. 1986. "Sample Size and Bentler and Bonett's Nonnormed Fit Index." *Psychometrika* 51: 375–377.

Bollen, Kenneth A. 1989. *Structural Equations with Latent Variables*. Hoboken, NJ: John Wiley.

Bollen, Kenneth A. 1993. "Liberal Democracy: Validity and Method Factors in Cross-National Measures." *American Journal of Political Science* 37(4): 1207–1230.

Bollen, Kenneth A. 2011. "Evaluating Effect, Composite, and Causal Indicators in Structural Equation Models." *MIS Quarterly* 35(2): 359–372.

Bollen, Kenneth A., and Robert W. Jackman. 1985. "Political Discourse and the Size Distribution of Income." *American Sociological Review* 46(5): 651–659.

Bollen, Kenneth A., and Pamela Paxton. 2000. "Subjective Measures of Liberal Democracy." *Comparative Political Studies* 33(1): 58–86.

Bowman, Kirk, Fabrice Lehoucq, and James Mahoney. 2005. "Measuring Political Democracy: Case Expertise, Data Adequecy, and Central America." *Comparative Political Studies* 38(8): 939–970.

Brinks, Daniel, and Michael Coppedge. 2006. "Diffusion Is No Illusion." *Comparative Political Studies* 39(4): 463–489.

Burkhart, Ross E., and Michael S. Lewis-Beck. 1994. "Comparative Democracy: The Economic Development Thesis." *American Political Science Review* 88(4): 903–910.

Center for Civil Society Studies. 2004. *Johns Hopkins Global Civil Society Index*. [online] Center for Civil Society Studies. Available at: http://ccss.jhu.edu/wpcontent/ uploads/downloads/2011/12/Civil-Society-Index_FINAL_11.15.2011.pdf [Accessed February 25, 2017].

Chambers, Simone. 2003. "Deliberative Democratic Theory." *Annual Review of Political Science* 6(June): 307–326.

Charron, Nicholas, and Victor Lapuente. 2010. "Does Democracy Produce Quality of Government?" *European Journal of Political Research* 49(4): 443–470.

Cheibub, José A., Jennifer Gandhi, and James Vreeland. 2010. "Democracy and Dictatorship Revisited." *Public Choice* 143(1–2): 67–101.

Christiane, A. et al. 2006. *Development Centre Studies Uses and Abuses of Governance Indicators*. Paris OECD Publishing.

Cingranelli, David, and David Richards. 2004. "The Cingranelli-Richards (CIRI) Human Rights Database Coding Manuel." Available at: http://ciri.binghamton.edu /documentation/ciri_coding_guide.pdf.

Cingranelli, David L., David L. Richards, and K. Chad Clay. 2014. "The CIRI Human Rights Dataset." Version 2014.04.14. www.humanrightsdata.com.

CIVICUS. 2013. *The CIVICUS 2013 enabling environment index*. [online] CIVICUS. Available at: www.civicus.org/downloads/2013EEI%20REPORT.pdf [Accessed February 17, 2017].

CIVICUS. 2017. *The CIVICUS civil society index*. [online] CIVICUS. Available at: http://civicus.org/index.php/what-we-do/knowledge-analysis/civil-society-index [Accessed February 17, 2017].

Clinton, Joshua D., and David E. Lewis. 2008. "Expert Opinion, Agency Characteristics, and Agency Preferences." *Political Analysis* 16(1): 3–20.

Collier, David, and Steven Levitsky. 1997. "Democracy with Adjectives: Conceptual Innovation in Comparative Research." *World Politics* 49(3): 430–451.

Collier, David, Fernando Daniel Hidalgo, and Andra Olivia Maciuceanu. 2006. "Essentially Contested Contests: Debates and Applications." *Journal of Political Ideologies* 11(3): 211–246.

Collier, Ruth Berins, and David Collier. 1991. *Shaping the Political Arena: Critical Junctures, the Labor Movement, and Regime Dynamics in Latin America*. Princeton, NJ: Princeton University Press.

Coppedge, Michael. 1999. "Thickening Thin Concepts and Theories: Combining Large N and Small in Comparative Politics." *Comparative Politics* 31(4): 465–476.

Coppedge, Michael. 2007. "Thickening Thin Concepts: Issues in Large-N Data Generation." In *Regimes and Democracy in Latin America: Theories and Methods*, ed. Gerardo L. Munck. Oxford: Oxford University Press.

Coppedge, Michael. 2017. "Rethinking Consensus vs. Majoritarian Democracy." Paper presented at the annual meeting of the American Political Science Association, San Francisco, August 31–September 3.

Coppedge, Michael, Angel Alvarez, and Claudia Maldonado. 2008. "Two Persistent Dimensions of Democracy: Contestation and Inclusiveness." *Journal of Politics* 70(3): 335–350.

Coppedge, Michael, Benjamin Denison, and Lucía Tiscornia. 2017. "Varieties of Democratic Diffusion: Colonial, Alliance, and Neighbor Networks." Paper presented at the conference on Varieties of Democracy in Central and Eastern Europe: Regional and Global Perspectives, Central European University, Budapest, March 9.

Coppedge, Michael, and John Gerring, with David Altman, Michael Bernhard, Steven Fish, Allen Hicken, Matthew Kroenig, Staffan I. Lindberg, Kelly McMann, Pamela Paxton, Holli A. Semetko, Svend-Erik Skaaning, Jeffrey Staton, and Jan Teorell. 2011. "Conceptualizing and Measuring Democracy: A New Approach." *Perspectives on Politics* 9(2): 247–67.

Coppedge, Michael, John Gerring, Staffan I. Lindberg, Svend-Erik Skaaning, and Jan Teorell. 2015. "Varieties of Democracy: Comparisons and Contrasts with Other Measurement Projects." *Varieties of Democracy (V-Dem) Project.*

Coppedge, Michael, John Gerring, Staffan I. Lindberg, Jan Teorell, David Altman, Michael Bernhard, M. Steven Fish, Adam Glynn, Allen Hicken, Carl Henrik Knutsen, Kyle Marquardt, Kelly McMann, Pamela Paxton, Daniel Pemstein, Megan Reif, Svend-Erik Skaaning, Jeffrey Staton, Eitan Tzelgov, Yi-tang Wang, and Briggitte Zimmerman. 2016a. Varieties of Democracy Codebook v5. Technical report. Varieties of Democracy Project: Project Documentation Paper Series.

Coppedge, Michael, Staffan I. Lindberg, Svend-Erik Skaaning, and Jan Teorell. 2016b. "Measuring High Level Democratic Principles using the V-Dem Data." *International Political Science Review* 37(5): 580–593.

Coppedge, Michael, and Wolfgang H. Reinicke. 1990. "Measuring Polyarchy." *Studies in Comparative International Development* 25(1): 51–72.

Cunningham, Frank. 2002. *Theories of Democracy: A Critical Introduction.* London: Routledge.

Dahl, Robert A. 1956. *A Preface to Democratic Theory.* Chicago: University of Chicago Press.

Dahl, Robert A. 1971. *Polyarchy: Participation and Opposition.* New Haven, CT: Yale University Press.

Dahl, Robert A. 1982. *Dilemmas of Pluralist Democracy: Autonomy vs. Control.* New Haven, CT: Yale University Press.

Dahl, Robert A. 1985. *A Preface to Economic Democracy.* Berkeley: University of California Press.

Dahl, Robert A. 1989. *Democracy and Its Critics.* New Haven, CT: Yale University Press.

Dahl, Robert A. 1998. *On Democracy.* New Haven, CT: Yale University Press.

Dahl, Robert A. 2006. *On Political Equality.* New Haven, CT: Yale University Press.

Dahlström, Carl, Victor Lapuente, and Jan Teorell. 2012. "The Merit of Meritocratization: Politics, Bureaucracy, and the Institutional Deterrents of Corruption." *Political Research Quarterly* 65(3): 656–668.

Dahlström, C., V. Lapuente, and J. Teorell. 2012. "Public Administration around the World." In *Good Government: The Relevance of Political Science*, eds. S. Holmberg and B. Rothstein. London: Edward Elgar.

Dahlum, Sirianne, and Carl Henrik Knutsen. 2017a. "Democracy by Demand? Reinvestigating the Effect of Self-Expression Values on Political Regime Type." *British Journal of Political Science* 47(2): 437–461.

Dahlum, Sirianne, and Carl Henrik Knutsen. 2017b. "What Counts as Evidence? Panel Data and the Empirical Evaluation of Revised Modernization Theory." *British Journal of Political Science* 47(2): 473–478.

Davenport, Christian. 2007. "State Repression and the Tyrannical Peace." *Journal of Peace Research* 44(4): 485–504.

Desbordes, Rodolphe, and Gary Koops. 2016. "Should We Care about the Uncertainty around Measures of Political-Economic Development?" *Journal of Comparative Economics* 44(3): 752–763.

Diamond, Larry, Jonathan Hartlyn, Juan J. Linz, and Seymour Martin Lipset, eds. 1989. *Democracy in Developing Countries: Latin America.* Boulder, CO: Lynne Rienner.

Diamond, Larry. 1999. *Developing Democracy: Toward Consolidation.* Baltimore: Johns Hopkins University Press.

Diamond, Larry. 2002. "Thinking about Hybrid Regimes." *Journal of Democracy* 13 (2): 21–35.

Diamond, Larry, and Leonardo Morlino, eds. 2005. *Assessing the Quality of Democracy.* Baltimore: Johns Hopkins University Press.

Diggle, Peter, Peter J. Diggle, Patrick Heagerty, Patrick J. Heagerty, Kung-Yee Liang, and Scott Zeger. 2002. *Analysis of Longitudinal Data.* Oxford: Oxford University Press.

Dixon, Robert G. 1968. *Democratic Representation: Reapportionment in Law and Politics.* New York: Oxford University Press.

Donchev, Dilyan, and Gergely Ujhelyi. 2014. "What Do Corruption Indices Measure?" *Economics and Politics* 26(2): 309–331.

Dryzek, John S. 2002. *Deliberative Democracy and Beyond: Liberals, Critics, Contestations.* Oxford: Oxford University Press.

Dryzek, John S. 2010. "Rhetoric in Democracy: A Systemic Appreciation." *Political Theory* 38(3): 319–339.

Dunn, John. 2005. *Setting the People Free: The Story of Democracy.* London: Atlantic Books.

Duverger, Maurice. 1954. *Political Parties: Their Organization and Activity in the Modern State.* New York: John Wiley.

Eckstein, Harry, and Ted Robert Gurr. 1975. *Patterns of Authority: A Structural Basis for Political Inquiry.* New York: John Wiley.

Elgie, Robert. 1998. "The Classification of Democratic Regime Types: Conceptual Ambiguity and Contestable Assumptions." *European Journal of Political Research* 33(2): 219–238.

Elkins, Zachary. 2000. "Graduations of Democracy? Empirical Tests of Alternative Conceptualizations." *American Journal of Political Science* 44(2): 293–300.

Elster, Jon. 1998. *Deliberative Democracy.* Cambridge: Cambridge University Press.

Fariss, Christopher J. 2014. "Respect for Human Rights Has Improved over Time: Modeling the Changing Standard of Accountability." *American Political Science Review* 108(2): 297–318.

Finer, Samuel E., ed. 1975. *Adversary Politics and Electoral Reform.* London: Anthony Wigram.

Finkel, Steven E., Anibal Pérez-Liñan, and Mitchell A. Seligson. 2007. "The Effects of U.S. Foreign Assistance on Democracy Building, 1990–2003." *World Politics* 59(3): 404–439.

Fish, M. Steven, and Matthew Kroenig. 2009. *The Handbook of National Legislatures: A Global Survey.* New York: Cambridge University Press.

Fishkin, James S. 1991. *Democracy and Deliberation: New Directions for Democratic Reform.* New Haven, CT: Yale University Press.

Foa, Roberto, and Jeffrey C. Tanner. 2012. "Methodology of the Indices of Social Development." Working Paper No. 2012-4. Rotterdam, Erasmus University, International Institute of Social Studies.

Ford, Henry Jones. [1898] 1967. *The Rise and Growth of American Politics: A Sketch of Constitutional Development*. New York: Da Capo Press.

Foweraker, Joe, and Roman Krznaric. 2000. "Measuring Liberal Democratic Performance: An Empirical and Conceptual Critique." *Political Studies* 48(4): 759–787.

Franzese, Robert J., Jr., and Jude C. Hays. 2008. "Interdependence in Comparative Politics: Substance, Theory, Empirics, Substance." *Comparative Politics* 41(4–5): 742–780.

Freeden, Michael. 1978. *The New Liberalism: An Ideology of Social Reform*. Oxford: Clarendon Press.

Freedom House. 2012. *Nations in Transit 2012: Methodology*. [online] Freedom House. Available at: https://freedomhouse.org/report/nations-transit-2012/methodology [Accessed February 15, 2017].

Fukuyama, Francis. 2014. *Political Order and Political Decay: From the Industrial Revolution to the Globalization of Democracy*. New York: Farrar, Straus, and Giroux.

Fuller, L. L. 1969. *The Morality of Law*. New Haven, CT: Yale University Press.

Gallie, W. B. 1956. "Essentially Contested Concepts." *Proceedings of the Aristotelian Society* 56: 167–198.

Galtung, Fredrik. 2006. "Measuring the Immeasurable: Boundaries and Functions of (Macro) Corruption Indices." In *Measuring Corruption*, eds. Charles J. G. Sampford, Arthur Shacklock, Carmel Connors, and Fredrik Galtung. Aldershot, UK: Ashgate.

Gasiorowski, Mark J. 1996. "An Overview of the Political Regime Change Dataset." *Comparative Political Studies* 29(4): 469–483.

Gassebner, Martin, Michael J. Lamla, and James R. Vreeland. 2009. "Extreme Bounds of Democracy." Working Paper 224. Zurich: KOF Swiss Economic Institute.

Geddes, Barbara, Joseph Wright, and Erica Frantz. 2014. "Autocratic Breakdown and Regime Transitions: A New Data Set." *Perspectives on Politics* 12(2): 313–331.

Gelman, Andrew, and Donald B. Rubin. 1992. "Inference from Iterative Simulation Using Multiple Sequences." *Statistical Science* 7: 457–511.

Gerber, Alan S., and Donald P. Green. 2012. *Field Experiments: Design, Analysis, and Interpretation*. New York: W. W. Norton.

Gerring, John. 2005. "Minor Parties in Plurality Electoral Systems." *Party Politics* 11(1): 79–107.

Gerring, John. 2012. *Social Science Methodology: A Unified Framework*. Cambridge: Cambridge University Press.

Gerring, John, and Rose McDermott. 2007. "An Experimental Template for Case Study Research." *American Journal of Political Science* 51(3): 688–670.

Gerring, John, Phillip Bond, William Barndt, and Carola Moreno. 2005. "Democracy and Economic Development: A Historical Perspective." *World Politics* 57(3): 323–364.

Gingerich, Daniel W. 2013. "Governance Indicators and the Level of Analysis Problem: Empirical Findings from South America." *British Journal of Political Science* 43(3): 505–540.

Gleditsch, Kristian S., and Michael D. Ward. 1997. "Double Take: A Reexamination of Democracy and Autocracy in Modern Politics." *Journal of Conflict Resolution* 41(3): 361–382.

Gleditsch, Kristian Skrede, and Michael D. Ward. 2006. "Diffusion and the International Context of Democratization." *International Organization* 60(4): 911–933.

Goertz, Gary. 2006. *Social Science Concepts: A User's Guide.* Princeton, NJ: Princeton University Press.

Goodin, Robert E. 1996. "Institutionalizing the Public Interest: The Defense of Deadlock and Beyond." *American Political Science Review* 90(2): 331–343.

Goodnow, Frank J. 1900. *Politics and Administration: A Study in Government.* New York: Macmillan.

Gordon, Scott. 1999. *Controlling the State: Constitutionalism from Ancient Athens to Today.* Cambridge, MA: Harvard University Press.

Gutmann, Amy, and Dennis Thompson. 1998. *Democracy and Disagreement.* Cambridge, MA: Belknap Press.

Habermas, Jürgen. [1981] 1987. *The Theory of Communicative Action.* Trans. Thomas A. McCarthy. Boston: Beacon Press.

Habermas, Jürgen. [1992] 1996. *Between Facts and Norms: Contributions to a Discourse Theory of Law and Democracy.* Trans. William Rehg. Cambridge, MA: MIT Press.

Hadenius, Axel. 1992. *Democracy and Development.* Cambridge: Cambridge University Press.

Hadenius, Axel, and Jan Teorell. 2005. "Assessing Alternative Indices of Democracy," Committee on Concepts and Methods Working Papers Series, August.

Hadenius, Axel, and Jan Teorell. 2005. "Cultural and Economic Prerequisites of Democracy: Reassessing Recent Evidence." *Studies in Comparative International Development* 39(4): 87–106.

Hadenius, Axel, and Jan Teorell. 2007. "Pathways from Authoritarianism." *Journal of Democracy* 18(1): 143–157.

Hamilton, Alexander, James Madison, and John Jay. 1992. *The Federalist Papers.* Cutchogue, NY: Buccaneer Books.

Hannan, Michael T., and Glenn R. Carroll. 1981. "Dynamics of Formal Political Structure: An Event-History Analysis." *American Sociological Review* 46: 19–35.

Hansen, Mogens Herman. 1991. *The Athenian Democracy in the Age of Demosthenes: Structure, Principal, and Ideology.* Oxford: Blackwell.

Hansen, Mogens Herman. 1989. "Athenian Democracy." *Classical Review* 39(1): 69–76.

Hartman, Erin, and F. Daniel Hidalgo. 2018. "An Equivalence Approach to Balance and Placebo Tests." *American Journal of Political Science* 62(4): 1000–1013.

Hawken, Angela, and Gerardo L. Munck. 2009a. "Measuring Corruption: A Critical Assessment and a Proposal." In *Perspectives on Corruption and Human Development,* eds. Anuradha K. Rajivan and Ramesh Gampat. New Delhi: Macmillan.

Hawken, Angela, and Gerardo L. Munck. 2009b. "Do You Know Your Data? Measurement Validity in Corruption Research." Unpublished transcript.

Heid, Benedikt, Julian Langer, and Mario Larch. 2012. "Income and Democracy: Evidence from System GMM Estimates." *Economics Letters* 116(2): 166–169.

Held, David. 2006. *Models of Democracy.* Redwood City, CA: Stanford University Press.

Heller, Hermann. 1930. *Rechtsstaat oder Diktatur?* Tübingen: Mohr.

Holmes, Oliver Wendell, and Sheldon M. Novick, ed. 1995. *The Collected Works of Justice Holmes: Complete Public Writings and Judicial Opinions of Oliver Wendell Holmes.* Chicago: University of Chicago Press.

Huntington, Samuel P. 1991. *The Third Wave: Democratization in the Late Twentieth Century*. Norman: University of Oklahoma Press.

Inglehart, Ronald, and Christian Welzel. 2005. *Modernization, Cultural Change, and Democracy: The Human Development Sequence*. New York: Cambridge University Press.

International Institute of Social Sciences. 2015a. "Indices of Social Development." Available at: www.indsocdev.org/faq.html [Accessed April 25, 2018].

International Institute of Social Sciences. 2015b. "Indices of Civic Activism." Available at: www.indsocdev.org/faq.html [Accessed April 25, 2018].

Jackman, Robert W. 1973. "On the Relation of Economic Development to Democratic Performance." *American Journal of Political Science* 17(3): 611–621.

Jackman, Simon. 2004. "Bayesian Analysis for Political Research." *Annual Review of Political Science* 7(1): 483–505.

Jackman, Simon. 2004. "What Do We Learn from Graduate Admissions Committees? A Multiple Rater, Latent Variable Model, with Incomplete Discrete and Continuous Indicators." *Political Analysis* 12(4): 400–424.

Johnson, Valen E., and James H. Albert. 1999. *Ordinal Data Modeling*. New York: Springer.

Karl, Terry. 1986. "Imposing Consent? Electoralism versus Democratization in El Salvador." In *Elections and Democratization in Latin America*, eds. Paul W. Drake and Eduardo Silva. San Diego, CA: Center for Iberian and Latin American Studies, UCSD.

Kaufmann, Daniel, and Aart Kraay. 2002. "Growth without Governance." *Economia* 3 (1): 169–229.

Kelley, Judith G. 2013. *Monitoring Democracy: When International Election Observation Works, and Why It Often Fails*. Princeton, NJ: Princeton University Press.

Kelsen, Hans. 1930. *Der Staat als Integration: Eine Prinzipielle Auseinandersetzung*. Vienna: Springer.

Kennedy, Jonathan. 2014. "International Crime Victims Survey." *The Encyclopedia of Criminology and Criminal Justice*.

Keyssar, Alexander. 2000. *The Right to Vote: The Contested History of Democracy in the United States*. New York: Basic Books.

King, Gary, and Jonathan Wand. 2007. "Comparing Incomparable Survey Responses: Evaluating and Selecting Anchoring Vignettes." *Political Analysis* 15(1): 46–66.

Knack, Stephen. 2007. "Measuring Corruption: A Critique of Indicators in Eastern Europe and Central Asia." *Journal of Public Policy* 27(3): 255–291.

Knutsen, Carl Henrik, John Gerring, Svend-Erik Skaaning, Jan Teorell, Matthew Maguire, Staffan I. Lindberg, and Michael Coppedge. 2019. "Economic Development and Democracy: An Electoral Connection." *European Journal of Political Research* 58(1): 292–314.

Knutsen, Carl Henrik, Jan Teorell, Tore Wig, Agnes Cornell, John Gerring, Haakon Gjerløw, Svend-Erik Skaaning, Daniel Ziblatt, Kyle Marquardt, Daniel Pemstein, and Brigitte Seim. 2018. "Introducing the Historical Varieties of Democracy Dataset: Patterns and Determinants of Democratization in the Long 19th Century." *Journal of Peace Research* 56(3): 440–451.

Lall, Ranjit. 2016. "How Multiple Imputation Makes a Difference." *Political Analysis* 24(4): 414–433.

Lambsdorff, J. G. 2007. "The Methodology of the Corruption Perceptions Index 2007." *Internet Center for Corruption Research* 12.

Leeson, Peter T., and Andrea M. Dean. 2009. "The Democratic Domino Theory: An Empirical Investigation." *American Journal of Political Science* 53(3): 533–551.

Lehoucq, Fabrice. 2003. "Electoral Fraud: Causes, Types, and Consequences." *Annual Review of Political Science* 18(6): 233–256.

Levitsky, Steven, and Lucan A. Way. 2010. *Competitive Authoritarianism: Hybrid Regimes after the Cold War*. New York: Cambridge University Press.

Lieberman, Evan S. 2005. "Nested Analysis as a Mixed-Method Strategy for Comparative Research." *American Political Science Review* 99(3): 435–452.

Lijphart, Arend. 1999. *Patterns of Democracy: Government Forms and Performance in Thirty-Six Countries*. New Haven, CT: Yale University Press.

Lindbolm, Charles E. 1977. *Politics and Markets: The World's Political-Economic Systems*. New York: Basic Books.

Lindstädt, René, Sven-Oliver Proksch, and Jonathan B. Slapin. 2015. "Assessing the Measurement of Policy Positions in Expert Surveys." Paper presented at the annual meeting of the American Political Science Association, San Francisco.

Lindstädt, René, Sven-Oliver Proksch, and Jonathan B. Slapin. 2016. "When Experts Disagree: Response Aggregation and Its Consequences in Expert Surveys." Working Paper. Available at: https://renelindstaedt.com/work-in-progress/.

Linzer, Drew, and Jeffrey K. Staton. 2015. "A Global Measure of Judicial Independence, 1948–2012." *Journal of Law and Courts* 3(2): 223–256.

Lipset, Seymour Martin. 1959. "Some Social Requisites of Democracy: Economic Development and Political Legitimacy." *American Political Science Review* 53(1): 69–105.

Lipset, Seymour Martin. 1960. *Political Man: The Social Bases of Politics*. Garden City, NY: Doubleday.

Locke, John. 1963. *Two Treatises of Government*. Cambridge: Cambridge University Press.

Lowell, Lawrence A. 1889. *Essays on Government*. Boston: Houghton Mifflin.

Lowi, Theodore J. 1969. *The End of Liberalism: The Second Republic of the United States*. New York: W. W. Norton.

Luebbuert, Gregory M. 1987. "Social Foundations of Political Order in Interwar Europe." *World Politics* 39(4): 449–478.

Lührmann, Anna, Marcus Tannerberg, and Staffan I. Lindberg. 2018. "Regimes of the World (RoW): Opening New Avenues for the Comparative Study of Political Regimes." *Politics and Governance* 6(1): 60–77.

Macpherson, C. B. 1977. *The Life and Times of Liberal Democracy*. Oxford: Oxford University Press.

Mainwaring, Scott, Daniel Brinks, and Aníbal Pérez Liñán. 2001. "Classifying Political Regimes in Latin America, 1945–1999." *Studies in Comparative International Development* 36(1): 37–65.

Mainwaring, Scott, and Aníbal Pérez Liñán. 2013. *Democracies and Dictatorships in Latin America: Emergence, Survival, and Fall*. New York: Cambridge University Press.

Mansbridge, Jane J. 1983. *Beyond Adversary Democracy*. Chicago: Chicago University Press.

Marquardt, Kyle, and Daniel Pemstein. 2018. "Estimating Latent Traits from Expert Surveys: An Analysis of Sensitivity to Data Generating Process." V-Dem Working Paper No. 83.

Marquardt, Kyle, and Daniel Pemstein. Forthcoming. "IRT Models for Expert-Coded Panel Data." *Political Analysis.*

Marquardt, K. L., D. Pemstein, C. Sanhueza Petrarca, B. Seim, S. L. Wilson, M. Bernhard, M. Coppedge, and S. I. Lindberg. 2017. "Experts, Coders, and Crowds: An Analysis of Substitutability." V-Dem Working Paper Series 2017, 53.

Marshall, Monty G., T. D. Gurr, and K. Jaggers. 2016. *Polity IV Project. Political Regime Characteristics and Transitions, 1800–2015. Dataset Users' Manual. Center for Systemic Peace.*

Martin, Andrew D., and Kevin M. Quinn. 2002. "Dynamic Ideal Point Estimation via Markov Chain Monte Carlo for the U.S. Supreme Court, 1953–1999." *Political Analysis* 10(2): 134–153.

Martin, Andrew D., Kevin M. Quinn, and Jong Hee Park. 2011. MCMCpack: Markov Chain Monte Carlo in R. Software.

Martínez i Coma, Ferran, and Carolien van Ham. 2015. "Can Experts Judge Elections? Testing the Validity of Expert Judgments in Measuring Election Integrity." *European Journal of Political Research* 54(2): 305–325.

McConnell, Grant. 1966. *Private Power and American Democracy.* New York: Alfred A. Knopf.

McHenry, Dean E., Jr. 2000. "Quantitative Measures of Democracy in Africa: An Assessment." *Democratization* 7(2): 168–185.

McMann, Kelly M. 2006. *Economic Autonomy and Democracy: Hybrid Regimes in Russia and Kyrgyzstan.* Cambridge: Cambridge University Press.

McMann, Kelly, Daniel Pemstein, Jan Teorell, and Brigitte Zimmerman. 2016. "Complementary Strategies of Validation: Assessing the Validity of V-Dem Corruption Index and Indicators." Varieties of Democracy Institute Working Paper.

McMann, Kelly, Daniel Pemstein, Brigitte Seim, Jan Teorell, and Staffan Lindberg. 2016. "Strategies of Validation: Accessing the Varieties of Democracy Corruption Data." V-Dem Institute Working Paper Series 2016:23, The Varieties of Democracy Institute, University of Gothenburg.

Melton, James, Stephen Meserve, and Daniel Pemstein. 2014. "Time to Model the Rating Process: Dynamic Latent Variable Models for Regime Characteristics." Paper presented at the annual meeting of the American Political Science Association, Washington, DC.

Meyer, Thomas. 2007. *The Theory of Social Democracy.* Cambridge: Polity Press.

Middleton, Joel A., Marc A. Scott, Ronli Diakow, and Jennifer L. Hill. 2016. "Bias Amplification and Bias Unmasking." *Political Analysis* 24(3): 307–323.

Miller, Michael K. 2012. "Economic Development, Violent Leader Removal, and Democratization." *American Journal of Political Science* 56(4): 1002–1020.

Montesquieu, Charles de Secondat. 1989. *Montesquieu: The Spirit of the Laws.* Eds. Anne M. Cohler, Basia Carolyn Miller, and Harold Samuel Stone. Cambridge: Cambridge University Press.

Montinola, Gabriella R., and Robert W. Jackman. 2002. "Sources of Corruption: A Cross-Country Study." *British Journal of Political Science* 32(1): 147–170.

Møller, Jørgen, and Svend-Erik Skaaning. 2010. "Beyond the Radical Delusion: Conceptualizing and Measuring Democracy and Non-Democracy." *International Political Science Review* 31(3): 261–283.

Møller, Jørgen, and Svend-Erik Skaaning. 2011. *Requisites of Democracy: Conceptualization, Measurement, and Explanation.* London: Routledge.

Møller, Jørgen, and Svend-Erik Skaaning. 2013. "Regime Types and Democratic Sequencing." *Journal of Democracy* 24(1): 142–156.

Munck, Gerardo L. 2009. *Measuring Democracy: A Bridge between Scholarship and Politics*. Baltimore: Johns Hopkins University Press.

Munck, Gerardo L. 2016. "What Is Democracy? A Reconceptualization of the Quality of Democracy." *Democratization* 23(1): 1–26.

Munck, Gerardo L., and Jay Verkuilen. 2002. "Conceptualizing and Measuring Democracy: Evaluating Alternative Indices." *Comparative Politics Studies* 35 (1): 5–34.

National Research Council, Committee on Evaluation of USAID Democracy Assistance Programs. 2008. *Improving Democracy Assistance: Building Knowledge through Evaluations and Research*. Washington, DC: National Academies Press.

Neumayer, Eric, and T. Plümper. 2016. "W." *Political Science Research and Methods* 4 (1): 175–193.

Nickell, Stephen. 1981. "Biases in Dynamic Models with Fixed Effects." *Econometrica: Journal of the Econometric Society* 1981: 1417–1426.

North, Douglass. 1993. "Institutions and Credible Commitment." *Journal of Institutional and Theoretical Economics* 149(1): 11–23.

Nussbaum, Martha C. 2011. *Creating Capabilities: The Human Development Approach*. Cambridge, MA: Harvard University Press.

Ober, Josiah. 1989. *Mass and Elite in Democratic Athens: Rhetoric, Ideology, and the Power of the People*. Princeton, NJ: Princeton University Press.

O'Donnell, Guillermo. 1994. "Delegative Democracy." *Journal of Democracy* 5(1): 55–69.

O'Donnell, Guillermo. 1998. "Horizontal Accountability in New Democracies." *Journal of Democracy* 9(3): 112–126.

O'Donnell, Guillermo. 2001. "Law, Democracy, and Comparative Politics." *Studies in Comparative International Development* 36(1): 7–36.

O'Donnell, Guillermo. 2007. *Dissonances: Democratic Critiques of Democracy*. Notre Dame, IN: University of Notre Dame Press.

O'Donnell, Guillermo, Philippe Schmitter, and Laurence Whitehead. 1986. *Transitions from Authoritarian Rule: Prospects for Democracy*. Baltimore: Johns Hopkins University Press.

Offe, Claus, and Ulrich Preuss. 1991. "Democratic Institutions and Moral Resources." In *Political Theory Today*, ed. David Held. Palo Alto, CA: Stanford University Press.

O'Loughlin, J., M. D. Ward, C. L. Lofdahl, J. S. Cohen, D. S. Brown, and D. Reilly. 1998. "The Diffusion of Democracy, 1946–1994." *Annals of the Association of American Geographers* 88: 545–574.

Park, Jong Hee. 2013. "A Change-Point Approach to Intervention Analysis Using Bayesian Inference." Working paper. Seoul National University.

Pateman, Carole. 1976. *Participation and Democratic Theory*. Cambridge: Cambridge University Press.

Paxton, Pamela. 2000. "Women's Suffrage in the Measurement of Democracy: Problems of Operationalization." *Studies in Comparative International Development* 35(3): 92–111.

Pemstein, Daniel, Kyle L. Marquardt, Eitan Tzelgov, Yi-ting Wang, and Farhad Miri. 2016. "The V-Dem Measurement Model: Latent Variable Analysis for Cross-National and Cross-Temporal Expert-Coded Data." The Varieties of Democracy Institute, University of Gothenburg, V-Dem Working Paper 2015:21.

Pemstein, Daniel, Kyle L. Marquardt, Eitan Tzelgov, Yi-ting Wang, Joshua Krusell, and Farhad Miri. 2018. "The Varieties of Democracy Measurement Model: Latent Variable Analysis for Cross National and Cross-Temporal Expert-Coded Data." V-Dem Institute Working Paper 21 (3rd ed.), University of Gothenburg.

Pemstein, Daniel, Stephen A. Meserve, and James Melton. 2010. "Democratic Compromise: A Latent Variable Analysis of Ten Measures of Regime Type." *Political Analysis* 18(4): 426–449.

Pemstein, Daniel, Eitan Tzelgov, and Yi-ting Wang. 2015. "Evaluating and Improving Item Response Theory Models for Cross-National Expert Surveys." Varieties of Democracy Institute Working Paper 1 (March): 1–53. 2014

Pemstein, Daniel, and Brigitte Seim. 2016. "Anchoring Vignettes and Item Response Theory in Cross-National Expert Surveys." Paper presented at the annual meeting of the American Political Science Association, Philadelphia.

Pevehouse, Jon C. 2002. "With a Little Help from My Friends? Regional Organizations and the Consolidation of Democracy." *American Journal of Political Science* 46(3): 611–626.

Pocock, John, and Greville Agard. 1975. *The Machiavellian Moment: Florentine Political Thought and the Atlantic Republican Tradition.* Princeton, NJ: Princeton University Press.

Powell, G. Bingham. 1982. *Contemporary Democracies: Participation, Stability, and Violence.* Cambridge, MA: Harvard University Press.

Przeworski, Adam, Michael E. Alvarez, José Antonio Cheibub, and Fernando Limongi. 1996. "What Makes Democracies Endure?" *Journal of Democracy* 7(1): 39–55.

Przeworski, Adam, and Fernando Limongi. 1997. "Modernization: Theories and Facts." *World Politics* 49(2): 155–183.

Przeworski, Adam, Michael Alvarez, José Antonio Cheibub, and Fernando Limongi. 2000. *Democracy and Development: Political Institutions and Well-Being in the World, 1950–1990.* New York: Cambridge University Press.

Putnam, Robert D., with Robert Leonardi and Raffaella Y. Nanetti. 1994. *Making Democracy Work: Civic Traditions in Modern Italy.* Princeton, NJ: Princeton University Press.

Ranney, Austin. 1962. *The Doctrine of Responsible Party Government.* Urbana: University of Illinois Press.

Raz, J. 1977. "Rule of Law and Its Virtue." *Law Quarterly Review* 93: 195–211.

Reich, Gary Matthew. 2002. "Categorizing Political Regimes: New Data for Old Problems." *Democratization* 9(Winter): 1–24.

Reiter, Dan. 2017. "Is Democracy a Cause of Peace?" *Oxford Research Encyclopedias.*

Ríos-Figueroa, Julio, and Jeffrey K. Staton. 2014. "An Evaluation of Cross-National Measures of Judicial Independence." *Journal of Law, Economics, and Organization* 30(1): 104–134.

Rock, Michael T. 2007. "Corruption and Democracy." United Nations Department of Economic and Social Affairs, DESA Working Paper No. 55.

Rodriguez, D. B., M. D. Mccubbins, and B. R. Weingast. 2009. "The Rule of Law Unplugged." *Emory Law Journal* 59: 1455.

Roodman, David. 2009a. "How to Do Xtabond2: An Introduction to Difference and System GMM in Stata." *Stata Journal* 9: 86–136.

Roodman, David. 2009b. "A Note on the Theme of Too Many Instruments." *Oxford Bulletin of Economics and Statistics* 71(1): 135–158.

Rose-Ackerman, Susan. 1999. *Corruption and Government: Causes, Consequences, and Reform*. New York: Cambridge University Press.

Ross, Alf. 1952. *Why Democracy?* Cambridge, MA: Harvard University Press.

Ross, Michael L. 2001. "Does Oil Hinder Democracy?" *World Politics* 53(3): 325–361.

Rothstein, Bo, and Jan Teorell. 2008. "What Is Quality of Government? A Theory of Impartial Political Institutions." *Governance* 21(2): 165–190.

Rousseau, Jean-Jacques. 1762/1984. *Of the Social Contract; or, Principles of Political Right and Discourse on Political Economy*. New York: Harper and Row.

Rueschemeyer, Dietrich, Evelyne Huber Stephens, and John D. Stephens. 1992. *Capitalist Development and Democracy*. Chicago: University of Chicago Press.

Salamon, L. M., H. K. Anheier et al. 1999. "Civil Society in Comparative Perspective." In *Global Civil Society: Dimensions of the Nonprofit Sector*, eds. L. M. Salamon, H. K. Anheier, R. List, S. Toepler, and S. W. Sokolowski. Baltimore: Johns Hopkins Center for Civil Society Studies.

Salamon Lester M., S. Wojciech Sokolowski et al. 2004. *Global Civil Society: Dimensions of the Nonprofit Sector*. 2nd ed. Greenwich, CN: Kumarian Press.

Sartori, Giovanni. 1970. "Concept Misinformation in Comparative Politics." *American Political Science Review* 64(4): 1033–1053.

Sartori, Giovanni. 1987. *The Theory of Democracy Revisited*. Chatham, NJ: Chatham House.

Sartori, Giovanni. 1997. *Comparative Constitutional Engineering*. 2nd ed. New York: NYU Press.

Saward, Michael. 1998. *The Terms of Democracy*. Cambridge: Polity Press.

Schattschneider, Elmer Eric. 1942. *Party Government*. New York: Holt, Rinehart, and Winston.

Schattschneider, Elmer Eric. 1960. *The Semisovereign People: A Realist's View of Democracy in America*. New York: Holt, Rinehart, and Winston.

Schedler, Andreas. 2002. "Elections without Democracy: The Menu of Manipulation." *Journal of Democracy* 13(2): 36–50.

Schedler, Andreas. 2012a. "Judgment and Measurement in Political Science." *Perspectives on Politics* 10(1): 22–36.

Schedler, A. 2012b. "The Measurer's Dilemma: Coordination Failures in Cross-National Political Data Collection." *Comparative Political Studies* 45(2): 237–266.

Schnakenberg, Keith, and Christopher J. Fariss. 2014. "Dynamic Patterns of Human Rights Practices." *Political Science Research and Methods* 2(1): 1–31.

Schumpeter, Joseph A. 1942. *Capitalism, Socialism, and Democracy*. New York: Harper.

Schumpeter, Joseph A. 1950. "The March into Socialism." *American Economic Review* 40(2): 446–456.

Seawright, Jason W. 2007. "Democracy and Growth: A Case Study in Failed Causal Inference." In *Regimes and Democracy in Latin America: Theories and Method*, ed. Gerardo Munck. Oxford: Oxford University Press.

Siaroff, Alan. 2003. "Comparative Presidencies: The Inadequacy of the Presidential, Semi-Presidential and Parliamentary Distinction." *European Journal of Political Research* 42(3): 287–312.

Sigman, Rachel, and Staffan I. Lindberg. Forthcoming. "Democracy for All: Conceptualizing and Measuring Egalitarian Democracy." *Political Science Research and Methods*.

Simmons, Beth A., and Zachary Elkins. 2004. "The Globalization of Liberalization: Policy Diffusion in the International Political Economy." *American Political Science Review* 98(1):171–189.

Sinclair, T. A., trans. 1962. "Translator's Introduction." In *Politics*, by Aristotle. Baltimore, MD: Penguin Books.

Skaaning, Svend-Erik. 2008. "The Civil Liberty Dataset: Conceptualization and Measurement." *Zeitschrift für Vergleichende Politikwissenschaft* 2(1): 29–51.

Skaaning, Svend-Erik. 2009. "Measuring Civil Liberty: An Assessment of Standards-Based Data Sets." *Revista de Ciencia Política* 29(3): 721–740.

Skaaning, Svend-Erik, John Gerring, and Henrikas Bartusevičius. 2015. "A Lexical Index of Electoral Democracy." *Comparative Political Studies* 48(12): 1491–1525.

Sofer, Tamar, David B. Richardson, Elena Colicino, Joel Schwartz, and Eric J. Tchetgen Tchetgen. 2016. "On Negative Outcome Control of Unobserved Confounding as a Generalization of Difference-in-Differences." *Statistical Science* 31(3): 348–361.

Stan Development Team. 2015. "Stan: A C++ Library for Probability and Sampling, Version 2.9.0." Available at: http://mc-stan.org/.

Starr, Harvey. 1991. "Democratic Dominoes: Diffusion Approaches to the Spread of Democracy in the International System." *Journal of Conflict Resolution* 35(2): 356–381.

Starr, Harvey, and Christina Lindborg. 2003. "Democratic Dominoes Revisited: The Hazards of Governmental Transitions, 1974–1996." *Journal of Conflict Resolution* 47(4): 490–519.

Steenbergen, Marco R., and Gary Marks. 2007. "Evaluating Expert Surveys." *European Journal of Political Research* 46(3): 347–366.

Steenbergen, Marco R., André Bächtiger, Markus Spörndli, and Jürg Steiner. 2003. "Measuring Political Deliberation: A Discourse Quality Index." *Comparative European Politics* 1: 21–47.

Sung, Hung-En. 2004. "Democracy and Political Corruption: A Cross-National Comparison." *Crime, Law and Social Change* 41(2): 179–193.

Tanner, Martin A. 1993. *Tools for Statistical Inference: Methods for the Exploration of Posterior Distributions and Likelihood Functions*. 2nd ed. New York: Springer.

Teorell, Jan. 2010. *Determinants of Democratization: Explaining Regime Change in the World, 1972–2006*. Cambridge: Cambridge University Press.

Teorell, Jan, Michael Coppedge, Staffan I. Lindberg, and Svend-Erik Skaaning. 2019. "Measuring Polyarchy across the Globe, 1900–2016." *Studies in Comparative International Development* 54(1): 71–95.

Teorell, Jan, Staffan Lindberg. 2019. "Beyond Democracy-Dictatorship Measures: A New Framework Capturing Executive Bases of Power." *Perspectives on Politics*. 17(1): 66–84.

Thomas, Melissa A. 2010. "What Do the Worldwide Governance Indicators Measure?" *European Journal of Development Research* 22(1): 31–54.

Treier, Shawn, and Simon Jackman. 2008. "Democracy as a Latent Variable." *American Journal of Political Science* 52(1): 201–217.

Treisman, Daniel. 2007. "What Have We Learned about the Causes of Corruption from Ten Years of Cross-National Empirical Research?" *Annual Review of Political Science* 10: 211–244.

Tsebelis, George. 2000. "Veto Players and Institutional Analysis." *Governance* 13(4): 441–474.

UNDP. 2004. *Democracy in Latin America: Toward a Citizens' Democracy*. New York: United Nations Development Programme.

USAID. 2012a. The 2011 CSO Sustainability Index for Central and Eastern Europe and Eurasia. [online] United States Agency for International Development (USAID). Available at: www.usaid.gov/europe-eurasia-civil-society/cso-sustainability-2011 [Accessed February 15, 2017].

USAID. 2012b. The 2011 CSO Sustainability Index for Central and Eastern Europe and Eurasia. [online] United States Agency for International Development (USAID). Available at: www.usaid.gov/africa-civil-society/2011 [Accessed February 15, 2017].

Waldron, J. 2002. "Is the Rule of Law an Essentially Contested Concept (in Florida)?" *Law and Philosophy* 21(2): 137–164.

Van Ham, Carolien, and Staffan I. Lindberg. 2015. "From Sticks to Carrots: Electoral Manipulation in Africa, 1986–2012." *Government and Opposition* 50(3): 521–548.

Vanhanen, Tatu. 1990. *The Process of Democratization: A Comparative Study of 147 States, 1980–1988.* New York: Crane Russak.

Vanhanen, Tatu. 1997. *Prospects of Democracy: A Study of 172 Countries.* London: Routledge.

Vile, M. J. C. 1998. *Constitutionalism and the Separation of Powers.* Indianapolis, IN: Liberty Fund.

Weber, Max. [1922] 1978. *Economy and Society: An Outline of Interpretive Sociology.* Berkley: University of California Press.

Welzel, Christian. 2007. "Are Levels of Democracy Affected by Mass Attitudes? Testing Attainment and Sustainment Effects on Democracy." *International Political Science Review* 28(4): 397–424.

Welzel, Christian, Ronald F. Inglehart, and Stefan Kruse. 2017. "Pitfalls in the Study of Democratization: Testing the Emancipatory Theory of Democracy." *British Journal of Political Science* 47(2): 463–472.

Western, Bruce, and Meredith Kleykamp 2004. "A Bayesian Change Point Model for Historical Time Series Analysis." *Political Analysis* 12(4): 354–374.

Whitehead, Laurence. 1986. "International Aspects of Democratization." In *Transitions from Authoritarian Rule: Comparative Perspectives*, eds. G. O'Donnell, P. C. Schmitter, and L. Whitehead. Baltimore: Johns Hopkins University Press.

Whitten-Woodring, Jenifer, and Douglas A. Van Belle. 2014. *Historical Guide to World Media Freedom: A Country-by-Country Analysis.* Washington, DC: CQ Press.

Wilson, Woodrow. [1879] 1965. "Cabinet Government in the United States." *International Review* 7 (August). Reprinted in *The Political Thought of Woodrow Wilson*, ed. E. David Cronon. Indianapolis, IN: Bobbs-Merrill.

Wilson, Woodrow. [1885] 1956. *Congressional Government.* Baltimore: Johns Hopkins University Press.

Wooldridge, Jeffrey. 2002. *Econometric Analysis of Cross Section and Panel Data.* Cambridge, MA: MIT Economic Press.

Xu, Yiqing. 2017. "Generalized Synthetic Control Method: Causal Inference with Interactive Fixed Effects Models." *Political Analysis* 25(1): 57–76.

Zakaria, Fareed. 2003. *The Future of Freedom: Illiberal Democracy at Home and Abroad.* New York: W. W. Norton.

Index